Four Years in the Cauldron

Four Years in the Cauldron

The Gripping Story of an Irishman
Making Sense of America

BRIAN O'DONOVAN

PENGUIN BOOKS

PENGUIN BOOKS

UK | USA | Canada | Ireland | Australia
India | New Zealand | South Africa

Penguin Books is part of the Penguin Random House group of companies
whose addresses can be found at global.penguinrandomhouse.com.

First published by Sandycove 2021
Published in Penguin Books 2022

001

Copyright © Brian O'Donovan, 2021

The moral right of the author has been asserted

Typeset by Jouve (UK), Milton Keynes
Printed and bound in Great Britain by Clays Ltd, Elcograf S.p.A.

The authorized representative in the EEA is Penguin Random House Ireland,
Morrison Chambers, 32 Nassau Street, Dublin D02 YH68

A CIP catalogue record for this book is available from the British Library

ISBN: 978–0–241–99365–1

For Joanna, Lucy and Erin

Contents

CONTENTS

Prologue

It was raining heavily in St Peter's Square. I had just finished a live TV report from a nearby rooftop overlooking the Vatican, speculating about who the next Pope might be. It was 13 March 2013 and Rome was alive with expectation. Cardinals had started voting the previous day but had so far failed to agree on a successor for Pope Benedict XVI, black smoke from the Sistine Chapel chimney indicating that a candidate had not yet been chosen.

An enormous press centre had been opened by the Vatican to assist the thousands of journalists who had come to Rome from around the world. When I'd arrived in the city a few days earlier, I had made my way there and had spoken to a very helpful priest who was the press officer on duty. He had explained to me that two votes would be taken in the morning and two votes in the afternoon, with the first smoke signal expected around 7.00 p.m. on the first evening of voting. On the second day of the conclave, a smoke signal would be expected at about noon, and again that evening.

This is great, I thought, as I worked out in my head how the schedule of events would coincide with the news programmes on TV3, the station I was working for at the time.

'And how long do you expect the whole process to take?' I asked the press officer. 'When will the cardinals make up their minds? Two, maybe three days?'

The priest smiled. 'Whenever the Holy Spirit tells them.'

That was the full extent of his advice.

So now, as the rain poured down, I wasn't too hopeful of today being the day. There had been suggestions from academics, historians and religious scholars that this could be a long papal conclave and that it could be several more days before a new Pope was elected. With that in mind, I was preparing to make my way back to my hotel for the evening. But on a whim, I decided to join the smoke-watchers who were huddled under umbrellas, just on the off-chance the experts were wrong.

At 7.06 p.m. the crowd suddenly erupted in loud cheers as the bells of St Peter's Basilica rang out. A group of locals standing next to me started shouting excitedly, 'Fumo bianco!' I didn't need a translation to know what was going on. Squinting through the raindrops, I could see it for myself: white smoke.

So much for all those predictions of a lengthy process, I thought as I rushed back to the rooftop camera position to prepare for my next live broadcast.

Whenever the Holy Spirit tells them.

Those words have always stayed with me. I had never covered a story like that before. As a broadcast journalist, your day is dictated by TV and radio deadlines. Forward planning and research are key when it comes to working out what is likely to have happened by the time of your next bulletin. Of course, the nature of breaking news is that there are always surprises and you must be prepared for the unexpected, but surely a structured, long-established process like the election of a Pope would come with a helpful timetable of events? Apparently not.

Surrounded by those ancient churches and squares, I was at the mercy of divine intervention. There were no political analysts or opinion polls that could project how this was going to end. Most of the experts who had made forecasts about frontrunners and timelines were proved wrong. We were all in the realm of the unknown. It was frustrating in one way, but it also brought a level of uncertainty to the story that was new and exciting. Little did I know then that it would be good practice for a tumultuous and unpredictable four years in Washington DC. That same feeling of living with the unknown, of searching for signs, would be the hallmark of my time reporting on America.

The 'smoke signals' came in the form of angry presidential tweets that would dictate my day and frequently send me racing to camera positions for last-minute live broadcasts. The normal rules were gone. I wasn't waiting for the Holy Spirit this time; but with Donald Trump in the White House, it was no easier to foresee what was going to happen next.

1. The Donald has landed

'Well, I guess they chose the wrong guy,' Donald Trump told me with a smile.

We were making small talk while the cameras were being set up ahead of a one-on-one TV interview. It was 2014 and at the time I was working as the Finance Correspondent for TV3 News. I mentioned that the station had the rights to the Irish version of his hit TV show *The Apprentice* but I added that, after four successful seasons, the series was no more.

'Why?' Mr Trump asked me. 'What happened?'

I said that I wasn't exactly sure why the show had been cancelled, that it had done well in the TV ratings. I then went on to mention that the host of the show, Bill Cullen, was in financial trouble. His car dealerships had recently gone into receivership.

'The guy who played your role on the show has got into some money trouble,' I said, prompting his response that the producers must have chosen the 'wrong guy'.

Donald Trump had been involved in multiple bankrupt-cies, how ironic that he would describe another businessman in this way, as if he himself were the model of financial suc-cess. It was a glimpse into what is at Donald Trump's core: a massive ego and sense of self that have convinced him he knows more about business than anyone else.

My 2014 interview with Mr Trump took place in Shannon Airport. He was visiting Ireland following the recent pur-chase of his golf resort in Doonbeg, county Clare. The self-proclaimed ultimate dealmaker had bagged himself a bargain, reportedly acquiring the luxury property for the knockdown price of €15 million after buying it out of receivership. As he stepped off his Trump-branded private Boeing 757, he was greeted on a red carpet by then Minister for Finance Michael Noonan and local officials. A harpist, a violinist and a singer were also on hand to mark his arrival. It was a VIP welcome for a man who was not yet US president. But he was still a big name, as a businessman and a reality TV star. He was accompanied by his sons Donald Jr and Eric and his daughter Ivanka. The journalists had to double-check the children's identities with the event organizers, as at that stage they were little known.

Before the one-on-one interviews, Donald Trump held a press conference for all the gathered media at Shannon airport's Gate 6. He spoke about his acquisition of Doonbeg and pledged to invest millions of euro in the property, creating hundreds of jobs in the process. 'I bought it for, well, you know what the number is. I would say I'll be doubling and tripling that number very quickly, to make it great.' If he had added the word 'again' to the end of that sentence, it would have been an interesting preview of things to come. 'Ireland is a special place and I love Ireland and I love the country and it was an opportunity that was presented to us, but I had been looking at this property for a long time,' he said. 'The hotel is one of the finest hotels anywhere in the world.'

Donald Trump was also asked repeatedly about a snail, of all things. *Vertigo angustior*, to be precise. The protection of this microscopic species had been problematic for the development plans of the resort's previous owners amid environmental and conservation concerns. Mr Trump vowed to be sympathetic when carrying out works at Doonbeg:

'The snail issue is an issue that will go on and we'll be very protective of it. We want to work together with certain environmental people, but they've been terrific and, as you know, we've already got lots of approvals.' But there were other approvals that Trump Doonbeg struggled with, particularly when it came to building a wall to protect the golf course from coastal erosion.

A planning row erupted over the proposal, with An Bord Pleanála (the independent planning appeals board) finally refusing permission to build the sea wall in March 2020. The authority said it was not satisfied that the development would not adversely affect sand-dune habitats at the site. Environmental campaigners, who had objected to the wall, welcomed the ruling, calling it a momentous victory that would protect local ecosystems that had been in place for thousands of years. When he bought Doonbeg, Donald Trump probably had no idea that an environmental row over native species of wildlife would last for six years, but these things tend to move at a snail's pace, so to speak.

It was a controversy that got plenty of media attention in the US for two reasons. First, it provided lots of nice headlines about 'Trump's Wall' and 'Build the Wall', references to his signature campaign promise to clamp down on illegal immigration across the US–Mexico border. Second, many of the articles were quick to point out that someone who had questioned the whole concept of climate change was being forced to take action to protect his property from rising sea levels and coastal erosion.

After questions about conservation and walls, the reporters moved on to a possible run for the White House in 2016. Donald Trump had first expressed presidential ambitions back in the 1980s. There was a theory that he made up his mind following the White House Correspondents' Dinner in 2011. He was a guest at the event and was the target of a series of jokes by President Barack Obama and the MC for the night, comedian Seth Meyers.

Mr Trump was mocked over his political ambitions, his TV shows and his 'birther theory', a false claim that Barack Obama may not have been born in the US. 'No one is happier, no one is prouder to put this birth certificate matter to rest than The Donald,' Barack Obama told the Correspondents' Dinner. 'That's because he can finally get back to focusing on the issues that matter – like, did we fake the moon landing? What really happened in Roswell? And where are Biggie and Tupac?'

The jokes continued and Donald Trump looked increasingly unhappy and humiliated. It has been suggested that the ordeal strengthened his resolve to run for president out of some sort of desire to get his own back on the Washington establishment. 'That evening of public abasement, rather than sending Mr Trump away, accelerated his ferocious efforts to gain stature in the political world,' wrote *The New York Times* in 2016. When asked about his presidential ambitions by reporters in Shannon in 2014, he claimed that he was already leading in many opinion polls, even though he had not yet declared whether or not he would enter politics.

The press conference ended and it was time for the one-on-one interviews. I was led into a small meeting room and my cameraman began setting up the lights and microphones. Donald Trump and his entourage entered, and we positioned him in front of the Irish and US flags that had been placed in the room.

As Finance Correspondent, it was my job to cover business and economic stories. In 2014, Ireland was coming out of a bleak recession and an EU/IMF bailout. The economy was recovering and lots of companies were expanding. Once a week, I would find myself at an Industrial Development Authority (IDA)-supported jobs announcement at a factory, call centre or technology park. An American billionaire CEO would jet in from Silicon Valley to hold a press conference. The fact that they were usually in their mid-twenties would depress everyone in the room and make us question what the hell we had done with our lives. We would listen and watch detailed presentations on growth projections, breakdowns of job numbers and timelines of when specific roles would be advertised. This was not the case with Donald Trump.

'How many jobs do you hope to create?' I asked him. 'Oh, many, many jobs,' came the vague reply. 'What level of investment are you planning?' I asked. 'Oh, a tremendous investment,' I was told. I was actually starting to miss the tedious PowerPoint presentations from all those twenty-something overachievers. I didn't know it then, but it was a vagueness that I, and the entire White House press corps, would have to get used to when it came to trying to get answers out of Donald Trump.

Our interview over, I grabbed the tape from the camera-man and rushed through the Departures area to the car park outside, where a satellite van was waiting. I was under time pressure to get the report edited and sent back for the even-ing news. Donald Trump and his family had also left the airport and were making their way to Doonbeg. A Trump visit is never without controversy and this time was no differ-ent. The Fine Gael-led government faced criticism over Michael Noonan's involvement in the event. Some commen-tators suggested that the red carpet, musicians and welcoming party were over the top, that the country was almost bowing and scraping in front of the Trumps. Michael Noonan was quick to dismiss the attacks. 'Would there be criticism if it was an IDA factory that was going into west Clare with three hundred jobs? This man says he's going to spend at least double the purchase price for investment down there,' he told RTÉ Radio 1's *News at One*. 'I've no connection with Donald Trump, but I can assure you if it was the IDA that was bringing a factory into Clare and I was invited to go down there and there were three hundred jobs in it, I'd be there.'

But I remember thinking at the time that this was *not* an IDA announcement. It was very different. There were no concrete numbers or projections, but there was plenty of glamour and hype. The whole event in Shannon Airport had been heavy on pomp but light on detail. I knew Donald Trump was a master at self-promotion and projecting an image of success and wealth. But, I wondered, could that be enough for a credible presidential run?

In June 2015, just over a year after his Irish visit, Donald Trump announced his intention to seek the Republican nomination. He famously descended the golden escalator in Trump Tower, New York, to launch his campaign. There were no traditional Irish musicians at the bottom of the steps to greet him on this occasion, instead he arrived to the sounds of Neil Young's 'Rockin' in the Free World'. In typical Trump fashion, he began his address by commenting on the crowd size at his launch event. It would later be reported that some of the cheering supporters were paid actors and that others were just curious passers-by.

'Our country is in serious trouble. We don't have victories any more,' Mr Trump told the crowd. He then went on to promise a 'great, great wall', not along the west Clare coast to protect his golf course, but along the Mexico border to clamp down on illegal immigration. 'When Mexico sends its people, they're not sending their best,' he said in a now infamous part of his speech. 'They're sending people that have lots of problems, and they're bringing those problems. They're bringing drugs, they're bringing crime, they're rapists. And some, I assume, are good people.'

The controversial comments only added to the widespread belief among the Washington establishment that Donald Trump's presidential ambitions were doomed before they even began and that his candidacy would go nowhere. What no one really grasped then was that beneath the polls, under the radar, America was choosing Trump. Just as his Shannon Airport visit looked nothing like a traditional jobs announcement, his Trump Tower event looked nothing like a traditional campaign launch. And that is what his supporters loved. He was an outsider. A successful billionaire and a 'non-politician' who would 'drain the swamp' and use his business savvy to run the country. He would speak his mind and not care whom he offended, even when it involved calling immigrants rapists and drug-dealers.

He was embraced by a large swathe of the electorate who had felt left behind by the very establishment Donald Trump was railing against. His presidency exposed a deep disunity within the US. It affected every aspect of life in America, and in many ways continues to do so. Donald Trump's loyal supporters celebrated his election win in 2016 and felt they finally had a president who cared about them. His many critics in the US, and around the world, never saw it coming. They could do little more than look on in shock and exclaim, to quote the man himself: 'Well, I guess they chose the wrong guy.'

2. The jinx

After ten enjoyable years in TV3, I left the station in 2015 and began working for RTÉ News. I was excited to start my new job and was instantly made to feel at home on the Foreign Desk in the newsroom. As the name suggests, the role involves covering international stories for TV, radio and online, and also working with Foreign Correspondents in the field. It was a busy time in the US, with the drama of Election 2016, the shock defeat of Hillary Clinton and the chaos of the new Trump presidency.

I was fascinated by all of it, so when the role of Washington Correspondent was advertised towards the end of 2017, I discussed the prospect of applying for the job with my wife, Joanna. At the time our daughters, Lucy and Erin, were only seven and four years old. Was this the right time for such a big change? Joanna, who has always had more of a 'travel bug' than I have, was delighted by the idea and we agreed that I should apply for the role. There were celebrations a few weeks later when I was successful. Then it was time for me to leave.

The Departures screen said the flight would be delayed by one hour, then two, then four. I should not have been surprised. Large mounds of snow lay piled all around the runways of New York's JFK Airport and although the blizzard was easing, the after-effects of the powerful winter storm had led to massive disruption along the eastern coast of the US.

There had been snow from Canada to Florida. States of emergency had been declared and hundreds of thousands of homes had lost power. It was January 2018 and a few hours earlier I had said goodbye to my family back in Dublin.

We had agreed that I would say my farewells to our two girls the night before because I would be leaving very early in the morning. I slowly crept down the stairs at dawn, trying not to wake them, secretly and selfishly hoping that maybe one of them would stir and come out to the landing and I would get to see them one last time, but that would have been unfair. There had been enough tears shed the night before.

They would be moving over to join me in the US in six months' time and I would be home for a visit in six weeks, but all that felt like an eternity away as I loaded several heavy suitcases into the back of the waiting taxi and left for the airport. I knew I would miss them terribly, but I also knew that it would be worth the upheaval as I embarked on the adventure of a lifetime having secured a dream job.

Friends who were familiar with America had told me not to be afraid to talk to random people. It might sound like a funny piece of advice, but I understood what they meant. Irish people, although known for being friendly and welcoming, can be shy and reserved around strangers, less likely to spark up a conversation with someone they haven't met before. Americans are more chatty, more open.

I put this theory to the test when I realized that I would have several hours to kill at the airport bar. There were plenty of others in my situation: flights delayed, stuck in the airport alone and looking to pass the time. The first person I chatted to was a middle-aged man who was fascinated to learn that I was headed to Washington to take up my new role as the TV and radio correspondent for the Irish public broadcaster. We chatted about his Irish roots until his flight was called. Unfortunately, mine was still delayed, but I did find a new person to chat to – an older lady from Long Island, New York. After we'd exchanged life stories, she asked where we would live when my family moved over. I said we couldn't decide between city or commuter belt.

'Go with the city,' she advised. 'You're going to be very busy over the next four years and your wife and kids will need neighbours and friends nearby.'

When her flight was called, I decided to check the status of mine. It had been delayed further. Three more hours passed and then the dreaded word appeared: Cancelled. As I was moving my entire life to Washington, I had a lot of luggage. I finally managed to locate the bulging bags, which had been abandoned in a pile in a distant Arrivals hall. The handle on one of my wheelie bags snapped as I tried to pull it through the terminal building, making an awkward situation even worse. I struggled into the snow-covered car park and took a taxi to Penn Station in Manhattan. From there, I boarded a train to Washington. It was 2.00 a.m. The train doors would not close properly and it was exceptionally cold.

At 5.30 a.m., I arrived in Washington's Union Station. I was exhausted and frozen, but at least I had finally made it to the city I would call home for the next four years. Worries about snowstorms, cancelled flights and broken luggage all evaporated when I walked through the station doors and was greeted by the Capitol Building in all its glory. It is my favourite Washington landmark, and on that freezing January morning it looked incredible. Bathed in yellow light, it stood like a beacon in the pre-dawn darkness. Little did I know that in the years to come, that symbol of American democracy would be the scene of two presidential impeachments and would be stormed by angry protesters. It would also play host to the inauguration of a new president, elected amid a raging pandemic and unprecedented racial unrest. I arrived in the US in a blizzard and the storms would continue to rage for the next four years.

I made my way, bleary-eyed, to the apartment where I would be staying until I found a house to rent. After a few hours' sleep, I walked to the RTÉ Washington bureau. It is in a great location, just a few blocks from the White House. It shares the office with other European broadcasters, on a floor operated by Eurovision. Yes, as in the Song Contest, but the group also has a news division – fewer sequins and cheesy dance routines but still plenty of celebrations of our European ties. I stepped out of the lift and was greeted by a wall of flags from all the nations that had offices on the floor. A sign on the opposite wall directed me where to go. *RTÉ – Irish Radio & TV* was listed on the directory among broadcasters from Spain, Germany, Russia, Switzerland, Norway, Sweden, Finland and Denmark. It resembled a multinational leader board and I wondered if the best stations would get awarded *douze points* by the viewers.

I walked into the RTÉ office and met two engineers who had travelled over from Dublin. They were busy installing new equipment in what would be my workplace for the duration of my stay. The bureau consists of two adjoining offices. One is an edit suite, with the computers and servers used to record video feeds, edit TV packages and transfer reports back to Dublin. The walls are decorated with campaign posters hung by the previous Washington correspondents. As I scanned the signs bearing the names Trump, Clinton, Obama, Romney, McCain and Bush, I wondered whose posters I would be hanging on the wall in three years' time.

The adjoining office has two desks: one for the correspondent and one for the cameraperson/producer. It was here that I met Patti Jette. She told me she was from Massachusetts and had been working in news and current affairs in Washington for several years. She had just been hired as a camerawoman by RTÉ, so we were both 'newbies'. We instantly clicked and ended up working that very first day when the editor of the *Six One News* asked us if we could cover a story for that evening's bulletin. The Golden Globe Awards were taking place that night in California. The bosses in Dublin stressed that I did not have to work if I was too tired or too busy unpacking, but Patti and I agreed that filming and editing a report would be the right way to kick off our first day. We decided to shoot a 'piece-to-camera' outside the White House. It would be the perfect location to talk about one of the big nominees that year, *The Post*, which told the story of the turbulent relationship between the media and the presidency.

The last time I had been at the White House was as a tourist seventeen years previously. This time, Patti was my guide. She knew exactly where to go for the best shot and how close we could get without attracting the attention of the Secret Service. As the report aired on TV that evening, there were lots of nice comments from family and friends back home. I breathed a sigh of relief that day one had been a success. The same could not be said for *The Post*, which failed to win an award. Perhaps we had jinxed it by highlighting the film in our report that day.

Patti and I hit the ground running on that first day and in the weeks that followed we kept running and running. Although the job title is 'Washington Correspondent', I was responsible for covering the whole of the United States. We criss-crossed the US, reporting on everything from an Irish famine exhibition in Connecticut to a visit by Taoiseach Leo Varadkar to Oklahoma and Texas. We interviewed undocumented Irish immigrants in Boston and spoke to the harbour master in Portland, Maine, who had been adopted from a Mother and Baby home in county Tipperary.

I had hung a large map of the US on the wall of the office and for each city we visited, I marked it with a red pin. In early March it was time to expand our horizons westward and travel to Los Angeles to cover the 2018 Oscars. That was a red pin I was eager to add to the map.

In her hit 'Do You Know the Way to San Jose' Dionne Warwick sang: 'LA is a great big freeway'. She wasn't wrong. It was my first time in the City of Angels and I was thankful that Patti was doing the driving as we weaved in and out of traffic along packed multi-lane highways. We had booked an Airbnb apartment close to the Oscars venue. It was nice, but it came with the world's smallest parking space, inside a tiny garage at the back of the property. Patti was worried about scratching our rental car every time we entered and exited.

There were dozens of movie industry events taking place in LA in the run-up to the Academy Awards. The Oscar Wilde Awards were hosted by the US-Ireland Alliance and honoured the contributions of Irish and Irish American people working in the film industry. The 2018 event was held in the Santa Monica offices of Bad Robot, the production company run by film director J. J. Abrams. The stars arrived on a green carpet. The big names that year included Colin Farrell, Barry Keoghan and Catherine O'Hara. Back then, I knew her from *Home Alone* and would only later discover her hilarious comedy series *Schitt's Creek*. Also attending that evening was *Star Wars* actor Mark Hamill. Patti, a big fan, was delighted to get her picture taken with Luke Skywalker.

It was time to move from the green carpet to the red carpet. The organizers of the Academy Awards insist that reporters and camera crews dress in black-tie attire while covering the event. For me, it was easy. I wear suits every day at work anyway, so I was just effectively replacing my tie with a dickie bow. Things were a little more complicated for Patti, who had to choose something stylish yet practical. A formal gown and high heels are far from ideal when lugging around a heavy camera. She pulled it off elegantly, but repeatedly used the words my wife always throws at me before big occasions: 'Things are so much easier for you men!'

There was strong Irish interest that year, across a number of categories. Saoirse Ronan was nominated for best actress for her role in the coming-of-age drama *Lady Bird*. London-Irish writer/director Martin McDonagh was nominated in the best original screenplay category for his movie *Three Billboards Outside Ebbing, Missouri*, which was also up for a best picture award. Wicklow-based Daniel Day-Lewis was nominated in the best actor category for *Phantom Thread*. Consolata Boyle was up for best costume design in the movie *Victoria & Abdul*, and Kilkenny's Cartoon Saloon had been nominated for the animated feature *The Breadwinner*, which told the story of a young girl in Taliban-controlled Afghanistan.

The awards were held at the Dolby Theatre in Hollywood. The venue is an impressive building and security was tight around the red carpet that led to its entrance. The surrounding streets were like another world, however, the antithesis of the celebrity glitz that the area is known for. Homeless people gathered in front of graffitied, shuttered storefronts. Tacky souvenir shops sold cheap trinkets.

'It's not as glamorous as I expected,' I told my wife on the phone, who was back home in Ireland. 'Hollywood is kind of rough,' I said.

'Oh, poor you!' came her sarcastic reply. 'At least it's warm there!'

Ireland was in the grip of the 'Beast from the East', a winter storm that had brought record snowfall and freezing temperatures. I may have been moaning about urban decay, but Joanna was worried about being snowed-in and the local shop running out of bread. She was also nervous about the central heating, hoping that our recently repaired boiler would hold out. 'Fingers crossed it'll be OK,' I said. A halfhearted, unhelpful reassurance, but it was the best I could do from 5,000 miles away. Thankfully, the boiler behaved itself and the family didn't starve. Ireland breathed a sigh of relief as the snow finally started to thaw, but unfortunately the country would not be celebrating any Oscar wins, as none of the Irish nominees was successful.

As with *The Post* at the Golden Globes, we joked that the 'Brian and Patti jinx' had struck again. It was the same bad luck, perhaps, that resulted in us handing back our rental car with a nasty scratch along the door. For three days Patti had skilfully manoeuvred it into and out of our tiny parking space, but as we pulled out for the final time, to go to the airport and return the car, we heard the crunching scrape of metal colliding with concrete. Oh well, what would a trip to Hollywood be without a little drama?

3. The Taoiseach and the President

During my first weeks in the US, Patti and I spent a lot of time on the road and in the air, travelling around the country, but things were also busy in Washington DC. Donald Trump came under fire for reportedly describing African nations as 'shithole countries', there was a government shutdown because Congress failed to agree a Budget, and reports started to emerge that the President had tried to dismiss Robert Mueller, the special counsel who was investigating links between the Trump campaign and Russia. There were also claims that Mr Trump's lawyer, Michael Cohen, had arranged 'hush money' payments to women to cover up alleged affairs with his client; the President made the unprecedented move of accepting an invitation to meet with the North Korean leader Kim Jong-un; and he also announced controversial trade tariffs on steel and aluminium imports.

There was a seemingly never-ending series of sackings and resignations from the White House. Members of Donald Trump's staff were frequently dismissed by tweet. 'Mike Pompeo, Director of the CIA, will become our new Secretary of State. He will do a fantastic job! Thank you to Rex Tillerson for his service!', Mr Trump tweeted on 13 March 2018. It was the first Rex Tillerson had heard of it. Later that year, the US President would tweet again about his former Secretary of State: 'Rex Tillerson didn't have the mental capacity needed. He was dumb as a rock and I couldn't get rid of him fast enough. He was lazy as hell.'

Covering the dramas and controversies of the Trump administration was never dull and always full of surprises, but it was time to switch my focus to another politician. For RTÉ's Washington Correspondent, the annual St Patrick's Day visit by the Taoiseach is one of the busiest times of the year. The Irish government typically tries to pack as much into the trip as possible, with visits to other US cities planned around the centrepiece White House meeting. It is a chance to meet Irish American groups and to celebrate cultural ties and shared histories.

In March 2018, Taoiseach Leo Varadkar and his entourage touched down in the US with a full schedule ahead of them. It began with the South by Southwest technology and arts festival in Austin, Texas, followed by a visit to the Choctaw Native American reservation in Oklahoma. There, Leo Varadkar thanked the community leaders for the goodwill and kindness shown to Ireland by their ancestors. In 1847, they had collected $170, the equivalent of several thousand dollars today, for famine relief. The donation was made just sixteen years after the start of the infamous 'Trail of Tears', when tribes were relocated from their lands, at a time when the Choctaw people were themselves living in poverty. In 2017, a sculpture was unveiled in Midleton, county Cork, to commemorate their generosity.

One of the best parts of the Taoiseach's annual visit is the fact that a cohort of Irish journalists also travels over to America to cover the trip. I always enjoyed catching up with colleagues and getting all the latest gossip from home in the worlds of media and politics. We boarded the press bus and were driven through the wide plains of Oklahoma. The reporters were entertained by our colleague Senan Molony – who was then Political Correspondent with the *Irish Daily*

Mail – and his song 'Brexit Shambles', a little ditty he had written about the mess that was Brexit. It was a welcome distraction from the flat landscape before us. Then, out of nowhere, a skyscraper appeared in the wilderness. It was a casino built by the Choctaw Nation, a lucrative source of income for the community. It was an impressive building that glinted in the morning sun. One of the journalists looked up at the building and joked: 'Look at the size of this place. I can't believe they only gave us $170!'

In a large function room, the Taoiseach watched traditional Choctaw music and dance performances. He then announced a scholarship for members of the community who wished to study in Ireland. That evening, we crossed back over the state line from Oklahoma into Texas. Leo Varadkar visited the location in Dallas where President John F. Kennedy was assassinated and was given a tour of the Sixth Floor Museum at Dealey Plaza, in the former Texas School Book Depository building. It is the spot from where Lee Harvey Oswald was accused of opening fire on JFK in November 1963. The museum was closed, but we got in after-hours and had the place to ourselves because we were with the Prime Minister of Ireland. A perk of travelling with a VIP, I guess, but the real access would come the following day at the White House, when Taoiseach Leo Varadkar met President Donald Trump for the first time.

The biggest opportunity for Ireland to get its voice heard in the US happens once a year, around St Patrick's Day. The tradition of a bowl of shamrock being presented to the US President dates back to the 1950s. Originally it was the Irish Ambassador who performed this duty, but over the decades it has evolved into a diplomatic opportunity that is the envy of small countries around the world.

The key event is the mid-morning, one-on-one Oval Office meeting with the President. That is followed by a lunch on Capitol Hill, hosted by the Speaker of the House, then it is back to the White House for a second meeting with the President for the presentation of the shamrock bowl. But before all that, the day begins with breakfast at the Vice President's residence at the Naval Observatory. During Leo Varadkar's time as Taoiseach, his vice-presidential meetings received more attention than usual. Mike Pence had controversial, conservative views on LGBT rights and in 2018 the world's media was waiting to see how he would interact with an openly gay prime minister. The night before the breakfast, however, it was announced that the meeting would be private. In a break from tradition, cameras would not be allowed inside the room.

Thankfully, the press would be allowed to attend the Taoiseach's meeting with President Trump. Before COVID-19 restrictions, the Irish press corps would join the White House media pool for the Oval Office meeting between the Taoiseach and the US President. The talks themselves were private, but journalists were permitted to attend what is known as the 'pool spray' at the start of the meeting. This is where the two leaders shake hands for the cameras, make brief statements and take questions from reporters.

After going through security, the journalists all gathered in a huddled group by a sliding door at the back of the White House press briefing room. It was important to be towards the front of the group to get a good position inside the Oval Office. You didn't want to be boxed in behind other reporters and photographers. That could make it harder to ask a question or, worse still, your camera might not get a decent shot of the President and the Taoiseach. It was the first time that both Patti and I were going to be inside the Oval Office and we were excited, if not a little nervous.

The door slid open and the press pack rushed through. We were held again outside the doors to the Oval Office and, in the confusion, Patti and I became separated. She was at the front of the pack, while I had been pushed to the back. The reverse would have been worse, as having a good camera position was the priority. I was holding a long boom pole with a microphone attached to the end. I would have to stretch it, and my arm, to the fullest extent to record what the VIPs said in their opening remarks.

Suddenly, Patti shouted from the front of the press pack. 'Brian, I'm not picking up any audio!' The microphone had stopped working. We were penned in tightly, shoulder to shoulder, with the other journalists. I struggled to bring the mic close to my face to examine it and as I did, it fell apart. The battery pack had become detached and as I reached out to screw it back together, the batteries dropped to the ground. The doors to the Oval Office swung open and the press pack started to move. 'Brian!' I could hear Patti call from the front of the group, 'We have no audio!' Risking being trampled by the stampede, I bent down and somehow managed to gather up the batteries from between the feet of my press colleagues. Reunited with Patti inside the Oval Office, she quickly reassembled the microphone and we were back in business.

By the time we got inside, Donald Trump and Leo Varadkar had already begun their chat, with the US President speaking about how he would like to visit Ireland soon. 'I have property there, and I may never get to see it again,' he said. He asked Mr Varadkar if he played golf. 'I don't,' he replied, 'but I'm always willing to learn so we can have you for a few rounds.' Donald Trump welcomed his guest with kind words: 'It's my great honour to have the very popular Prime Minister of Ireland with us. And we're having some good talks about trade and about military and about cyber and all of the other things that we're talking about. The relationship is outstanding and only getting better.'

I covered three of Donald Trump's St Patrick's Day Oval Office meetings and they were all somewhat of a rollercoaster. Usually, by the time we got into the room, the remarks were already underway and then the questions would come thick and fast from the assembled media. The US press would pepper President Trump with queries about the issues of the day. We, the Irish media, would shout questions about Mr Trump's views on issues of relevance to Ireland, such as Brexit, which was indeed a bit of a 'shambles' back then.

In 2018, after polite chats about golf and visits to Ireland, questions moved to Russia, staff changes in the Trump administration and the President's relationship with Justin Trudeau, Prime Minister of Canada. After five minutes it was all over and we were escorted out to the sound of shouts from White House staff of, 'Thank you, press, time to go!' Outside I turned to Patti and asked if everything went OK from her end. 'Did the microphone work? Were you happy with your position?' She looked worried. 'I got bumped around a bit and I need to double-check that the footage is OK,' she said. She was worrying needlessly. The recording was perfect. We rushed back to the RTÉ office to edit our report for the *Six One News*.

Encounters with Donald Trump always had the potential for controversy, gaffes or drama but, from the Taoiseach's perspective, the Oval Office meeting had gone well. The day was not over yet, however. The next event was the St Patrick's Day lunch on Capitol Hill hosted by the Speaker of the House

Paul Ryan. Leo Varadkar made a speech during which he said that, while Minister for Tourism, he had been contacted by a businessman by the name of Donald Trump who had recently purchased a property in west Clare. The businessman was concerned about a wind-farm development planned for the area. Mr Trump objected to the construction of the project, which had been proposed by Clare Coastal Wind Power. Leo Varadkar told the lunch guests that he had approached Clare County Council after Mr Trump had phoned him directly. With the US President looking on, he claimed that he 'endeavoured to do what I could do about it'. The planning permission was later declined, he added. 'I do think it probably would have been refused anyway, but I am very happy to take credit for it, if the President is going to offer it to me,' said Mr Varadkar. The room erupted with laughter.

Back home in Ireland, controversy was erupting. Critics said it was improper for a government minister to intervene with a local authority on behalf of a private businessman. It made Michael Noonan's welcoming party in Shannon Airport look tame by comparison. The planning permission story rumbled on for that day and into the next and threatened to overshadow what had otherwise been a very successful visit to Washington.

My fellow journalists and I moved on to New York to cover the next leg of the Taoiseach's US trip. Leo Varadkar issued a clarification. He had not, in fact, contacted Clare County Council at all. He had contacted Fáilte Ireland, the tourism authority, about the matter. He said that following the controversy over his remarks the day before, he had asked his staff to go back and check the record. This showed, Mr Varadkar said, that he had not reached out to Clare County Council either verbally or in writing as Minister for

Tourism, and that it was within the remit of Fáilte Ireland to look at planning applications to see if they would have a negative impact on tourism.

Asked if it was an error of judgement to have told such an anecdote on the international stage, Mr Varadkar replied, 'It was that sort of an occasion, where people were telling stories and anecdotes and jokes.' He defended his actions by saying, 'I did what any tourism minister would do.' Opposition politicians had earlier criticized Mr Varadkar, with Labour Party leader Brendan Howlin saying that the whole controversy was a sign of 'Leo losing the run of himself'. So, did Leo lose the run of himself?

Three years after the saga, I asked him what he thought about it now, looking back. 'Of course, I regret it. I was at the lunch, got caught up in the moment, made a silly joke about something that was kind of half true that I didn't really remember anyway. It kind of blew up and marred the visit a little bit. Sadly, there are many moments in my political life like that – just some stupid thing that you said or did that if only you could delete that ten seconds you would, but there's no point beating yourself up about it,' he told me.

Aside from his dealings with Donald Trump, Leo Varadkar had tried to cultivate a relationship with Vice President Mike Pence in the hope of gaining support within the US administration for Ireland's Brexit position. In 2018, Mr Pence had excluded the media from his St Patrick's Day meeting with the Taoiseach, but it was a different story the following year. Not only was the press given access, but Mike Pence also invited Leo Varadkar's partner, Matt Barrett.

The Naval Observatory is a gated compound in Northwest Washington DC, on a stretch of Massachusetts Avenue known as Embassy Row. There are several large houses on the property and the most impressive is the Vice President's residence. It is a white mansion with a round turret and a wraparound porch. As it was a breakfast meeting, the media had to assemble at the gates of the compound before dawn to go through security checks. We were then escorted to the rear of the mansion where we waited in a tented area, alongside a covered swimming pool, until the VIPs were seated inside the building. Reporters and camera crews then crowded around a doorway leading into the dining room to hear the opening remarks. Leo Varadkar used the breakfast meeting as an opportunity to make a speech about equality and inclusion.

'I stand here as leader of my country, flawed and human, where I am judged by my political actions and not my sexual orientation, my skin tone, gender or religious beliefs,' he said while Mike Pence looked on. Leo Varadkar told me that he always found Mr Pence to be a very polite gentleman who had a genuine connection to Ireland. 'My objective with him was to try to build a relationship that might help tilt the White House and State Department a little more in our favour when it came to issues like Brexit, and it was worth trying. I invested a lot in it but, ultimately, it didn't work.'

He recalled Mike Pence's visit to Ireland in September 2019. Following a lunch meeting in Farmleigh House in the Phoenix Park, the Vice President said Ireland and the European Union should 'negotiate in good faith with Prime Minister Johnson and work to reach an agreement to respect UK sovereignty and minimize disruption to commerce'. It was a blow to Leo Varadkar's charm offensive.

'It ended with that speech he made in Farmleigh. We were sitting right beside him and he more or less told us to cut a deal with Boris Johnson. They did take sides and they took the side of Boris Johnson on Brexit. I don't think it was an anti-Irish thing. It was an anti-EU, anti-multilateralism, pro-Brexit thing. I did invest a lot in that relationship and it didn't work. It is not to say it wasn't the right thing to do,' he said.

Leo Varadkar doesn't regret the time he spent cultivating a relationship with Mike Pence, but he did get a mixed reaction from people over his decision to take his partner to their meetings. 'The invite was there and it was sincere. Maybe he did that to soften his image and if so, fair enough. He is a professional politician and that's what politicians do sometimes. I used it to make a statement about equality that I wanted to make and make it in America. It was generally well received by a lot of people, but it was divisive in America among LGBT groups and among our LGBT friends. Some said: "Fair play, you went in there with your partner and said what you needed to say." Others said: "No, this guy is a pariah. You should have boycotted him." So it was kind of divided in that sense.'

The polarization of America, on so many issues, was laid bare during the Trump era, so perhaps it was no surprise that there were also divisions over how Leo Varadkar should have dealt with a controversial Vice President. The annual St Patrick's Day visit to Washington is an opportunity to celebrate ties between the US and Ireland, but also a chance to explore Irish American heritage and to assess how Irish identity is perceived in the US. Despite efforts to project an image of a modern, progressive Ireland, many Americans continue to have traditional views of 'Irishness'. For some, it is born out of romantic nostalgia for a country that no longer exists, for others it comes from a willingness to embrace negative stereotypes of the 'drinking and fighting Irish'.

4. The fighting Irish

The National Gallery of Art in Washington DC is one of the city's most stunning museums, housing works by the likes of Leonardo da Vinci, Monet, van Gogh and Picasso. In April 2018, I found myself with some spare time and decided to pay a visit. I needed cheering up. Just a few hours before, I had said an emotional goodbye to my family at the airport.

I had been RTÉ's Washington Correspondent for almost four months at that stage, but Joanna and the girls had not yet moved over and would not be doing so until the end of the school year. There were visits back and forth and they had just spent the Easter holidays with me in Washington, but it would be several weeks before we'd see each other again.

The ornate halls of the National Gallery, adorned with their extraordinary works of art, helped take my mind off things as I got lost in the worlds of the paintings, but I was quickly brought back to reality by the shrill ring of my phone. I had forgotten to put it on Silent and it echoed through the cavernous museum, prompting angry looks from fellow visitors and gallery staff.

I fumbled to get it out of my pocket and rushed towards an exit to take the call. It was the newsroom in RTÉ. 'Conor McGregor is in trouble in New York and the police are looking for him,' my editor told me. 'For what?' I asked. 'We're not sure, smashing up a bus, we think,' came the reply. 'Can you do a live report into the *Nine O'Clock News* in thirty minutes?' Leonardo would have to wait. I now had to focus on a mixed martial artist.

I jumped into a taxi, hoping to make it from the gallery to the RTÉ studio in time. All the while, I was frantically looking for information about the alleged offence with multiple calls to the NYPD. I made it back to the studio with minutes to spare and with enough details gathered for my live report.

In the hours that followed, Conor McGregor turned himself in, was charged with assault and criminal mischief and was slated to appear in court in Brooklyn. Patti and I got an early morning train for the three-and-a-half-hour journey to New York to cover the court appearance, and I remember that we both wondered if we would be the only media there. Obviously, this was a big story back home in Ireland, but was it a big deal here in the US?

It was. There was a massive media presence outside Brooklyn Criminal Court, as well as crowds of fans carrying posters, signs and flags. I hadn't realized it until that moment, but Conor McGregor was a huge star in the US. Arguably, he was the most famous Irishman in America at the time.

There was a long wait for the hearing to be called and when it was, as is often the case with first appearances, it was over in minutes. Conor McGregor spoke just once, to confirm he understood the judge's instructions. The court heard that he was captured on surveillance cameras at the Barclays Center arena in Brooklyn throwing an object at the window of a bus carrying a group of MMA fighters. He was released on bail of $50,000, with his lawyer telling the court that his client had no criminal record and was not a flight risk because he was 'the most visible face on the planet'.

McGregor was due to appear in court again, on the same charges, in July 2018 and as we discussed going back to New York to cover it, Patti made her announcement. 'I'll stay for that big McGregor court hearing in July because I don't want to leave you in the lurch,' she told me, 'but that will be my last story. I'll be finishing up after that.' It was not a total surprise to me. In the weeks leading up to Patti's resignation, I could sense something was not right. She was unhappy at work. She was not enjoying the hectic, day-to-day news coverage in the way I was, and in the way she once had. It was nothing to do with Conor McGregor. In fact, I suspect that story came as a welcome relief for her.

Away from the court cases and the Oscars' red carpet, the vast majority of our time was spent covering the Trump administration. And, for Patti, that was a problem. She started to hate the rhetoric, the lies, the anger and the divisions. She'd had enough of news and needed a change. She felt bad for leaving, but I understood, and we parted as friends. We had a front-row seat on the chaos, but the difference was that I was in the US as a guest, and I knew my family and I would return home to Ireland when the roller-coaster ride was over. When American colleagues and neighbours said things like, 'I don't know what's happening to our country' or 'Things have never been so divided', it reminded me that while I was covering it, they were living it. Patti decided to move to Hawaii, to become a photographer and a tour guide. She wanted to be far away from Donald Trump's angry tweets and constant controversies.

But, as promised, she was there with me for Conor McGregor's July 2018 court appearance, when he was sentenced to five days of community service for throwing a metal handcart at a bus. After pleading guilty to a reduced charge of disorderly conduct, as part of a plea deal, he was ordered to undergo an anger management programme. Speaking outside the court, Conor McGregor thanked the judge and the district attorney's office and paid tribute to his family, friends and fans for their support.

Patti and I took a taxi from the Brooklyn Courthouse to Penn Station in Manhattan to get our train back to Washington. On board, we chatted about her departure. 'We'll need to organize a going-away party,' I said, but when we compared calendars, it proved difficult to find a date. 'I'll be back in a minute,' I said as I rose from my seat. I went to the train's dining-car and bought beers and snacks. We ate, drank and laughed the whole way back to Washington. A train was perhaps the perfect venue for a farewell party for a pair of co-workers who had spent so much time on the move.

After Patti's departure, I started working with a new cameraman, Kutaba Rashid. Originally from Iraq, he had been living in the US for many years. Although my co-worker had changed, many of the stories we covered remained the same. In March 2019, Conor McGregor was in trouble again. It meant I was on the move once more, this time to Miami Beach, Florida, where the UFC star had been charged with robbery and criminal mischief after being accused of smashing another man's phone. The case was subsequently dropped after the alleged victim withdrew his complaint.

I didn't just report on Conor McGregor's court cases, I also covered his fights in Las Vegas. Billed as the biggest bouts in UFC history, they took place in the massive T-Mobile Arena, just off the famous Las Vegas strip. On my first visit, I booked a hotel for me and Kutaba that was 'just across the street' from the venue, according to Google Maps. 'Across the street' ended up being across a six-lane highway and although we could see the arena in front of us, we ended up having to get taxis as there was no way to walk there. In America, the car is king.

That was something that was on full display at the arena's VIP entrance, where lines of limousines, stretch Humvees and sports cars were dropping off celebrities and millionaires. Of all the shows on in Vegas, a Conor McGregor fight was always the hottest ticket in town. Inside the arena, when there was a break between fights, the cameras would seek out the Hollywood A-listers and sports stars sitting in the front rows and broadcast their faces on the big screens to the cheers of those gathered. Matt Damon, Mel Gibson and Rory McIlroy were among those in attendance.

In January 2020, Conor McGregor defeated Donald 'Cowboy' Cerrone after just forty seconds due to a technical knockout. Standing in the middle of the octagon, McGregor thanked his fans and dedicated his win to the Irish people and his mother: 'I've etched my name in history one more time, for the Irish people and for my Ma back home.'

I had to leave the arena quickly and make my way to a large media tent that had been set up in the car park of the venue. There were hundreds of journalists and photographers from around the world waiting to speak to the victorious McGregor. He fielded a series of questions about his win and as the press conference was wrapping up, Kutaba and I made our way towards the table where he was sitting at the top of the room in the hope of getting a one-on-one interview with him. 'A quick word with RTÉ?' I shouted as he prepared to leave the tent. 'Ah, I recognize you off the telly,' he said to me as he walked over. 'I love US politics and I watch your stuff all the time.' He was wearing a blue three-piece suit with a red flower in his lapel. He was holding a bottle of 'Proper 12' Irish whiskey, a brand he had launched in 2018. I began our interview by asking him what his message was for his Irish fans.

'I'm very grateful for the support of the Irish people. I love my country dearly and have carried the tricolour with me with pride throughout my career. The Irish people are very proud of my successes and I was happy to represent them tonight.' I then asked a follow-up question, wondering what he would say to those many Irish people who were disappointed with his behaviour outside the octagon, following his various court appearances. 'The Irish people celebrate my successes but at the same time, they call me out if I let them down. That affects me and motivates me to be the man that I want to be. I want the Irish people to be proud of me. I know some of the things have not been right and I owned up to that and we move on.'

Outside the arena, I spoke to Irish fans who had travelled over for the fight. They were delighted with McGregor's win and not worried about his legal issues. At first, I thought it would be easy to spot the Irish people – just look for the ones wearing green jerseys or wrapped in tricolours. But that described almost everybody there and I soon realized that the vast majority of them were Americans. They showed their support for their favourite UFC star, not by wearing a Conor McGregor T-shirt, but by wearing an Ireland T-shirt. To them, they were one and the same. McGregor was Ireland and Ireland was McGregor.

For a while, taxi-drivers, waiters and many people I encountered in daily life would say, 'Oh yes, where Conor McGregor comes from', when I mentioned that I was Irish. McGregor himself had done much to foster his Irish image. On fight nights, he would emerge into the arena, wrapped in a tricolour, to the sound of Sinéad O'Connor's rendition of 'The Foggy Dew'. He used this 'Irishness' to market his whiskey, which proved popular in the US. However, many

Irish people were uncomfortable with the fact that Conor McGregor had become a representative for Ireland in the US. He had criminal convictions on both sides of the Atlantic and seemed to be perpetually surrounded by controversy.

His status as an informal ambassador for 'Brand Ireland' did not sit well with those in official circles and that unease came into sharp focus in March 2019. McGregor turned up unexpectedly at the St Patrick's Day parade in Chicago and marched among the VIPs, just a few feet away from Taoiseach Leo Varadkar. It was an awkward moment for the Irish government, which was keen to avoid Mr Varadkar being photographed alongside a man who only days before had been charged with a criminal offence in Florida.

I was covering the parade that day and the fact that Conor McGregor had unexpectedly turned up was a big story. I had to re-edit my TV report. I stayed behind while Kutaba went on ahead to the Taoiseach's next engagement – a boat ride on the Chicago River, which had been dyed green for St Patrick's Day. We agreed that I would meet him at the dock in a few minutes. It was vital that we didn't miss the trip as the Taoiseach was due to address the media on board and we wanted to get his reaction to the surprise appearance of Conor McGregor.

I sent my report and started to make my way towards the pier, but there was a problem. The walk along Michigan Avenue should have taken only a few minutes, but I couldn't move through the thousands of people who had gathered to watch the parade. They were packed shoulder-to-shoulder. I tried to weave my way through the crowd as best I could, but it was difficult as I was holding a heavy camera tripod. 'Excuse me, sorry, can I get by, please?' I tried to be as a polite as I could, but a police officer spotted me and shouted at me to stop pushing, threatening to arrest me! All the while, my phone was buzzing with calls and texts from Kutaba and from the Taoiseach's handlers, telling me that they were preparing to leave.

I eventually made it through the crowd and onto the dock just as the boat was about to depart. On board, we got the Taoiseach's reaction to the unexpected arrival of Conor McGregor. He said he hadn't spoken to the MMA fighter. He was asked if it was appropriate for a man who had made numerous court appearances to be in a parade representing Ireland. 'I think that is up to the organizers of the parade to decide who they want to march. I don't think he was representing the country, that's kind of what I was doing,' he said.

Looking back on it, Leo Varadkar told me that it was one of those things they really didn't have a lot of control over. If they'd had a proper heads-up from the organizers that McGregor was going to be there, they would have been better prepared. 'To a certain extent, you have to be polite about these kinds of things. What we wanted to do was avoid a photograph of the two of us marching together and I think we did manage to avoid that. There was never a picture of the two of us side-by-side and that was the objective there,' he told me.

The intertwining of Conor McGregor with Irish identity had not escaped the former Taoiseach's notice. 'I remember on personal trips to America, people would say to me: "Oh you're from Ireland?" and Conor McGregor would come to mind as quickly as *Riverdance* and Guinness. Even the President of Mongolia, he was a boxer or a martial artist too, and he mentioned Conor McGregor when I met him. He's not as famous as Bono, but he's way up there internationally in terms of people who are associated with Ireland, and I guess it kind of ties into the idea of the "fighting Irish" so it's not an image of Ireland that I warm to, but you have to accept that it's out there.'

Other politicians have attempted to embrace McGregor's star power. The Trump administration had looked at the possibility of recruiting McGregor for an ill-fated $300 million coronavirus advertising campaign ahead of the 2020 presidential election. The taxpayer-funded ads were supposed to 'defeat despair' about the pandemic and promote a positive mood before voters went to the polls. Democrats launched an investigation, claiming the campaign would be used to boost President Trump's poll numbers. The House of Representatives Oversight Committee obtained documents relating to the matter, which included a list of dozens of celebrities who might be recruited to appear in these advertisements. The file, which was called the 'PSA Celebrity Tracker', included details about the demographics that each actor or sports star represented and whether they were supporters of Donald Trump.

According to this document, Conor McGregor would appeal to the general public as well as to 'super-spreaders', people who would be less likely to wear masks and practise social distancing. It added that he had in the past voiced public support for President Trump. In January 2020, he tweeted that Mr Trump was a 'Phenomenal President. Quite possibly the USA goat [greatest of all time]. Most certainly one of them anyway, as he sits atop the shoulders of many amazing giants that came before him.' Donald Trump tweeted his best wishes to the Dublin fighter following his victory over 'Cowboy' Cerrone. 'Congratulations on your big UFC win,' he wrote. My wife used to joke that I spent 50 per cent of my time covering Donald Trump, and 50 per cent covering Conor McGregor. For a while, it was as if those two worlds had collided.

Donald Trump was popular among UFC fans. The president of the UFC, Dana White, campaigned for him and appeared at his rallies. In the run-up to Election 2020, Donald Trump Jr hosted a 'Fighters Against Socialism' bus tour that featured UFC stars urging fans to re-elect the President. When I attended Trump rallies, it was not unusual to see Conor McGregor T-shirts among the crowd and references to his name would almost inevitably follow when I introduced myself as Irish. The fighting, whiskey-drinking 'Irishness' embodied by Conor McGregor may have appealed to many Americans, perhaps even to the President himself, but the Irish government was keen to portray a different image of the country in the US.

A good example of this was the campaign to secure a seat on the United Nations Security Council in New York. United Nations ambassadors were taken to a U2 concert and a performance of *Riverdance*. An 'Irish village' was set up at the UN headquarters showcasing the best of Irish music, culture and food. Conor McGregor was nowhere to be seen. Bono was there, though. He delivered a speech and spent time signing autographs and taking selfies with the UN ambassadors. The charm offensive clearly worked. Ireland won enough votes to claim a seat on the Security Council.

There is another angle to 'Irishness' in America that might not be widely appreciated in Ireland, and that is the shared history that exists with African Americans. Beyoncé, Shaquille O'Neal and Barack Obama all have Irish roots, and it is believed around 38 per cent of African Americans have some Irish ancestry. Dennis Brownlee established the African

American Irish Diaspora Network in 2019 to help connect people who are interested in exploring this heritage. It all began when he started researching his own Irish roots.

'When I was growing up in the sixties, my mother would tell me that we had some Irish ancestry. She was proud of that and wanted to share it with me, but at the time . . . I was more interested in my African heritage, my African American identity and what was happening in the civil rights and black power movement and all that. I put it to the side, never thought about it much,' he said.

Later in life, Dennis moved to Washington DC and became good friends with his neighbour Stella O'Leary, president of Irish American Democrats. 'She implored me to explore my Irish roots and even bought me an ancestry DNA kit. She introduced me to the Irish American community in Washington and made me feel very welcome. We also started thinking about how to commemorate the 175th anniversary of the visit of Frederick Douglass to Ireland.'

Born into slavery, Douglass escaped and went on to become a leading voice in the US abolitionist movement. In 1845 he toured Ireland, giving lectures and selling books, and he was profoundly influenced by his time there. He became friends with Daniel O'Connell, the champion of Catholic Emancipation. Douglass recalled that while in Ireland, he was treated as a man and not as a colour. 'I can truly say, I have spent some of the happiest moments of my life since landing in this country. I seem to have undergone a transformation. I live a new life,' he wrote of his time in Ireland.

The history of relations between African Americans and the Irish also has a more negative side, however. Working-class Irish immigrants and their black neighbours competed for work and social status in nineteenth-century America. In 1863, an Irish-dominated mob killed dozens of people, mostly African Americans, in three days of riots in New York.

According to Dennis Brownlee, 'The relationships Frederick Douglass had in Ireland were very different to the relationships he had with Irish people in America when he returned. Daniel O'Connell admonished the Irish in America for retreating from their moral high ground that had been established in Ireland to fight slavery throughout the world and fight for human rights.'

For some African Americans, an exploration of their Irish roots means confronting the fact that many Irish were slave-owners. This is, as Brownlee points out, a challenging aspect of the shared history: 'It is a difficult discussion for all black people who have heritage that is not entirely African because so many of those relationships were as a result of rape, slavery and abuse. In many black households the origin of the non-black aspect of the family's heritage was suppressed and not talked about because it was so painful. But while that negative aspect of the relationship was true, there were also many neighbourhoods in the nineteenth century where African American communities and Irish communities lived side-by-side in very positive ways, and there were a significant amount of intermarriages between African Americans and Irish Americans, so not all of those relationships were the result of oppression and abuse.'

Dennis Brownlee said he was overwhelmed by the response he has received from the African American community since setting up his network, which he believes will have benefits on both sides of the Atlantic. 'Ireland is changing. Seventeen or 18 per cent of people weren't born there. The complexion of Ireland has changed. Ireland has a lot that it can provide to the African American community and vice-versa. We are trying to connect African American entrepreneurs with business opportunities in Ireland, a country that is the English-speaking bridge to the EU.'

In May 2020, African American Irish dancer Morgan Bullock spoke out about the racist abuse she had received after a video of her performing went viral. Critics accused her of trying to appropriate a culture that was not her own by performing Irish dance, of trying to embrace a tradition that, for some reason, she had no right to.

'I'd never even thought of that being a response I would get because throughout the years, travelling to Ireland, I've always been met with love and support from Irish people and I've fallen in love with the culture,' Morgan told presenter Joe Duffy on *Liveline* on RTÉ Radio 1. 'I think that people are failing to recognize the difference between cultural appropriation and cultural appreciation. And I think what I'm really doing is appreciating the Irish culture. I'm participating in it in a very respectful way, I would say.' Morgan said that most of the negative comments came from people in the US, not in Ireland. It was Americans who seemed to have an issue with who should be taking part in Irish dancing and what an Irish dancer should look like.

The Irish Ambassador to the US, Dan Mulhall, believes there is a growing awareness in America of the diverse country that Ireland has become: 'Younger Americans have a better route of understanding Ireland because of travel, and many are proud of the changes that have occurred in the country. It may not be that old, traditional, sentimental view of Ireland, but instead perhaps an admiration for a country that is progressive and outward looking.'

America, the world's ultimate melting pot of cultures and nationalities, continues to battle with its own issues of identity, race and equality. There are some in the US who still embrace the traditional, simplistic view of 'Irishness' embodied by a whiskey-drinking UFC fighter who gets into trouble with the police. However, an evolving, modern Ireland is being highlighted more and more in America. An image of a nation that is far more representative of what the country looks like today, whether that is a young black woman dancing an Irish jig, or a gay prime minister of Indian heritage who came to Washington and spoke of tolerance and acceptance while the world was watching.

5. Punching above their weight

Forging new links in the US and presenting the modern face of Ireland have become key elements of the country's diplomatic efforts. The Irish Embassy in Washington has built up a network of contacts in the White House and on Capitol Hill and uses behind-the-scenes diplomacy to lobby hard for Irish causes.

During my time in Washington, Irish diplomats secured a big win when the US announced that it was lifting sanctions on the Russian parent company of Aughinish Alumina, based in Limerick. There had been fears for the future of the plant and its 450 workers. During their Oval Office meeting in 2019, Leo Varadkar thanked Donald Trump for his help on the matter: 'Hundreds of jobs were threatened as a result of the Russian sanctions and, with the help of the administration, we were able to save those jobs, so thank you very much for that.' Donald Trump replied by giving the impression that it was all a big secret, gesturing towards us reporters and saying, 'They don't know about that.' Leo Varadkar laughed and said, 'They do now!' For President Trump, the easing of Russian sanctions wasn't something he wanted to broadcast from the rooftops, but the cat had been out of the bag for some time, particularly among Irish officials, who were keen to spread the word.

The Irish lobby came close to securing another victory on E3 visas. A bill that would have given Irish workers access to thousands of US work permits every year was passed by the

US House of Representatives on two separate occasions, in 2018 and again in 2020, but it failed to get the unanimous support that was required in the US Senate. During his visit to Shannon, Donald Trump had said he was supportive of the measure and that he had spoken to the one Republican senator, Tom Cotton of Arkansas, who had blocked the bill. 'We almost made it last time. It was one vote, you know that . . . And I spoke to the one vote, who's a great senator, by the way. And we think we're going to be successful. He's a terrific person. He doesn't mean to do any harm, he was telling me he loves Ireland, actually. So I think we're going to be in good shape.' Despite the President's reassurances, the E3 visa bill was not passed before the end of his term.

That was a setback, but Irish diplomats are regarded by many as among the best in Washington. Donald Trump's former acting Chief of Staff, Mick Mulvaney, told me that he was once asked by a British think-tank if the Irish were better diplomats than the British. 'I knew it was a loaded question, but I looked at the guy and said: "I know I'm not supposed to answer that question directly, but the simple answer is yes." Because it's true, the Irish are just better diplomats than most people and they do punch above their weight in Washington. If you look at the access and the contacts that a small country of five million people has, to put it in context, roughly the same size as New Zealand and I'm not sure if anyone knows who the New Zealand Ambassador is, but everyone knows the Irish Ambassador, Dan Mulhall, and everybody knew Anne Anderson before him. Leo Varadkar was able to come in and meet with dozens of people and sometimes I'd slip up and call him by his first name, which I knew was disrespectful, but that was just the nature of the relationship. It is a close tie.'

Leo Varadkar told me that he hates the phrase 'countries punching above their weight', but that it really is true in Ireland's case. 'The level of access we have to the corridors of power and the boardrooms largely because there is a group of people in Irish America who are now doing very well for themselves, powerful people in business and politics who really do care about the "Old Country" and look for nothing in return, that is not common,' he said.

The Irish influence has not just been felt in the White House, diplomats and officials also have access to the corridors of power on Capitol Hill. In 2021, the Friends of Ireland caucus in the US Congress marked the 40th anniversary of its establishment. The bipartisan group was founded by Irish American politicians, including Senator Ted Kennedy, Senator Daniel Moynihan and the Speaker of the House, Tip O'Neill, who wanted to support peace in Northern Ireland. Democratic Congressman and co-chair of the caucus, Richard Neal, told me that the whole idea of setting up the group was to generate a competing narrative of what could happen peacefully on the island of Ireland: 'It was a direct challenge to much of the gun-running that had been taking place in the United States. For those of us who attended certain events back in those days, frequently at the end of the evening there was a passing around of a hat and while it was advertised as being money for the families in the North, everybody had some idea of how that money was really being used and it was being used for armaments. So, the response was to find a peaceful avenue to channel the grievance that many of us who supported the nationalist position felt, but to do it through the argument for reconciliation.'

The culmination of US involvement in the Northern Ireland peace process was the Good Friday Agreement in 1998.

'I have always congratulated Bill Clinton for standing up to his own State Department,' Richard Neal said. 'It was difficult to convince them that there could be a competing argument when it came to the island of Ireland. They took the position that it was a matter that was internal to the United Kingdom and we took the position that it was a matter of international human rights and it was what eventually brought about the Good Friday Agreement.'

He recalled an evening at the British Embassy in Washington when the Friends of Ireland were invited to British Prime Minister Tony Blair's last public engagement in the US: 'Tony Blair said that the US–UK alliance had been great, but that the one area we disagreed on was Northern Ireland. He thanked the Friends of Ireland for their help getting through the grim moments and the hard days. I was witnessing history, a British prime minister thanking the Friends of Ireland.'

Ireland's top diplomat in Washington, Ambassador Dan Mulhall, said he always found the Friends of Ireland caucus to be extraordinarily open and helpful when it came to listening to Ireland's point of view because they recognized that their predecessors had played an instrumental role in bringing about the Good Friday Agreement and were determined to protect that Agreement through the Brexit process. 'The Friends of Ireland has made an enormous contribution. One of its founding members was then Senator, now President Joseph Biden, so that is a sign of how far back it goes. It goes back to Tip O'Neill, Ted Kennedy and those great Irish Americans who started a tradition of Congressional interest and involvement in the Northern Ireland peace process,' Dan Mulhall told me. 'Move the clock forward to recent years and we see the Friends of Ireland caucus taking a strong position on the Good Friday Agreement and maintaining an open border on the island of Ireland. They weighed in to prevent a hard border being imposed as a consequence of Brexit.'

Concerns about Northern Ireland in the US had eased due to the success of the peace process, but they were reignited once again with Brexit. The House of Representatives Ways and Means Committee is in charge of overseeing trade deals and, as its Chairman, Richard Neal warned repeatedly that there would be no US–UK trade deal if Brexit threatened the Good Friday Agreement or led to the return of a hard border. It was a message echoed by fellow senior Democrats, including the Speaker of the House Nancy Pelosi and then Senate Minority Leader Chuck Schumer. Fears over Brexit and its impact on the peace process subsided following agreement on the Northern Ireland protocol contained within the Brexit Withdrawal Agreement, but in September 2020 there was another dramatic twist in the Brexit journey when the British government announced plans to amend the agreement. It sent shockwaves through the UK, Ireland and all the way to Capitol Hill.

'My phone exploded,' Nancy Pelosi told me, when news broke that Britain was looking to change the deal. I spoke to her after her meeting with UK Foreign Secretary Dominic Raab, who had come to Washington to seek US support for Britain's Brexit position. Speaker Pelosi told me that she had been given assurances by Mr Raab that there would be no construction of physical barriers at the border. In their meeting she had once again warned the UK that there would be no trade deal with the US if Brexit threatened the Good Friday Agreement.

Dominic Raab had found a more sympathetic ear in his

meetings with the Trump administration. After his talks with the US Secretary of State Mike Pompeo, the two men held a joint press conference in which Mr Raab claimed that the threat to the Good Friday Agreement was coming from the EU's politicization of the issue. Mike Pompeo told reporters that the US trusted the UK on Brexit: 'I am confident they'll get it right. We've made clear the importance of the Good Friday Agreement.'

During Dominic Raab's visit to Washington, there was a shot across the bow from Democratic presidential candidate Joe Biden, who warned that the Good Friday Agreement could not become a casualty of Brexit. 'Any trade deal between the US and UK must be contingent upon respect for the Agreement and preventing the return of a hard border. Period,' he tweeted. It was an intervention that was welcomed by the government in Dublin and by the Irish diplomats in Washington.

An Irish official told me that while there was disappointment that the Trump White House appeared to be siding with Boris Johnson on Brexit, there was no great surprise: 'The problem was that no one in the US administration at a political level seemed to have any real understanding of what Brexit was about apart from a knee-jerk dislike by President Trump of the EU, which seemed to be due to the European Union's size and economic clout. The only official who 'got' Brexit was John Bolton and he was very much in sync with the British Embassy on this. We always knew we needed Congress to try to keep the US on the right side of the Brexit debate.'

While the US Vice President Mike Pence was telling Ireland to work with Boris Johnson, senior Democrats were voicing their support for the Good Friday Agreement and the Northern Ireland peace process. It created an impression that Republicans were on one side and Democrats on the other. Not so, insisted Mick Mulvaney, who would go on to become the US Special Envoy for Northern Ireland.

'The personality of Donald Trump and the press coverage of him may have coloured that impression, but after the 2020 election, while I was still Special Envoy for Northern Ireland, it became clear that the policy was not going to change much at all,' he told me. 'I used to joke, there's only two things that are bipartisan in Washington right now, antipathy towards China and favourability towards the island of Ireland. The Good Friday Agreement, in particular, has tremendous bipartisan support. We don't pick sides between the Irish and the British.'

Dan Mulhall worked closely with the Trump administration and met the President on several occasions. 'Diplomats don't get to design the field of play, we play the field as we find it. I came here eight months into the Trump administration so my job was to connect with the administration and to find people I could deal with. I did that and so did my colleagues, that's our job. Our job is not to have biases or preferences in political terms. Our job is to observe the political realities and work within them to extract the best possible outcome for Ireland. I think we have managed, under both Republicans and Democrats, over the last forty years to have a positive relationship with the US.'

Dan Mulhall said he always found Donald Trump in their various meetings to be very friendly and someone who spoke fondly of Ireland. 'I was with him when he visited Ireland and when he stayed at his property in Doonbeg. I usually met him in the company of the Taoiseach [Varadkar], who had managed to build a good rapport with the President. That was important because President Trump was

46

someone who prized the personal connections with leaders and if he liked a leader and got on well with them, that helped a lot.'

'How different will the relationship with the White House be under the Biden administration?' I asked the Ambassador in 2021. 'I think the understanding of us on behalf of President Biden will be something different and special because of his lifelong immersion in Irish affairs, in his Irish heritage and his Irish identity. I think the White House door has always been open, but maybe the welcome on the mat will be a little different,' he said.

I first interviewed Joe Biden in September 2018, a few months before he announced his run for president. I met him at the Irish Ambassador's official residence, a redbrick mansion located in Washington's exclusive Kalorama neighbourhood. Just two doors down there is an enormous house owned by the Amazon billionaire Jeff Bezos. Technically, it is two enormous houses that have been connected. The adjoining mansions used to be a textile museum. In 2016, Jeff Bezos paid $23 million for the 27,000 square foot property. He embarked on an extensive renovation project to turn the museum into the largest home in Washington.

Aside from the Irish Ambassador, his other distinguished neighbours included Barack and Michelle Obama, who rented a nearby mansion after they left the White House. Ivanka Trump and Jared Kushner also lived in the area for a while. The couple were accused of refusing to allow their Secret Service agents to use any of the six bathrooms inside their luxury home. Instead, US taxpayers had to pay $3,000 a month to rent a basement apartment, with a bathroom, from a neighbour of the Kushners. The White House denied that the family had blocked access to their facilities, insisting that it was the decision of the Secret Service not to allow the agents inside.

Perhaps they could have popped around to Jeff Bezos' sprawling mansion where there are twenty-five bathrooms, as well as two elevators, eleven bedrooms, a ballroom, a wine cellar and a cinema. When the renovations of the property were completed in early 2020, the billionaire threw a big party with a guest list that included Bill Gates, Mitt Romney, Ben Stiller, Ivanka Trump and Jared Kushner.

But while Jeff Bezos' palace was still a construction site, there were plenty of other VIPs turning up at neighbouring homes for various parties and events. Joe Biden was at the Irish Ambassador's residence in the autumn of 2018 for the launch of the four-volume *Cambridge History of Ireland*. I had covered several events at the residence before, but this was by far the most crowded. A former Vice President rumoured to be considering a run for the White House was always going to attract big numbers and the room was packed as Mr Biden took to the podium to deliver an address. With Donald Trump's clampdown on border security very much in the news at the time, Joe Biden used his speech as an opportunity to highlight the important role played by immigrants in the emergence of modern America.

He made reference to his own Irish roots, which he traces to counties Mayo and Louth, and said that immigrants had 'made us who we are', adding that there was a passion that 'runs through the bloodstream of Americans and Irish Americans alike. When you know suffering, when you know pain, when you have gone through difficulties, when you've been through the short end of the power spectrum, you understand, you have insight, you have empathy that I think is greater than most people ordinarily have. I really believe that. I believe that is part of what we inherited from our parents. Everyone, no matter who they are, is entitled to be treated with dignity. Xenophobia steps in every once in a while . . . but we always overcome it.' Joe Biden described the current treatment of immigrants in the US as a disgrace and said the W. B. Yeats quote, 'a terrible beauty is born', could be applied to modern-day America.

Dan Mulhall had hosted Joe Biden in his home on several occasions. 'He's always extremely gracious and extremely friendly. Very often I find in my career, when you invite a celebrity to an event, they come for ten minutes, they shake hands, they make themselves visible and then they go to another event. Every time President Biden has come to this house, he has stayed for a couple of hours, he hasn't rushed away, and I could tell he took genuine pleasure in being in an Irish Embassy because it was a reflection of his identity as an Irish American . . . when he was here for the launch of the *Cambridge History of Ireland*, he spoke with great passion and sentiment about his Irish upbringing in Scranton and his grandfather and his mother.'

After Joe Biden's speech, he spent an hour shaking hands and taking selfies with the guests. His staff had told us that he would not be doing media interviews, which was met with a giggle and the words 'Yeah, right' from one US journalist. Biden has a reputation as someone who likes to talk and is not camera-shy. Indeed, he spoke to everyone at the event that night, whether they were guests or reporters, much to the annoyance of his handlers, who were trying to escort him from the room.

There was a large group of US journalists there, more than I had expected. They asked him about his presidential ambitions and whether he would be running for the Democratic nomination, to which he gave vague, non-committal answers. The reporters had also come that night to ask Joe Biden about his thoughts on the allegations of sexual assault that had recently been made against Donald Trump's Supreme Court nominee Brett Kavanaugh. The US media were particularly interested in Mr Biden's views on the matter because of its similarities to another controversy, twenty-seven years earlier. Joe Biden was the Chairman of the Senate Judiciary Committee and in 1991 he oversaw the confirmation hearings for Supreme Court Justice Clarence Thomas, who had been accused of sexual harassment by Anita Hill. The young African American woman testified before the hearings and was grilled by an all-male, all-white panel of senators. Joe Biden was criticized for his handling of the matter, accused of insensitivity and of failing to take the allegations seriously. He later apologized to Anita Hill.

Almost thirty years later, he told reporters at the Irish Ambassador's residence that the Kavanaugh allegations had brought back all the 'complicated issues that were there' back in 1991. He said that any woman's public claims of assault should be presumed to be true. 'For a woman to come forward in the glaring lights of focus, nationally, you've got to start off with the presumption that at least the essence of what she's talking about is real, whether or not she forgets facts, whether or not it's been made worse or better over time,' he said.

His handlers eventually prised him away from the US journalists. As he neared the exit, I took my opportunity to get a quick interview with him. What better way to open a conversation with Joe Biden than with a reference to Irish poetry? 'You quoted Yeats and spoke about a *terrible beauty* in your speech,' I said. 'Do you really think things are that bad in this country right now?'

'I think this idea that a terrible beauty has been born is more appropriate today than at any time in American history,' he replied. 'America should just stand up, man, and there's no reason why America shouldn't be leading the world again. We just need to get our confidence back.' 'Are you the one to lead that change, are you going to run for president?' I asked. 'Whoever does, I am going to help,' he said as he was ushered out the door by his handlers.

The election was still two years away and it was impossible to predict who the Democratic nominee would be. One thing was certain, though – whoever was chosen to run against President Donald Trump would have a serious fight on their hands.

6. 'See you at the Starting Gate'

'The core values of this nation, our standing in the world, our very democracy, everything that has made America, America, is at stake. That's why today, I'm announcing my candidacy for President of the United States.'

In April 2019, a few months after my interview with him at the Irish Ambassador's Residence, Joe Biden formally announced his run for the presidency. In a video message he referred to the white supremacist rally in Charlottesville, Virginia, in August 2017 and Donald Trump's handling of the aftermath: 'He said there were some very fine people on both sides. With those words, the President of the United States assigned a moral equivalence between those spreading hate and those with the courage to stand against it. And in that moment, I knew the threat to this nation was unlike any I had ever seen in my lifetime.' He described the election as a 'battle for the soul of this nation'.

Joe Biden was joining an already crowded field of candidates for the Democratic nomination. The 76-year-old became the instant frontrunner in the opinion polls, but critics suggested his age was a problem. He also had to address allegations that he had made women feel uncomfortable because of unwanted touching. He denied that he had acted inappropriately but said that he would be more considerate in the future: 'Social norms are changing. I understand that, and I've heard what these women are saying. Politics to me has always been about making connections, but I will be more mindful about respecting personal space in the future.'

'Welcome to the race Sleepy Joe,' Donald Trump tweeted when Mr Biden announced his candidacy. 'I only hope you have the intelligence, long in doubt, to wage a successful primary campaign. It will be nasty – you will be dealing with people who truly have some very sick & demented ideas. But if you make it, I will see you at the Starting Gate!'

By this time, I was working with a new cameraman, Murray Pinczuk. He was born and raised not far from Washington DC. In a city filled with 'blow-ins', my new co-worker was a true native. I had been introduced to him by my former colleague Patti. They had worked together on several TV projects over the years and now I was receiving the benefit of his long experience and calm demeanour.

When the news broke that Joe Biden was entering the presidential race, Murray and I were in the Williamsburg neighbourhood of Brooklyn, filming a report about an outbreak of measles among the Orthodox Jewish community in the area. Although it is a suburb of New York, walking through Williamsburg was like being transported to another place and another time. Traditional Jewish music played from open storefronts, the signs over businesses were written in Yiddish and almost everyone we encountered on the street was dressed in the distinctive clothing associated with Orthodox Judaism.

A group of young boys approached us, their sidelocks, or *payot*, curling out from under their hats. 'Are you Jewish?' they asked us. I replied no; Murray told them that he was. 'What's your name?' they asked and when he told them it was Murray, they were confused. 'No, what's your Jewish name?' they asked. 'It's Moshe,' he replied, 'but I don't use that name.' Now I was the one who was confused. After the boys left, Murray explained that many Jewish people have a Hebrew name that is different from their everyday name and used only in a religious context. The boys we had met were Hasidic Jews and would use their Hebrew names all the time, which was why they could not understand why my cameraman was not going by 'Moshe'.

Many of the locals we encountered were unhappy with the media intrusion that had become a feature of their district since it had been dubbed the 'measles epicentre' of the US. They didn't like the negative attention and we were met with some hostility as we tried to interview residents on the street. Joe Biden's announcement of his candidacy forced us to abandon our measles story for another day and switch focus to the breaking news. With the deadline for the *Six One News* bulletin back home in Ireland fast approaching, there was no time to find a different location for our live report, so we set up our tripod, camera and lights on the side of the street in Williamsburg.

It is a conspicuous operation and it attracted plenty of comments, not all of them positive. 'Why are you here?' one young man asked aggressively. 'To talk about the measles and make us look bad,' another said. 'Actually, we're doing a report on Joe Biden,' I replied. Which, at that exact moment in time, was not a lie. 'Oh, is Joe Biden coming here today?' came the confused response. The confusion increased when I said he wasn't, but perplexity is preferable to annoyance on the street, so I didn't enlighten them any further. We were left alone as I reported on Mr Biden's presidential bid. Many Irish viewers were no doubt also left confused, wondering where on Earth we were reporting from with the passers-by in the background wearing traditional clothing, including tall furry black hats known as *shtreimels*.

Joe Biden's first campaign rally was at a trade union event in Pittsburgh, Pennsylvania. It was a clear signal of intent and a look ahead to his election strategy. Donald Trump had defeated Hillary Clinton in 2016 by winning over blue-collar workers in the Rust Belt areas of Pennsylvania, Michigan and Wisconsin. These traditionally Democratic voters had felt let down by their party and gave their backing to Mr Trump. Joe Biden was determined to win them back. 'If I'm going to be able to beat Donald Trump in 2020, it's going to happen here,' Mr Biden told his Pittsburgh rally. 'Donald Trump is the only president who has decided not to represent the entire country. We need a president who will work for all Americans.'

As a representative from Philadelphia, Democratic Congressman Brendan Boyle understands the politics of Pennsylvania better than most. He apologized for the mess as we arrived in his office on Capitol Hill for an interview. The walls had just been repainted and stacks of framed photos, paintings and certificates were piled up on the furniture and on the floor. Just three framed photos were left on display, and Joe Biden was in two of them. In late 2018, just after the midterm elections, Brendan Boyle had visited Mr Biden in his office to try to convince him to run for the White House.

'Democrats had won back the House for the first time in a decade,' he told me. 'I was concerned that there was a narrative in the media that essentially the Democratic Party had changed so much that it wouldn't nominate Joe Biden. I knew that was false because I went out personally campaigning for a number of Democratic colleagues and I saw how Joe Biden was popular in suburban Philadelphia, rural Iowa, in small towns, large towns, in African American, white,

Asian and Latino areas. I also felt that after the 2018 mid-terms there were some Democrats who thought beating Trump was going to be easy. And I kept saying, no, he has a built-in base, this election will be close.

'I sat down with Joe Biden in his office and had a long conversation with him. I said, I'm sorry to put pressure on you because it's always a big decision and there are a lot of sacrifices any time you run for office. I told him that if Donald Trump wins a second term, the United States of America will be a very different country and will be permanently changed as a result. I urged him to run. I thought he would be our best candidate against Trump and the best candidate to win the nomination and I wanted him to hear that in case there were others in his ear who were telling him the opposite.'

When Joe Biden announced his candidacy in April 2019, Brendan Boyle endorsed him immediately. In the early Democratic primaries, however, his candidate was struggling, and friends and reporters were telling Congressman Boyle that it was all over.

'There is no question that after New Hampshire, things looked pretty tough. But I knew once we got to Nevada and South Carolina the race would look different, and more of the remaining contests would look like those states than Iowa and New Hampshire. I didn't think it would turn around so quickly. I thought he would win South Carolina and take the lead on Super Tuesday and then it would be a contest, but it happened so much faster. He won on Super Tuesday, the world shut down for COVID and then it was all over, he was the nominee.'

Joe Biden did not have big, traditional rallies because of the pandemic, but of the few campaign events he did hold, many were in the key swing state of Pennsylvania. Congressman Boyle gestured to one of the three, upright photos in his office. His young daughter was standing in front of Joe Biden on a street, both wearing masks. 'That's the most special memory I have from the campaign. It's outside my office in Northeast Philadelphia, two days before Election Day. I had invited President Biden to do a campaign event in the area. He was very gracious. He mentioned that I was the first member of Congress to endorse him and that's the kind of guy he is, he didn't forget that. It is a very special memory for me that just two days before Election Day, he was there, interacting with my family and my supporters. Four days after Election Day, on the Saturday, finally the votes came in from Philadelphia and it was our city that put Pennsylvania over the top for Joe Biden, and then it was our state that clinched the victory for him.'

'So what sort of a person is Joe Biden?' I asked Brendan. He began his answer by calling him Joe, before correcting himself and referring to him as the President. 'He wears his heart on his sleeve. He is a very nice, caring, empathetic guy. What you see is what you get and he is exactly the same in private as he is in public. He's also very knowledgeable about public policy. Just a wonderful person and, I have to say, you couldn't have more of a contrast between the last person in the Oval Office and this one.'

Brendan Boyle is the only member of the US Congress with a parent who was born in Ireland. His father, Frank, migrated from Donegal in 1970. Pride in his Irish roots is something Brendan shares with Joe Biden. 'There is a lot on the plate of any American president, but we have someone who is knowledgeable about Ireland, who personally cares about it and that goes for an awful lot,' he said.

Back in 2019, while this most Irish of candidates was

announcing his White House run, Ireland was preparing for a visit from the sitting President, Donald Trump. In the weeks leading up to the trip there was confusion over whether or not he was actually coming, when exactly he was going to come and where he would be staying. Plans were being put in place for the visit from the Irish side, but the US had yet to make any formal announcement about the trip. Calls and emails to the White House press office were met with 'no comment' or 'no updates to announce at this stage'.

The only way I was going to get a direct answer was to ask the man himself. Before coronavirus restrictions reduced the level of access to the President, journalists from America and from around the world would line up on the South Lawn of the White House in the hope of getting a quick word with Donald Trump. In Ireland we call these short, impromptu media opportunities 'doorsteps', in the US they call them 'gaggles', but these particular encounters became known as 'chopper talk'. That is because they took place as Mr Trump was about to board the presidential helicopter, Marine One. He would speak to reporters as the chopper waited nearby, its engines roaring and rotor blades spinning. The whole thing was a circus. Dozens of journalists, camera crews and photographers packed into a tiny space, cordoned off by a rope, everyone shouting their questions at once. You're not just competing with other reporters, your voice also needs to be heard over the noise of the helicopter. It offered cover for Donald Trump because if he didn't like a question, he could just move on to the next, claiming he couldn't hear. After I had two failed attempts to get my question answered on two separate days, my wife Joanna suggested I shout the word Doonbeg. 'Who knows,' she said, 'maybe hearing the name of his Irish golf course will grab his attention?'

It was a hot day in late May and the media pack had already been standing in the baking sun for some time before the President finally emerged from the White House to board his helicopter. As he passed the waiting reporters, he stopped and answered questions about the Mueller Report, Russia, China, Venezuela, Israel, John McCain, election interference, abortion and, thankfully, Ireland.

'Are you going to be travelling to Doonbeg when you visit Ireland?' I shouted.

As Joanna had predicted, the mention of his own golf course caught his attention. He made eye contact with me and walked in my direction.

'Well, we're going to be staying at Doonbeg in Ireland because it's convenient and it's a great place. But it's convenient. We'll be meeting with a lot of the Irish officials, and it'll be an overnight stay. And I look forward to that.' In his answer to me, he had used the word 'convenient' twice. Was it a case of 'the lady doth protest too much'? Was the President anticipating the inevitable backlash from the media as he prepared, once again, to spend US taxpayers' money at one of his own resorts?

'What will you be discussing with the Taoiseach?' I asked in a follow-up question.

'A lot of the things that you would think,' came his rather non-committal reply. It brought back memories of those vague Trumpian answers in Shannon Airport five years earlier.

Donald Trump's visit to Ireland in June 2019 was brief, with few public engagements, and there were mixed views about the substance of the trip. In advance of the visit the White House said the President and the Taoiseach would discuss 'a range of bilateral issues as well as shared international interests and priorities', adding that they would 'pick up on some of the issues they discussed' during their St Patrick's Day meeting in March. Critics of the US President said the visit was just an opportunity for him to play golf at his Doonbeg resort. Others argued that it was about far more than that. It was a chance to celebrate US–Irish relations and provided an opportunity for Irish officials to speak directly with the most powerful administration in the world.

There was controversy ahead of the visit over where the meeting between Donald Trump and Leo Varadkar would take place. The US side was pushing for Doonbeg, the Irish government suggested Dromoland Castle in county Clare. They settled on Shannon Airport.

'I wasn't overly pushed about where I met him but my people, more so the civil servants than anyone else, thought it wouldn't be a great look for me to be in his resort, so they looked at alternatives, like Dromoland,' Leo Varadkar recalled. 'I think I suggested Shannon as the easiest, most obvious, convenient place. I was never pushed about that sort of stuff, but your protocol people look out for you on that and determine that it would be a bad idea to be in a Trump resort, whatever about attending a dinner there, but that the actual meeting should happen elsewhere. I doubt Donald Trump was wasting much time or ruminating on where he met me either. I'd say he was just told by his people: "Your man can't come to Doonbeg, so meet him at the airport instead."'

Mick Mulvaney told me that the controversy over the US President staying at Doonbeg, and potentially holding his meetings there, was a 'tempest in a teapot' and something they had become used to in the Trump administration.

'There is so much that goes into the planning of a meeting between world leaders,' he told me. 'There are all sorts of mundane things to think about. Do we have to shut down all the roads in county Clare? Is there somewhere to land a helicopter? Is there a facility large enough for all the support staff? It was just another logistics conversation, but because, in large part, it was Donald Trump, it became a controversy. I absolutely see why this controversy exists. A president spending taxpayers' money at his own facility. I get that, but we were going to spend the money at one place or another and it's about choosing the very best place to stay. And if you know anything about Doonbeg, it is remote and it is easy to seal off from the area around it. When it's the President of the United States, security is paramount. If we had put him in the Shelbourne Hotel in the centre of Dublin, they would have closed off every road around [St] Stephen's Green for the duration of his stay and that would have been a tremendous inconvenience and created ill-will that wasn't necessary. Yes, there were criticisms, but I can assure you there was method to the madness and, ultimately, we were very comfortable with the decision.'

Donald Trump might not have shut down Dublin city centre, but the visit to Ireland did highlight what a polarizing figure he was. In the US, I had encountered a level of admiration from his staunch supporters matched only by the level of disdain from his detractors. I saw that replicated during his Ireland visit, with locals in Doonbeg celebrating his arrival, while protesters gathered in Shannon and Dublin.

Demonstrators marched outside the airport as the Taoiseach and the US President met inside. The two leaders sat at one end of a meeting room while members of the media pushed to get as close as we could to hear the remarks.

'Probably you'll ask me about Brexit because I just left some very good people who are very involved with Brexit, as you know,' Donald Trump said at the start of the meeting. 'And I think it will all work out very well, and also for you with your wall, your border.'

Leo Varadkar quickly replied, 'I think the one thing we want to avoid, of course, is a wall or border between us.' He had never been shy about correcting Donald Trump or offering contrarian views in front of the cameras. I asked Leo Varadkar if he thought this annoyed the President.

'I'm not sure he was all that bothered. I think that is just the way he is,' he said. 'To the extent that he knew who I was, I did get the impression that he kind of liked me, so that probably gave me a bit more latitude. He did take a dislike to other people and he didn't take a disliking to me. My main objective with Donald Trump was to ensure he didn't dislike us because this was a man who could do you real harm if he took a dislike to you or your country.' I recall that on more than one occasion Mr Trump had referred to Leo Varadkar and himself as 'becoming fast friends'.

'And what about Donald Trump's knowledge of Ireland and Irish issues?' I asked Leo Varadkar. 'I think it's fair to say that he would not have had a detailed knowledge of the political history of Ireland, partition, our membership of the EU, use of the euro, etc. That would have been very different to Joe Biden, Barack Obama or Hillary Clinton, all of whom would have an encyclopaedic knowledge of Ireland and the EU.'

Mick Mulvaney, Donald Trump's former acting Chief of Staff, said his former boss was always very interested in the UK and Ireland. 'This was in large part because of his ancestry. His mother was from Scotland, so he always had a close interest in that part of the world. I think it was fair to say he was as interested in Northern Ireland as he was in the

Republic. He would talk to me very regularly about the history of Northern Ireland and was familiar with Gerry Adams and some of his history, like his famous trip to Washington DC a generation ago. Obviously when it comes to the Republic, he is heavily invested there and has spent a lot of time there. Doonbeg is one of his most famous and high-profile properties. Briefing President Trump about Ireland was entirely different to, let's say, briefing him about India, where you would be starting from scratch. He was very familiar with and very interested in Ireland and I hope the Irish recollection of his trips will be generally positive.'

Mick Mulvaney accompanied Donald Trump on his June 2019 visit to Ireland. 'My memory was meeting the Taoiseach at the airport and there was a very warm welcome. You would always expect that from the Irish. Donald Trump can be a very divisive figure, but that was all put aside as we were received in a small holding room in Shannon Airport where we met with the Taoiseach and his team. The President was struck by the warmth and genuineness of the reception.'

I asked Mick Mulvaney what Donald Trump was like as a boss. 'Did he shout at you? Did he get angry? Were you ever afraid of him? Did you row?'

'Yes, all of the above, I guess!' he replied. 'It was a very dynamic relationship. I've worked with and for similar people in my history, it's one of the reasons I enjoyed the job as much as I did. It was not surprising. I didn't know Donald Trump very well, I'd only known him for two years when I took the job, but that gave me an advantage over my predecessors. Reince Preibus had only known him for a few months, John Kelly had only known him for a few months. I'd worked with him in the cabinet for two years, so I knew what I was getting into. I would describe him as this: he was always tough, sometimes combative, but never unreasonable.'

During the 2019 St Patrick's Day visit, the 'Brexit shambles' had become even more shambolic and was dominating the news agenda back home in Ireland. It also dominated proceedings at that year's Oval Office meeting between Donald Trump and Leo Varadkar and was the first thing mentioned by the President when he welcomed his guest. 'It's a great honour to have the Prime Minister of Ireland here. As you know, he's in a very complicated position right now because of Brexit. You're going to have to tell me what's happening. You're going to have to, perhaps, tell the world what's happening because I'm not sure anybody knows,' Mr Trump said.

Looking back on his various meetings with Donald Trump, Leo Varadkar told me that their conversations were always very interesting and that Mr Trump was always very personable. 'I know he doesn't drink, but he's the kind of guy you might go for a drink with if he did. He was always very friendly and always made you feel very welcome, but he was the big personality. It felt like you were the next guest on his talk show. A combination of appearing on a talk show and going in to see a king in his court. You sit there beside the king and all his courtiers are there. He'd have several cabinet members and senior advisers with him, people I wouldn't drag into a meeting with another head of government, and he'd point to them for a reply and say things like: "You sort that out!" Something I'd never experienced with any other heads of state or government.'

Leo Varadkar saw Donald Trump as someone who could be witty and was liable to make fun of his guests. 'He was very different to someone like Mitch McConnell, who was quite formal by comparison. I remember when we were talking about our tax rules, and how they benefit us and American companies, and we would be ready to answer the President's questions and he'd go, "Ah, it's OK, I know you don't want to talk about that, we can talk about something else."'

'He wouldn't be a man for detail, but he liked to get to the point,' Leo Varadkar told me. But sometimes, those points could be a little random and unexpected. While making small talk, Donald Trump was liable to bring up anything, whatever happened to be on his mind. 'He would often be focused on a particular thing on a particular day. One day it was Beto O'Rourke. He had seen one of his videos and Beto, like a lot of American politicians, does a lot of pointing. I don't know if they get training in pointing school or something. But [Donald Trump] said, "You see the way he's pointing? That means he's crazy." It was similar to Bernie [Sanders]. He thought he was crazy because he did a lot of pointing in his videos.'

One Irish official I spoke to who was also in those Trump–Varadkar meetings described them as odd and unpredictable. 'Donald Trump never followed an agenda. He jumped around from topic to topic and clearly had never been briefed or read any papers. He didn't know any details and just flew by his pants and street smarts, which were considerable, though no substitute for facts. Mr Trump's favourite tactic seemed to be to ask the Taoiseach what he thought about something and then pretty much repeat back what Leo Varadkar had said, in his own words. It always reminded me of the kid who had not done his homework.'

Also sitting in on those Oval Office meetings was Mick Mulvaney. He recalled beer being mentioned on one occasion. 'Early on, John Kelly, another Irish American, was the

Chief of Staff and I was in the meeting as the head of the Office of Budget Management. We were discussing trade and the President was talking with the Taoiseach about the things we trade in. When Leo mentioned Guinness, the President looked at John Kelly and me and said, "If these two guys die, then sales of Guinness to the US would be in real trouble!"' No doubt there was lots of laughter from the assembled audience as they prepared for the next guest on the Trump talk show.

But while the President was busy with foreign trips and hosting world leaders, Election 2020 was fast approaching, and the Democrats were getting ready to pick their candidate.

7. All eyes on Iowa

Iowa farmer Aaron Lehman crawled through a tiny door into an enormous grain silo to check his harvest. It was a tight squeeze, and things were getting even tighter. The crop he was inspecting had been hit hard by the trade war between the US and China. As a grower of corn and soybeans, Lehman felt the brunt of tariffs and falling exports. He, like many of his fellow farmers in Iowa, was struggling to make ends meet.

'Farmers have been meeting with landlords, bankers and suppliers, trying to cut costs. It's a tough time right now,' he told me. He was the president of the Iowa Farmers' Union and described it as a stressful time for members. 'They are reporting high debt ratios and bankruptcies. The stress hotlines that farmers can phone are getting lots and lots of calls.' Many farmers who had supported Donald Trump in the 2016 election were thinking about where to go next. 'The approach the President takes with our trade partners has been so acidic. Instead of making trade friends, we are making trade enemies all over the world,' Lehman said.

Donald Trump won Iowa in 2016 and managed to win it again four years later. The state attracted a lot of attention in early 2020, for a different reason. The Iowa caucuses kicked off the Democratic primary season. It was only the start of a long process, but the winner of Iowa traditionally receives a boost in media coverage and funding, providing plenty of momentum as the primary season gets underway. Candidates who do badly in the state often see their money and support evaporate quickly and are forced to pull out of the running. Since 2000, the winner of the Iowa caucus has eventually gone on to become the Democratic nominee – but not in 2020.

A winter election in Ireland always leads to warnings of dark evenings and cold weather for canvassers, but campaign workers in Iowa have to brave sub-zero temperatures in the run up to the state's caucus. While the conditions might be freezing, Iowa is traditionally where the race for the White House starts to heat up.

It was a crowded field and all the candidates spent a lot of time in the small farm state. The Democratic voters of Iowa were spoiled. They had their pick of events where they could hear speeches from those vying for their party's nomination, and they could also meet household names like Joe Biden and Bernie Sanders. A billionaire named Tom Steyer was also quite well known at the time. He had spent millions of dollars on TV ads in his bid for the Democratic nomination. I went along to one of his campaign events. It was taking place in a small office building on the outskirts of Des Moines that one could easily miss were it not for the large, branded campaign bus parked outside between high mounds of snow. It was early February, just before the pandemic hit, and in a scene that would soon become unimaginable, dozens of members of the media and supporters were packed into a tiny room. It was before the term 'social distancing' had entered the daily lexicon and we were just glad to come in from the cold.

Enthusiastic canvassers, who were wearing blue hoodies emblazoned with the candidate's name, started cheering when Tom Steyer arrived. He was wearing his signature red tartan tie, which was seen so often on the campaign trail that it ended up with two Twitter accounts of its own. Social media users would ask why a billionaire appeared to own only one tie. Steyer explained that he wore Scottish tartan ties every day. 'You gotta dress up for a fight,' he told the *Washington Post* in a profile piece back in 2013.

After delivering his speech at his campaign event in Des Moines, the candidate embarked on a rather bizarre motivation-building exercise by getting all his supporters to chant: 'I believe that we will win, I believe that we will win!' Perhaps the power of positive thinking helped Tom Steyer make his billions, but it wasn't working in politics. Iowa holds caucuses as opposed to a primary. Voters physically show up in a town hall or a school gym and listen to canvassers promoting their candidate. They then move to a particular part of the room to show their support for their chosen nominee. If a candidate doesn't have enough supporters to meet the threshold, the voters reconvene and go to those candidates who are still in play. Tom Steyer was struggling in the polls, so I asked him who he would like his supporters to back if he was eliminated.

'Look, my job is to go out and talk to as many people as possible in Iowa and meet them face-to-face and that is exactly what I am going to do. We want to come out of here with momentum going into the early primary states. That is all I'm focused on and I haven't thought of one other thing,' he told me.

Some of those attending Tom Steyer's campaign rally still hadn't made up their minds about who they'd be voting for. 'I am going to see every candidate, to hear what they have to say,' a woman told me. 'It has been fascinating to be up close, to meet them and to see them, unvarnished.'

The Iowa caucus is an unusual beast and a sight to behold.

The Precinct 62 caucus was held in a basketball arena in Drake University in Des Moines. Democratic voters filled the seats that lined the basketball court in the centre of the hall. The announcer welcomed everyone and paid tribute to the youngest voters in the room – those who had recently turned eighteen. There was also a special mention for the oldest caucus-goer present, 96-year-old Marie.

The atmosphere was warm and friendly as the business of the night got underway. Voters were instructed to move and sit in areas associated with their candidate of choice. Counters then passed through the crowds, tallying the numbers. Husband and wife David Fautsch and Elizabeth Talbert were backing different candidates. David was a Pete Buttigieg supporter, but Elizabeth was voting for Senator Elizabeth Warren. Did it lead to arguments over the dinner table? 'Not at all, we're a "beat Trump" family, whoever the candidate is,' Elizabeth told me.

The caucus was well organized and efficient, a far cry from the chaos and confusion that were to follow. Problems reporting data from precincts around Iowa led to massive delays. It took days to finally declare a winner, and even then the outcome was vague. Pete Buttigieg won the most delegates, but Bernie Sanders won the popular vote. Joe Biden, the frontrunner in the polls, had a poor showing, but that was not clear on the night of the vote because of problems with the count.

Joe Biden's election night event was taking place at the same university, in a building in another part of the campus, and I went along to hear his address to supporters. His campaign had not got off to the start he wanted but, as all candidates do, he put on a brave face as he and his wife, Jill, bounded onto the stage. They smiled and pointed at people in the crowd while Jackie Wilson's 'Higher and Higher' blared from the speakers. He told the audience that he felt good, but that it was going to be a long night. 'The Iowa Democratic Party is working to get the raw results straight. Indications are it will be close. We will walk out of here with our share of delegates. We do not know what it is yet, but we feel good about where we are, so we go on to New Hampshire, Nevada, South Carolina, and well beyond. We are in this for the long haul,' he told his cheering supporters. I was hoping to shout a question at Joe Biden at the end of his speech, but I had no chance of being heard over the deafening music. The volume of Jackie Wilson was turned up 'higher and higher' as he left the stage.

Iowa was quickly followed by New Hampshire, and again Joe Biden failed to live up to his frontrunner status. He had a disastrous showing, coming in fifth place behind Bernie Sanders, Pete Buttigieg, Amy Klobuchar and Elizabeth Warren. He didn't even hang around in New Hampshire for the results to come in. At his primary-night event he addressed supporters via a live-stream from South Carolina. 'Now we are moving on to Nevada and South Carolina and beyond,' he said. 'We'll see you in the general,' he added, but at that point it looked like Joe Biden had a major fight on his hands to reach the general election.

He had a better performance in the next contest, in Nevada, coming second to Bernie Sanders. Then it all changed with South Carolina. Congressman James Clyburn, the highest-ranking African American in the US House of Representatives, endorsed Joe Biden four days before the South Carolina primary. It was a crucial vote of confidence. Biden needed a win in South Carolina or his campaign would be over. He called the state his firewall and was relying on a strong showing from

African American voters. An endorsement from one of the most prominent black politicians in the US could not have come at a better time.

'I want the public to know that I am voting for Joe Biden. South Carolina should be voting for Joe Biden,' James Clyburn said at a news conference. 'I know Joe. We know Joe. But most importantly, Joe knows us,' he added. 'I know his heart. I know who he is. I know what he is. I know where this country is. We are at an inflection point. I am fearful for the future of this country. I'm fearful for my daughters and their future, and their children and their children's future. It is time for us to restore this country's dignity, this country's respect. That is what is at stake this year. And I can think of no one better suited, better prepared. I can think of no one with the integrity, no one more committed to the fundamental principles to make this country what it is, than my good friend, my late wife's great friend, Joe Biden.'

The endorsement rescued the Biden campaign, and he would go on to win South Carolina with a massive 48 per cent share of the vote, well ahead of Bernie Sanders on 20 per cent and billionaire Tom Steyer on 11 per cent. The man who had chanted 'I believe that we will win' back in Iowa had pulled off a better-than-expected performance, but it wasn't enough to rescue his bid for the nomination and he dropped out of the race.

Next came Super Tuesday, the biggest single day of the Democratic primary season. Voters cast their ballots in fourteen US states and in the US territory of American Samoa. Democrats abroad also began voting. The early states of Iowa, New Hampshire, Nevada and South Carolina were important for candidate momentum and profile, but at this point of the contest it was all about delegates.

At least 1,991 pledged delegates were needed to win the Democratic nomination on the first ballot at the party's convention. On Super Tuesday there were a massive 1,357 delegates up for grabs, that was more than one-third of the total delegate count. Big states were voting, like California, where 415 pledged delegates were available, and Texas with its 228 delegates.

To put those numbers in context, only around 150 delegates had been allocated up to this point. The Vermont senator Bernie Sanders was leading in the delegate count, but only just. Joe Biden wasn't far behind, thanks to his convincing win in South Carolina. He was hoping that the victory would give him a big Super Tuesday boost and see him do well in other states with large African American populations, like Tennessee, Alabama, North Carolina and Virginia.

But when it came to the two biggest states up for grabs, California and Texas, Bernie Sanders was ahead in the polls. A progressive candidate to the left of the Democratic Party had become the frontrunner because there were so many moderates running on the other side, splitting the vote. There needed to be dropouts so that centrist voters could unite behind one candidate to take on Sanders.

That had started to happen in the days leading up to Super Tuesday. Pete Buttigieg and Amy Klobuchar suspended their campaigns and, along with former candidate Beto O'Rourke, all endorsed Joe Biden. It was starting to look like a two-horse, Bernie–Biden race, but not quite. The big question was, how would Michael Bloomberg do?

The billionaire former mayor of New York had skipped the early voting states and had instead pumped hundreds of millions of dollars of his own money into campaigning in Super Tuesday contests. Virginia was one of the biggest states voting that day, with 99 delegates up for grabs. An Arlington high-school cafeteria had been converted into a polling station and I was covering the election from there. In the corner of the room there was an old piano. At a quiet moment, during a long day, an election worker started playing the theme tune from the *Charlie Brown* cartoon series, a light-hearted soundtrack for the voters who had gathered to cast their ballots in the race for the Democratic nomination. Despite the child-like background music, the Democrats I spoke to that day were all united in a very serious mission: to get Donald Trump out of office.

Jackie Johnson told me that she was an Elizabeth Warren supporter but had switched her allegiance in recent days because she wanted to back a candidate who could win the nomination and the White House. 'I voted for Mike Bloomberg. These are challenging times, and a challenging approach is what we need,' she said. Martina Smith had also voted for Michael Bloomberg: 'I'm not sure he's the right person, but I felt he's the strongest to stand up to Trump and I'll vote for a rabid dog before I'll vote for Donald Trump!'

Joe Biden was hoping that those all-important endorsements he had received from former candidates would give him a boost. Virginia couple John Kettering and Sharon Perales had been backing Amy Klobuchar until she dropped out. 'I voted for Joe Biden, after my candidate endorsed him last night. It was a last-minute change for me,' Sharon said. Derrick Malis voted for Bernie Sanders: 'He's a socialist and so am I [and] I think he'll bring transformation to this country.'

Although I had met quite a few Michael Bloomberg supporters at the Virginia polling station, it was not indicative of a wider trend. Having spent millions of dollars campaigning in Super Tuesday states he managed to pull off only one victory, winning the tiny US territory of American Samoa (pop. *c.* 55,000). He suspended his campaign and endorsed Joe Biden, who was celebrating a strong Super Tuesday performance, winning nine states, including a surprise victory in Texas. There was some good news for his main rival, Bernie Sanders, who came out with a projected win in the biggest Super Tuesday state, California.

There was no denying that Biden now had the 'Joementum' and that not enough voters were 'feeling the Bern' (sorry, but these were election slogans we had to get used to!). Bernie Sanders remained in the race for a few weeks after Super Tuesday but suffered more defeats in the primaries that followed. In mid-March 2020, the world was turned upside-down as the pandemic hit, schools and businesses were closed and in-person campaign events had to be cancelled. One of Bernie Sanders' strengths was delivering barnstorming speeches to packed rallies, and he was far better at it than Joe Biden. But such gatherings could no longer happen. Bernie Sanders suspended his campaign. He said that his path to winning the Democratic nomination was 'virtually impossible', adding that he did not want to put more effort into a doomed campaign just as the coronavirus pandemic was starting to take hold. 'I cannot in good conscience continue to mount a campaign that cannot win, and which would interfere with the important work required of all of us in this difficult hour,' he said in a live-streamed video from his home.

He congratulated Joe Biden but did not explicitly endorse him, calling him 'a very decent man who I will work with to move our progressive ideas forward'. The senator said that he would keep his name on the ballot in states that had not yet voted in order to continue winning delegates, so he could advance his platform at the Democratic Convention. 'Then together, standing united, we will go forward to defeat Donald Trump, the most dangerous president in modern American history,' he said.

Joe Biden paid tribute to his former rival, saying he had 'created a movement', and he encouraged Sanders' loyal supporters to back him instead. 'I hope you will join us. You are more than welcome. You're needed,' he said. Donald Trump also tried to entice some of Sanders' followers, tweeting: 'Bernie people should come to the Republican Party.'

The election line-up was now finalized. It would be Trump versus Biden.

8. The dinner

She was the Taoiseach's Secret Service detail, tasked with protecting Leo Varadkar while he was in Washington DC.

'Excuse me, where will the media be sitting?' she asked.

I turned and saw a woman with shoulder-length blonde hair wearing a black pants suit. She and another agent wanted to ask me questions about the layout of the room. I had arrived early with my cameraman, Murray, and we were among the few people in the venue at the time, so they obviously thought we were involved in setting up the event. I explained my limited knowledge of the seating plan before spotting a diplomat from the Irish Embassy and calling him over, knowing that he would be far better equipped to answer their questions. The female agent thanked me for my time. We then both paused and almost in unison said: 'Don't I know you?'

She had been our daughters' babysitter when we'd first moved to Washington. At the time, she was a student at one of the universities near our home and we knew that she hoped to pursue a career in law enforcement when she completed her studies. Our girls were very fond of her and we were all disappointed when it became clear she would no longer be available for babysitting as she moved on to begin her career.

We didn't know which law enforcement agency she had joined until I saw her there, securing the room ahead of the arrival of the VIP she was there to protect. My daughters' babysitter had now become the Taoiseach's babysitter. It was one of those bizarre, head-scratching moments that makes you think, only in Washington! But it would not be the strangest part of that night. More was to follow. It was Wednesday, 11 March 2020 and we were at the Ireland Funds Gala Dinner, one of the main events of the annual St Patrick's Day celebrations in the US.

That year, one of the guests of honour was the Speaker of the House Nancy Pelosi. Also present was the acting White House Chief of Staff Mick Mulvaney. Needless to say, the Taoiseach's Secret Service agents weren't the only bodyguards in the room. And what a room it was. The Gala Dinner was being held in the National Building Museum, an enormous redbrick structure that once housed the US Pension Bureau. It was built in the 1880s, its designers drawing on influences from the Roman palaces of the Renaissance era. The interior of the building is dominated by a grand central space called the Great Hall, which has a fountain and a series of enormous columns that support the ornate ceiling. It is a truly stunning venue that once a year plays host to the crème de la crème of Irish America.

The Ireland Funds is a philanthropic network that promotes peace and development throughout the island of Ireland by raising money for projects north and south of the border. Its annual Gala is a black-tie dinner that sees the biggest names in business and politics coming together to celebrate St Patrick's Day and honour US–Irish relations. In the past, it has been addressed by Presidents, Vice Presidents, senior members of Congress and Taoisigh. There is Irish-themed entertainment and the menu is always filled with tastes of home, such as Clonakilty black pudding, smoked salmon and Irish beef specially imported for the event. In previous years, the tables were packed and tickets were in high demand, but in 2020 something felt different. There were fewer tables in that cavernous room and some of the ones that had been set up were completely empty. Even before the announcement of major coronavirus restrictions, the pandemic had started to make people rethink their travel plans and avoid big public gatherings.

The theme of that year's Gala was 'A Celebration of Irish America's Commitment to Peace and Reconciliation'. The Republican Congressman Peter King, who was the co-chair of the Friends of Ireland caucus on Capitol Hill, received a Special Recognition Award. Nancy Pelosi was honoured with a Distinguished Leadership Award and was presented with a beautiful painting of the Capitol Building.

Speaker Pelosi had just finished her acceptance speech when phones started to ping. Guests rose from their tables and huddled in groups. The VIPs, including the Taoiseach and the Speaker, were swiftly escorted out of the room. Donald Trump had just delivered an 'address to the nation' from the Oval Office. It was a sombre eleven-minute speech from the location that US Presidents use to announce bad news or to offer reassurance at times of crisis. Mr Trump made Oval Office addresses on only a handful of occasions during his presidency. This was one of those rare times, and it began the way all those big speeches do, with the words: 'My fellow Americans'.

Sitting at the Resolute Desk with his hands clasped, Donald Trump went on to claim that the US response to the pandemic had been the best in the world. 'At the very start of the outbreak we instituted sweeping travel restrictions on China and put in place the first federally mandated quarantine in over fifty years. We declared a public health emergency

and issued the highest level of travel warning on other countries as the virus spread its horrible infection.' But then, in
true Donald Trump fashion, it was time to play the blame
game. 'The European Union failed to take the same precautions and restrict travel from China and other hotspots. As a
result, a large number of new clusters in the United States
were seeded by travellers from Europe. After consulting with
our top government health professionals, I have decided to
take several strong but necessary actions to protect the health
and well-being of all Americans.' And then came the key part
of his address: 'To keep new cases from entering our shores,
we will be suspending all travel from Europe to the United
States for the next thirty days. The new rules will go into
effect Friday, at midnight.' It was a dramatic shift from a man
who only weeks before had dismissed the virus as a 'flu that
would soon go away.

The President said the travel ban would not affect the UK,
even though coronavirus case numbers were soaring there at
the time. He made no reference to Ireland, so it was unclear
if we were included on his list of banned countries. I was
sitting at the press table with a group of journalists who had
travelled over from Dublin to cover the Taoiseach's visit.
They were checking their phones for updates, worried about
the immediate implications of the travel ban. Would there be
a reciprocal announcement from the EU? Could it affect
them getting home? It was a confusing, chaotic time with
lots of questions. The Taoiseach had been taken to a private
room on an upper floor and the journalists started gathering
at the bottom of the stairs in the hope of getting his reaction
to the travel ban announcement.

While we waited for Leo Varadkar to reappear, the US
Department of Homeland Security issued further details

about the travel ban. It contained some badly needed clarifications. The Irish people gathered at the St Patrick's Day dinner in Washington DC weren't the only ones who were confused. The President had misspoken in his speech and suggested that the restrictions would also apply to goods and cargo, but this was not the case. The Homeland Security statement also clarified that the ban would not affect US citizens travelling back from Europe. This had not been obvious from the President's address and had sparked panic among Americans who were abroad and fearful that they would not be allowed to return home. There was one other important clarification – well, important to us, at least. Ireland was not on the list of banned countries. The ban related to nations within the 26-country Schengen Zone.

Donald Trump's prime-time TV address was supposed to calm the nation and give the impression that he was in control of the worsening crisis, but instead it sparked confusion, widespread panic and sent financial markets tumbling.

The President's acting White House Chief of Staff Mick Mulvaney was not at his side while he delivered this pivotal address because he was at the Ireland Funds Gala Dinner. 'Obviously, the President's announcement didn't take me by surprise. I knew it was coming,' Mick Mulvaney told me, as he recalled the events of that night. 'I had visited Ireland, Northern Ireland and Britain the previous month. The media portrayed it as a visit about 5G and Huawei, but that wasn't accurate. One of the things I was there to discuss was the coronavirus and to try to encourage the Europeans to get the Italians to stop their direct flights from China that had no restrictions on them. We were worried about the virus getting out of China into Italy in mid-February and history would show us that's exactly how it ended up in Northern

Italy and that's how it got to the continent of Europe. We had seen this coming for several weeks,' he said.

He told me that while the Oval Office address was a big announcement and there was a lot of activity around it, it was not chaotic. 'You don't realize people you see on television who are, for want of a better word, famous and work for governments are in fact ordinary human beings. In my case, I had a daughter at Trinity College Dublin, so in my own head I'm wondering how I am going to get my daughter home. At the same time, I had just been announced as the Northern Ireland Special Envoy. I had a breakfast the next morning with representatives from Northern Ireland, so I'm thinking about that and how we were going to handle health and safety for that meeting. Was everybody going to be able to attend and what would it mean more broadly for the relationships I was trying to establish for that role? So yes, very active, I wouldn't say chaotic, but certainly it was not ordinary times.'

After waiting for several minutes for the Taoiseach to descend the steps and possibly speak to the media, we were informed that he had already left the building and would be holding an early morning press briefing the following day. He would deliver an address outside Blair House, a mansion across the street from the White House where visiting foreign leaders stay. We assumed that the media briefing would involve Mr Varadkar giving his reaction to President Trump's travel restriction announcement, but that would not be the case.

It had been a dramatic night and it was time to go, but not before my phone pinged once again. What now? I thought. It was a notification from the White House. The annual shamrock ceremony, which was due to take place the following day, had been cancelled because of coronavirus concerns.

The Irish Embassy quickly clarified that the one-on-one meeting between Leo Varadkar and Donald Trump planned for the following day would go ahead. Usually that would be followed by a large gathering that would see hundreds of people packed into the East Room of the White House for the official presentation of the shamrock bowl. In mid-March 2020 a new term started to enter common use, 'super-spreader event', and there was no denying that the shamrock ceremony would fall into that category. It could not go ahead.

Leo Varadkar remembers well the dramatic developments that unfolded at the Gala Dinner that night. The announcement of the travel ban didn't come as a big surprise to him. 'We had a heads-up that that was going to happen and then the news started filtering through to the dinner,' he told me. 'But I remember being whisked away. Martin Fraser, the Secretary General of the Government, came up to me and said, "We have to go", and I was whisked off, something that very rarely happens in politics, but it was like a scene from a movie, where you get whisked away through the kitchens or something to this private area upstairs. It was not because of Donald Trump's travel ban, it was because NPHET [the Irish National Public Health Emergency Team] were meeting in the Department of Health at the time. [Tánaiste and Minister for Foreign Affairs] Simon Coveney and [Minister for Health] Simon Harris were holding the fort for me back home and they'd come to the point where they felt we had hit exponential growth and wanted to recommend the first set of major restrictions, including the closure of schools and all the measures I announced the next day on the steps of Blair House. So that's why we were whisked away and had to leave.'

By now it was late at night, but the work for the next

morning's announcement was just beginning. Leo Varadkar and his team started writing his speech. This was an unprecedented moment. Donald Trump had delivered his address to the nation that evening, the following morning it would be the Taoiseach's turn.

'Did you get any sleep that night?' I asked Leo Varadkar. 'I did, not a huge amount. Maybe three or four hours. When it comes to the big speeches, I like to write them myself.' He wrote the first draft and then members of his team put the finishing touches to the address. 'They turned it into a much better thing, which I then delivered the next day. So it was all pretty dramatic. Most of the time, being Taoiseach is just like having a normal job, you go into work, have your meetings, send your emails, but there are a few of those moments that are like something straight out of a movie. And that really was one of those times.'

I got just a few hours' sleep myself that night and woke at 5.00 a.m. to make my way to the Taoiseach's address. It was 10.00 a.m. back home in Ireland and news had already been leaked that the Irish government was getting ready to announce the closure of schools and crèches. RTÉ was running a special TV news programme, hosted by Bryan Dobson, to cover the announcement.

The sun was starting to rise over Washington as we arrived at the White House outer perimeter. As sniffer dogs checked our equipment and we passed through metal detectors, I was being interviewed live over the phone by Bryan Dobson, who was back in the studio in Donnybrook.

A podium had been set up in front of Blair House and staff were moving a large Irish flag into position as we arrived. Murray clicked his camera onto its tripod and unfurled microphone cables while I called RTÉ in Dublin to check that they were receiving our live signal. The special pro-gramme would cut to the Taoiseach's address as soon as he began speaking. Amid the cables, lights, flags and micro-phones someone had placed a hand-sanitizing station close to the podium. We were entering a very new world.

March weather in Washington is unpredictable. Some days are mild, offering a preview of the sweltering summer to come, but there can also be reminders of the freezing winter that only began its thaw a few weeks before. That morning it was cold and the gathered journalists stomped their feet to stay warm, our breaths visible in the icy air as we chatted about what the Taoiseach was likely to say. The wait felt like an eternity as I looked up at the mansion. Blair House is known as the President's Guest House. It is an impressive townhouse across the street from the White House and is named after Francis Preston Blair, an influential newspaper editor who lived in the house in the mid-1800s. No doubt, as a newspaper man, he would have appreciated the fact that in 2020 the biggest story in Ireland was playing out on the steps of his former home.

The US government bought Blair House in 1942 at the urging of President Franklin D. Roosevelt, who wanted somewhere for visiting dignitaries to stay. Up to then, for-eign leaders would often spend a night at the White House during their trips to Washington. Winston Churchill was famously intercepted by the US First Lady Eleanor Roosevelt while making his way to the President's private quarters at 3.00 a.m. Churchill, with his signature cigar in hand, said he was hoping to wake President Roosevelt to continue their conversation, but he was persuaded to wait until breakfast. It was not long after that incident that the purchase of Blair House was approved and the days of letting prime ministers and princes sleep a few doors down from the president were over.

We got a two-minute warning from the Taoiseach's team and I called Dublin again to tell them to get ready. The glass-panelled door swung open and Leo Varadkar descended the steps to deliver his address. 'Am I OK to start?' he asked the assembled media and we nodded. 'Good morning, every-one,' he began. 'I need to speak to you about coronavirus and COVID-19.'

He made reference to the actions the government had taken up to that point, but clearly things were changing fast. 'Yesterday, the World Health Organization formally described this as a pandemic and the European Centre for Disease Prevention and Control updated its guidelines advising us all to act early to be effective. Our own National Public Health Emergency Team met last night and has issued new advice to government. We are acting on that advice today. Schools, colleges, and childcare facilities will close from tomorrow. Where possible, teaching will be done online or remotely. Cultural institutions will close. Our advice is that all indoor mass gatherings of more than one hundred people and out-door mass gatherings of more than five hundred people should be cancelled.'

People were encouraged to work from home, if they could. 'We have not witnessed a pandemic of this nature in living memory. This is uncharted territory,' Mr Varadkar said. 'I know that some of this is coming as a real shock and it is going to involve big changes in the way we live our lives. I know that I am asking people to make enormous sacrifices. We're doing it for each other.'

He concluded his five-minute address with a note of optimism. 'Ireland is a great nation. And we are great people. We have experienced hardship and struggle before. We have overcome many trials in the past with our determination and our spirit. We will prevail.' As soon as he finished speaking, we started to shout questions, but the Taoiseach ignored them. He turned and walked back inside Blair House.

I called Dublin to make sure the live feed was clean. I offered to re-feed the speech if there had been any glitches or break-up of the picture. 'No, it's all good,' the programme editor replied. 'We need to go live to you in five minutes for some analysis,' he added. I grabbed the microphone that just minutes before had carried the Taoiseach's words back to a worried nation 3,000 miles away and got ready for my live report.

A year on from that dramatic moment in Irish history, I asked Leo Varadkar what was going through his mind as he walked down the steps of Blair House to deliver his address. 'It was a speech like nobody had ever done before, at least not for generations, it was a real national emergency moment. The journalists didn't really know what I was going to say, so it was quite dramatic in that sense. One thing that was on my mind is that I was in DC and I was keen to get back home. I wanted to get the business done there and get home as soon as possible to take charge of the situation.'

But before he could return home, Leo Varadkar had one more job to do in Washington: his meeting with Donald Trump in the Oval Office. I also had an appointment in the West Wing that day. I had managed to secure a one-on-one interview with Mick Mulvaney. On an ordinary day, this would have been a major news story, but this was no ordinary day. The Taoiseach had just made his big speech and he was about to become the first foreign leader to meet the US President since his shock announcement the night before of a European travel ban.

The world as we knew it was changing in ways nobody could have predicted. The word 'coronavirus' had been in the news for weeks but it had felt like a distant threat in faraway lands. Now, it was at our doorstep. More restrictions and lockdowns would be announced in the weeks that were to follow as world leaders, and the wider public, struggled to cope with a devastating pandemic.

9. Shamrocks and sniffer dogs

After Leo Varadkar's Blair House address, Murray and I made our way across the street to the White House. Mick Mulvaney had arranged for our interview to take place just before the Oval Office meeting between the President and the Taoiseach, but the timings were tight. I was checking my watch throughout the painfully slow security procedures, which involved multiple ID checks, bag searches, sniffer dogs and metal detectors. Eventually we were through and were escorted along a pathway that skirts the North Lawn of the White House.

We walked past the area known as Pebble Beach, which is a row of small tents from where TV reporters do their live broadcasts. It is used by all the main US networks and by broadcasters from around the world. I was booked to file a live report from there later that day into the RTÉ *Nine O'Clock News*. The area used to be grassed, but it became damaged and muddied from reporters and camera crews walking across it every day. It was then covered in gravel, hence the nickname 'Pebble Beach'. The gravel is now gone, replaced by concrete, but the nickname has stuck.

On all my previous visits to the White House I turned left as I approached the main building and entered the James S. Brady Press Briefing Room. This is located in a long, single-storey building that connects the West Wing to the main mansion. It is where the daily White House press briefings take place and, interestingly, it is built over what was once an indoor swimming pool. It has led to lots of witty references over the years about presidents and press secretaries 'struggling to stay afloat' or being 'out of their depth' as they stood at the podium trying to answer tough questions from the media.

On this occasion, I did not turn left for the briefing room. Instead, we continued straight ahead and were led into the main West Wing lobby. There, I met two diplomats from the Irish Embassy whom I knew well. 'What are you guys doing here?' I asked. 'Dropping off the shamrock bowl,' they replied. The presentation ceremony had been cancelled so instead the shamrock, in its crystal bowl, would be placed on a table between the President and the Taoiseach for the duration of their Oval Office meeting. It was a reminder to me that the big event was fast approaching and that the clock was ticking. I hoped that Mick Mulvaney would be ready for us soon, otherwise I would have to cut our interview short. The minutes felt like hours as I watched the hands of an antique clock hanging on the wall.

'Mr Mulvaney will see you now,' a staff member told us. 'Thank God,' Murray and I exclaimed with relief. 'Wait a minute, you can't bring that into the Chief of Staff's office,' a Secret Service agent said, pointing to our equipment. 'Your gear hasn't been swept.' We both assured him that it had, describing the lengthy process of sniffer dogs, metal detectors and searches that we had just been through. 'No, that was just to get onto the grounds. If you're going into the West Wing offices, you have to be swept again,' he insisted. Even some of the White House staff seemed a little sceptical about this, but the agent was adamant and radioed for a K9 unit and a search team to be sent our way. 'It could be a half hour before they get here,' he told us. The same could not be said for the Taoiseach, who was just ten minutes away. It looked like my interview with the acting White House Chief of Staff was about to be scuppered by an overly cautious Secret Service agent. Just then, a member of Mick Mulvaney's team appeared in the lobby and told us that he was happy to move our appointment to later in the day. We could come back after the Oval Office meeting.

Murray and I talked through our new timetable of events while gathering up our equipment, but we were told to speed things up by the White House staff. 'The President will be coming through here in the next few minutes to greet the Taoiseach and you can't be here,' we were told. We quickly grabbed our things and made our way to the briefing room, where the rest of the Irish reporters were waiting. 'Where were you guys?' they wondered. 'Oh, don't ask!' I replied with a frustrated eye-roll. But before I could complain about the Secret Service agent we'd encountered we were informed that the Taoiseach had arrived and that we should get ready to make our way to the Oval Office.

Inside the room, we all crowded around the furniture where the VIPs were sitting, stretching out phones, microphones and boom poles as far as our arms could reach. It was my third Oval Office St Patrick's Day meeting. I made my way to what I had learned was one of the better positions. It was next to the arm of a large couch just to Donald Trump's left. It was important to be within earshot of the US President so he could hear my questions above the shouting of all the other reporters in the room. As I reached my spot, I noticed the bowl of shamrock sitting on a table between the two leaders.

'Well, thank you all very much,' Donald Trump began. 'It's an honour to be with the Prime Minister of Ireland. We've known each other now for quite a while, and we have a great relationship and a great relationship with Ireland.' Leo Varadkar thanked his host for the invite and described some of the COVID-19 restrictions he had announced across the street just a few hours earlier. Without making an explicit reference to Donald Trump's travel ban, the Taoiseach then spoke about the importance of working with other countries. 'It is a virus that has gone pandemic. It is all over the world. It knows no borders, knows no nationalities. And I think we all need to work together in the world on this. And America, in particular, you're the richest country in the world. You've got great scientists, great companies, great universities, and we need them working on treatments, working on tests, and working on a vaccine, because that's what will get us on top of this.'

As soon as he finished speaking, I was able to get in with the first question. There was still confusion over exactly which countries were included in Donald Trump's travel ban and I was hoping to get some clarity from the man himself. 'Mr President, can you confirm if Ireland will be excluded from your European travel ban you announced last night?'

'Well, they know, and I think it was made very clear last night who is and who isn't. And we'll be discussing that. We'll be discussing some other moves that we're going to be making. And I think it's going to work out very well for everybody. But it's a world problem, and you do need separation in some cases. You have some areas that are very heavily infected, and you have some areas that aren't, frankly. But we do need separation for a little period of time, in some cases,' he replied.

Donald Trump hadn't directly answered my question and hadn't definitively said whether travel from Ireland would be banned. Leo Varadkar interjected to clarify matters: 'Just to say that the President has excluded Ireland from the travel ban. And one of the things that we have in Ireland is American border security. I went through it myself yesterday, and they were asking the right questions – whether people had been to China, things like that. So that puts us slightly in a different position.'

It was Donald Trump's first media availability since his address to the nation the night before, so the large group of US reporters in the Oval Office were keen to get more details about his plan to tackle the pandemic, calling out questions about China, the economy, restricting outdoor gatherings and declaring a national emergency. An Irish colleague managed to get a question in: 'Mr President, will Irish citizens always be welcome to America throughout this coronavirus pandemic?'

'Always. Always. Always. Just like your Prime Minister, always. They are not only welcome, they are loved.'

The US reporters wrested control of the press briefing back from the Irish and started firing questions about Iran, Brazil, Japan and the Democratic primaries. My location over the President's left shoulder was paying off, I managed to ask a second question. 'You've broken with tradition today, President Trump. You're not going to Speaker Pelosi's annual lunch. Can you tell us why?' I asked. 'No, I won't be going. No, I have other things to do. I'm very busy,' came his sullen reply.

A few days earlier, I had reported that Donald Trump would be skipping the traditional St Patrick's lunch on Capitol Hill hosted by the Speaker of the House Nancy Pelosi. It was always held immediately after the Oval Office meeting and was normally attended by both the Taoiseach and the US President. At that time, however, relations between Donald Trump and Nancy Pelosi had hit a new low. At his State of the Union address the previous month, he had refused to shake her hand and she had ripped up a copy of his speech. Ahead of the Speaker's lunch, the White House issued me with a statement, which read: 'Since the Speaker has chosen to tear this nation apart with her actions and her rhetoric, the President will not participate in moments where she so often chooses to drive discord and disunity, and will instead celebrate the rich history and strong ties between the United States and Ireland at the White House on March 12th'.

The Speaker's office issued a strongly worded statement of its own: 'There has never been stronger support in the Congress and in the country for the US–Ireland bilateral relationship. One would think that the White House could set petty, partisan politics aside for this historic occasion.'

Judging by his grumpy, short answer, I got the impression that Donald Trump did not like the fact that I had asked him about Nancy Pelosi in the Oval Office. Leo Varadkar, on the other hand, seemed amused by his response and a wide smile appeared across his face as the President moved on to the next question. 'Mr President, are you OK with shaking hands with foreign prime ministers when they visit?' he was asked. This was the start of the pandemic, so the world was still getting used to bumping elbows and fists.

'Well, we didn't shake hands today,' the President said, gesturing towards Leo Varadkar. 'And we looked at each other and said, "What are we going to do?" You know, it's sort of a weird feeling. So we settled on this.' The two leaders each clasped their hands in a prayer-like manner and bowed, Donald Trump comparing it to greetings in India and Japan.

'It almost feels impersonal. It feels like you're being rude,' remarked the Taoiseach. 'But we just can't afford to think like that for the next few weeks.' Of course, it would be a lot longer than 'a few weeks' before people could start shaking hands again, but at that stage no one could predict the scale of the global crisis that was about to unfold. Whether or not to 'press the flesh' with people we met would be the least of our worries.

We left the Oval Office, and when the Taoiseach had departed the White House for Capitol Hill, we returned to the West Wing lobby for our interview with Mick Mulvaney. There was a different Secret Service agent on duty, and we asked him where we should wait while he called the sniffer dogs and search team. 'No need for that,' came his reply. 'You were already searched on the way in.' That figures, I thought.

We were led to the Chief of Staff's office, which is down the corridor from the Oval Office. Obviously, it isn't as large and well decorated as the room where the Commander in Chief sits, but it is still impressive. It is a corner office with tall windows on two walls. A large fireplace, plush carpets and paintings gave the space the feel of an old-world living room, but desks, a conference table and stacks of documents and files left no doubt that this was very much a working office. A dark mahogany door swung open and we were greeted by Mick Mulvaney. I reached out my arm for a handshake. 'Oh, I don't think we're doing that any more,' he said. I apologized for my absentmindedness and we bumped elbows instead.

As Murray set up the lights and the camera, I surveyed the large office. It was just as well there was plenty of space as Mick Mulvaney told me that he was currently sharing it with the man who would soon be succeeding him as White House Chief of Staff, Mark Meadows. Mr Mulvaney had just been announced as the US Special Envoy to Northern Ireland.

'Surely that is a demotion?' I began our interview. 'Anything is a demotion from White House Chief of Staff,' he replied, 'short of becoming president or perhaps vice president. The job of chief of staff is one that one never has for life, the average is fourteen months, which is almost exactly how long I was in the job.'

Mr Mulvaney is proud of his Irish roots, which he has traced back to county Mayo. He told me that he asked Donald Trump for the Northern Ireland job and insisted that he was leaving the White House on good terms with the President: 'He came to me and said you've served the administration and the country very well and he asked if there's anything I'd like to do. I said, Northern Ireland Envoy.' It was a position that had been vacant since Donald Trump took office and Mick Mulvaney was taking it on at a crucial time, with Brexit negotiations underway and looming talks on a future trade deal between the US and the UK.

Mick Mulvaney's time as acting White House Chief of Staff hadn't been without controversy. In October 2019, at the height of the investigations leading up to Donald Trump's first impeachment, he was asked about conditions being attached to military aid for Ukraine. 'We do that all the time with foreign policy,' Mr Mulvaney responded. 'Get over it! There's going to be political influence in foreign policy.'

Now, as he prepared to leave the White House, I asked him if he regretted those comments. 'What I was saying was that we use foreign aid to try to get foreign countries to do what we want them to do. It was misinterpreted as doing something regarding our election and that was not my intention.' He was about to vacate his large West Wing office but although he would no longer be down the corridor from the President, Mick Mulvaney said he would still have a direct line to the White House. 'I can pick up the phone next week or next month if I'm in Belfast and call the President of the United States directly. I'm not sure there are other envoys who've been able to do that,' he said. As it transpired, however, Mick Mulvaney wasn't able to do that either. Not because the President wouldn't answer the phone, but because the Northern Ireland Envoy couldn't travel to Belfast due to coronavirus travel restrictions. He ended up making just one trip to Ireland and the UK as Envoy.

The travel restrictions that upset Mick Mulvaney's plans, and those of millions of others around the world, were constantly changing in those early weeks. Ireland had escaped Donald Trump's travel ban in his initial address to the nation in March 2020, but just days later that would change. It was the Saturday after a busy week of covering the Taoiseach's visit to Washington. Leo Varadkar had left the US, but there was another big story about Ireland for me to report.

The dishwasher in our house had died a few days previously and we had scheduled the delivery of a new one for Saturday, thinking things might be a little quieter and that there would be a better chance of me being at home. The day before, our daughters' school had closed because of the pandemic. We assumed this was a temporary measure, little did we know then that it would remain shut for a year. It was a scary, uncertain time and we decided to keep our girls inside and not let them play on the street with their friends, much to their frustration as it was a beautiful, sunny day. I was watching CNN in our living room as Donald Trump took to the podium in the White House press briefing room. With that, the doorbell rang. It was the dishwasher delivery men. I called for my wife, but she was upstairs dealing with two very upset girls who could not understand why they could no longer go outside and play with their friends. I opened the door and directed the delivery men where to go, while keeping an eye on Donald Trump's press conference. He was asked if Ireland and the UK would be added to his European travel ban. 'We're looking at it very seriously because they have had a little bit of activity, unfortunately. We actually have looked at it already and that is going to be announced,' he said.

'Joanna, I have to go into the office,' I shouted upstairs. 'Excuse me, sir,' the dishwasher installer called from the kitchen. 'There is a problem with the electrics. I'm going to have to install a new power outlet and it's going to cost extra and . . .' I stopped him and informed him that as we were renting the property, I'd have to call our landlady. I dialled her number while trying to put on my suit and trying to keep an eye on the TV. I handed my phone to the workman so he could talk directly to the landlady just as Vice President Mike Pence took to the podium.

'Where are the girls?' Joanna called from upstairs. 'I thought they were up there with you?' I replied. The delivery men had left the front door open and Lucy and Erin had taken it as an invite to go outside and play on the street with the neighbourhood children.

As Joanna dashed out to find them, Mike Pence was announcing that the US travel ban was being extended based on the 'unanimous recommendation' of health officials. He said: 'The President has made a decision to suspend all travel from the United Kingdom and Ireland, effective midnight Monday. Americans in the UK and Ireland can come home, but they will be funnelled through specific airports and processes.' Joanna was doing some funnelling of her own. She had found the girls at the end of our street eating hotdogs with the neighbours. 'So much for keeping them indoors,' she said as she led their ketchup-covered faces through the door.

'Have you seen my phone?' I asked, eager to call an Uber to take me to the office. I needed to do a live report into the *Six One News* and the deadline was fast approaching. 'I don't know where it is,' Joanna replied and the ensuing search for the device only added to everyone's stress levels. I then realized that my phone was still being used by the dishwasher installer, who was scribbling my landlady's credit card number on a piece of paper.

It was a chaotic and stressful morning at the end of a chaotic and stressful week. Reunited with my phone, I made my way to the office to report on the travel ban announcement. Only two days earlier, in the Oval Office, the Taoiseach had claimed that Ireland was in a 'different position' from our European neighbours because of our airports' US preclearance facilities. Donald Trump had vowed that Irish citizens would 'always' be welcome in the US. How quickly things had changed.

When I returned home that evening, my thoughts turned to what the travel ban would mean for us as a family. We would be able to fly to Ireland, but if we did, we would not be allowed back into the US. We, like everyone else in the world that week, realized that the days of getting on planes were over, at least for now. Joanna's cousin, Jennifer, was in Washington at the time, studying at American University. With the college closed, and amid growing uncertainty over how she might get back home, she decided to leave the US early. On St Patrick's Day 2020, Jennifer joined us for a roast dinner with all the trimmings. It was both a celebration of our national day and her farewell meal. Her flight home to Dublin was due to leave the following day.

Before we sat down to eat, we turned on the RTÉ Player to watch Leo Varadkar's address to the nation. He was back in Ireland and this time he was speaking from Government Buildings, not from the steps of Blair House. 'This is a St Patrick's Day like no other,' he began. 'A day that none of us will ever forget. Today's children will tell their own children and grandchildren about the national holiday in 2020 that had no parades or parties but instead saw everyone staying at home to protect each other. In years to come, let them say of us, when things were at their worst, we were at our best.'

He went on to outline that the restrictions and closures he had announced in Washington the week before were likely to last much longer and to be expanded. He urged people to avoid unnecessary travel, to work from home and to practise social distancing. 'In short, we are asking people to come together as a nation by staying apart from each other.' He then went on to praise the healthcare workers on the frontlines. 'Not all superheroes wear capes, some wear scrubs and gowns. All of our healthcare workers need us to do the right thing in the weeks ahead. This is the calm before the storm, before the surge. And when it comes, and it will come, never will so many ask so much of so few.'

As in his address in Washington the week before, the Taoiseach struck a note of optimism as he concluded his speech: 'Tonight, I send a message of friendship and of hope from Ireland to everyone around the world this St Patrick's Day. *Lá Fhéile Pádraig shona daoibh*,' he said.

It was a strong speech, probably Leo Varadkar's best. Joanna and Jennifer wiped tears from their eyes. I moved to the kitchen, pretending to check on dinner so I could do the same. The Taoiseach's message was one of unity and coming together, but at that moment home had never felt so far away. As I set the table, I thought back to the black-tie dinner we had sat down to in the lavish surroundings of the Building Museum less than one week before. It was like a different world, where people could come together, gather in groups, hug and shake hands. But the dramatic events that unfolded that night, and in the days that followed, were the first in a series of unthinkable developments that would alter the world we knew in unimaginable ways. It also marked the beginning of a tumultuous year in the US. A year of protest, unrest and division, when everything became political, even the wearing of a face mask.

The Ireland Funds Gala Dinner would be the last night out Joanna and I would enjoy for a very long time. As for everyone else, there were no more dinners, no more reasons to get dressed up and no more calls to the babysitter. Just as well, I suppose, that she had gone off to become a Secret Service agent.

10. An invisible enemy

I turned forty in late March 2020. Joanna had organized what would have been a wonderful celebration involving a surprise visit to Washington by my parents followed by a surprise trip to New Orleans. But the real surprise came when we realized, just like the rest of the world that year, that celebrations of special occasions had to be cancelled because of the coronavirus. Mom and Dad could not fly and our trip could not happen.

We decided to make the best of my birthday with a walk in nearby woods followed by a takeaway from a local restaurant. It was a far cry from the festivities that were planned, but it was nonetheless a great day. Something was wrong, though. That evening I noticed a niggling sore throat that wouldn't go away. Over the days that followed I started to feel worse, with 'flu-like symptoms and a high temperature.

In the early stages of the pandemic, it was almost impossible to get tested for COVID-19 in Washington DC. Testing kits were in short supply and the infrastructure that would be set up in the months that followed was not yet in place. I called my doctor, who said I should isolate for the appropriate time and wait until the symptoms subsided, which I did. As a family we had been very careful about our interactions and practised social distancing and mask-wearing. If it was COVID-19, where had I caught it? The medical advice at the time was that symptoms typically first started to show around five days after exposure to the virus. That makes sense, I thought. Five days before I had been in a hospital Emergency Room.

It was a Saturday and we wanted to do something outdoors with the children. We drove to Hains Point, the tip of a long park that juts into the water at the confluence of Washington's two rivers, the Potomac and the Anacostia. It is lined with cherry trees and at that time of the year they were in full blossom. It is a beautiful sight for which Washington is famed. Every year, trees all around the city burst into life with shades of pink and white.

Fearing there would be a shortage of parking spaces we left the car in the first spot we saw, even though it was quite a distance from our final destination – a playground at the end of the Point. When we finally reached it, we realized there were plenty of parking spaces and I decided to go and get the car to spare the girls from having to make the long walk back, and to spare Joanna and I from having to listen to them complain about it! As I made my way back, I watched a Donald Trump press conference on my phone. He was giving an update on his administration's COVID-19 response, which in those early days of the pandemic was haphazard, to say the least. Things would not improve a whole lot in the months that followed.

I knew my phone battery was running low and that watching a live press conference via the White House Twitter account was draining the power even further, but I also knew that I would be able to recharge the phone as soon as I reached the car. President Trump was delivering his usual flow of hope and optimism, promising that the virus would soon be defeated. 'Every American has a role to play in defending our nation from this invisible, horrible enemy. It really is. It's an invisible enemy and we will be successful, very successful, hopefully very much sooner than people would even think,' he said, before touting the possible benefits of the anti-malaria drug hydroxychloroquine as a treatment. 'Right now, this to me would be the greatest thing that could happen. This would be a gift from heaven. This would be a gift from God, if it works.'

My viewing of the press conference was interrupted by a phone call from Joanna, who was at the playground. She sounded upset. 'Get back here quick . . .' was all I heard before the phone went dead as the battery ran out of power. I rushed to the car and started charging the device. My drive to the playground was delayed by traffic, with lots of people out enjoying the cherry blossom. When I finally got there, I saw my daughter Erin with blood gushing from her face. She had fallen and had a nasty gash on her cheek, under her left eye. The wound was wide and bleeding heavily. We knew it would require a trip to the Emergency Room. Because of the complicated and extortionately expensive US healthcare system, we had been warned never to just turn up at a hospital or we could be hit with a bill of thousands of dollars that would not be covered by our insurance plan. Instead, we had been advised to always call our insurance provider first and be directed where to go. We did just that and were given an immediate appointment at a nearby facility.

I dropped my wife and older daughter home first, as only one family member would be allowed to accompany Erin due to COVID-19 restrictions. With coronavirus cases rising in Washington at that time, I expected bedlam at the admissions desk, but instead we encountered a quiet, pristine waiting room. The coronavirus cases were being admitted in another part of the building and we were dealt with quickly. Erin didn't require stitches, but the wound did have to be treated with adhesive strips and medical glue. The doctor assured us that scarring should be minimal. The whole hospital visit lasted around twenty minutes.

Then five days later, I started feeling ill with a sore throat, fever, cough and shortness of breath. The lack of testing at that time meant I never found out if it was COVID-19 or not, and of course I will never know for sure where I picked it up. After a few days of isolation, I began to improve. Once I was well again, I started working from home while still in quarantine. Live reports from my bedroom sparked comment on social media about the room's decor, but it wasn't uncommon to see TV reporters broadcasting from inside their homes. The viewers didn't know I was doing those reports from inside my house because I suspected I might have COVID-19. Whatever it was, thankfully I came through it and, more importantly, those around me did not fall ill.

I called the people I had been in contact with in the days leading up to my illness. Fortunately, it was a short list: my cameraman, Murray, and a man we had interviewed by the name of Mark Kirwan. Mark is originally from Tipperary and now runs two Irish pubs in the US, businesses he was forced to close because of the pandemic. But while his bars had taken a hit, his day job as a Washington DC police officer had never been busier, enforcing the lockdown that was underway in the US capital.

While Mark's police work had ramped up because of the outbreak, his other career had been decimated. His two Irish pubs, Kirwan's On The Wharf in Washington DC and Samuel Beckett's in nearby Arlington, Virginia, were both shut down at the start of the pandemic, resulting in more than one hundred staff being laid off. 'It was very difficult for me to face the employees, not just to tell them that I had to lay them off but also not being able to tell them when they could come back,' Mark said. His two pubs continued to provide takeaway and delivery services in the hope of keeping the business afloat and he got plenty of support from his police colleagues. Mark also delivered free food to local hospitals and police stations for those on the frontlines of the coronavirus fight. 'We were trying to give something back to the community and also let them know that we were still here so that when we reopened again, they would come back.'

Mark Kirwan was one of the many, many Irish people I spoke to as part of my job. While the White House was my regular beat, as Washington Correspondent I also covered stories that involved Irish people either living in, or visiting, this vast country. These could be tales of hope and triumph or, more often than not, stories of tragedy and loss. Criminal trials involving people from Ireland could run for months, or even years, with multiple court appearances and hearings. COVID-19 had a big impact on the criminal justice system and resulted in new twists and turns in some of the cases I had been covering.

In August 2015, Limerick man Jason Corbett was beaten to death at his home in North Carolina. His wife and her father, Molly and Thomas Martens, were arrested and charged, but claimed they acted in self-defence. In August 2017, a jury found them guilty and they were convicted of second-degree murder. It was the first story I covered in the US, back before I had taken up the role of Washington Correspondent.

It came about because I was in New Jersey visiting my brother, who was on holiday there with his family. News broke that the Martens trial had finished earlier than expected and that the jury had retired to consider its verdict. As I was just a two-hour flight away from North Carolina, I was dispatched by RTÉ to cover the case.

I have reported on many trials over the years and I know that the duration of jury deliberations is impossible to predict. They can be over in a matter of hours or can take several days. I switched off my phone as the plane took off, wondering how long I would be in North Carolina waiting for a verdict. Not long at all, as it turned out. When I switched my phone back on two hours later, it buzzed with text messages. The jury had come back with two guilty verdicts. A local cameraman picked me up at the airport and in less than an hour we pulled up outside the Davidson County Courthouse in the city of Lexington, just in time for our live report into the *Nine O'Clock News*.

That didn't mark the end of my involvement with the case. In February 2020, Molly and Thomas Martens won an appeal against their convictions and a retrial was ordered. They remained in jail while the decision was considered by a higher court. In April, lawyers for Mr Martens argued that he should be released from prison because of coronavirus concerns. They told a court hearing that the seventy-year-old retired FBI agent was at an elevated risk of contracting a serious case of COVID-19 due to his age. At the time, there had been several coronavirus outbreaks in US prisons and some inmates were being released to home confinement in a bid to address the problem. Given that Thomas Martens was serving a sentence for murder, prosecutors objected and he remained behind bars. A year later, in April 2021, he and his daughter were released after the North Carolina Supreme Court upheld the decision to grant a retrial.

Another case I had spent several months covering was that of 26-year-old Dublin man Steven O'Brien. He had been jailed in New York for a fatal assault on Longford native Danny McGee. The 21-year-old died after being punched outside a pub in Queens on Thanksgiving Day in November 2018. Steven O'Brien had pleaded guilty to the assault and received a six-month prison sentence as part of a plea deal. He began his jail term in January 2020 but was released in March as part of an effort by authorities in New York to combat a coronavirus outbreak in the city's prison system. Hundreds of prisoners were being let out early in a bid to stop the spread of the virus.

Those being released were typically serving less than year-long sentences and with only a few weeks or months left to serve. Even though Steven O'Brien had just started his sentence, he qualified for early release and was a free man. I had met Danny McGee's mother, Colleen, at Steven O'Brien's sentencing hearing in Queens. She had travelled over from Ireland for the court appearance and a heart-breaking victim impact statement was read out on her behalf. She said her sense of loss would never go away and that life would never be the same without her son.

'The impact of Danny's death on me is immeasurable. As his mother, there is no one in this world who loves him as much as I do or misses him as much as I do,' the statement read. She was deeply disappointed that the man convicted of her son's fatal assault had received a sentence of just six months. His early release only added to her distress, even though she acknowledged that anger would not bring her son back. The 'big news' about the pandemic filled the headlines, but everywhere there were stories like this, telling of the hidden impact of COVID-19 in all manner of ways on people's lives.

The news of Steven O'Brien's early release broke on

26 March 2020, the day of my fortieth birthday. As I wrote up the article, I started to notice my sore throat and I cast my mind back to our visit to the Emergency Room five days before.

Since then, the small cut on my daughter's face has healed well and traces of it will probably be gone soon. When she is older, she's unlikely to remember the fall in the playground that came at the start of an unprecedented period of turmoil for the entire world. Maybe she will remember not being able to go to school or not being able to visit her grannies, grandads and cousins. Hopefully, when she has grown up, words like 'coronavirus', 'COVID' and 'herd immunity' will have faded from our collective memories, just like the little scar beneath her left eye.

11. 'Positively toward the negative'

At the start of the pandemic, the rate of COVID-19 cases ballooned quickly across the US, with record numbers of infections and deaths. Donald Trump's handling of the outbreak came in for sharp criticism amid downplaying and promises of quick-fix cures. The President gave nightly press conferences from the White House briefing room. Billed as coronavirus updates, they usually descended into extended rants from Mr Trump about whatever was on his mind. He used the podium to attack political rivals, clash with the media or wonder aloud about how the biggest test of his presidency, the coronavirus, would magically disappear.

The election was just months away, but traditional campaign rallies and public addresses all had to be cancelled due to the pandemic. However, these nightly press conferences gave Donald Trump a prime-time TV audience, and he loved it. He boasted on Twitter about the TV viewership figures for them, tweeting on 29 March: 'Because the "Ratings" of my News Conferences etc. are so high, "Bachelor finale, Monday Night Football type numbers" according to the New York Times, the Lamestream Media is going CRAZY.'

At that time, it gave the President a big advantage over his opponent, Joe Biden, who was cocooning inside his home in Wilmington, Delaware. He had set up a TV studio in the basement to do media interviews, and he did plenty of them, but he couldn't compete with the prime-time audiences the President was commanding. Due to COVID-19 restrictions,

I was unable to attend the White House press briefings in person. Social distancing meant a greatly reduced number of journalists were allowed inside the room. Instead, like indulging in the latest box set or Netflix series, I monitored 'The Trump Show' from home.

It became a nightly ritual. The TV would go on at 5.00 p.m. or 6.00 p.m. every evening to watch the White House briefing. Dinner and playtime with the children were structured around it, although it was difficult to plan the evening as the press conferences often started late and could go on for more than an hour. Usually, it was just as easy to eat in front of the TV and have a side order of press briefing with my spaghetti bolognese. Although on the evening of 23 April 2020, I nearly choked on my meal when I heard the President's latest musings on the pandemic.

He took to the podium in the James S. Brady Press Briefing Room and began his address by giving an update on the economic stimulus plan being debated by Congress. He then moved on to highlight falling case numbers in some states. He spoke about vaccine trials and increased deliveries of personal protective equipment (PPE) for frontline medical workers. He was keen to talk about phased reopening plans for the economy. Throughout the pandemic, Donald Trump had always prioritized lifting restrictions on businesses and schools. 'We cannot let the cure be worse than the problem itself,' he would say. In Bob Woodward's book *Rage*, Mr Trump admitted deliberately downplaying the seriousness of the virus: 'I wanted to always play it down. I still like playing it down, because I don't want to create a panic.'

As I indulged in a second helping of spaghetti bolognese, the President introduced a new member of his coronavirus team. Bill Bryan was in charge of the Science and Technology

Directorate at the Department of Homeland Security. He and his staff had been researching ways of killing the coronavirus and Donald Trump told us that he had some exciting results to share. 'I think it's going to be something that nobody has ever heard. It'll be brand-new information and very important information,' the President said. Mr Bryan then described the effect of sunlight on the coronavirus: 'Our most striking observation to date is the powerful effect that solar light appears to have on killing the virus, both on surfaces and in the air. We've seen a similar effect with both temperature and humidity as well.'

Next came the D word – disinfectants.

'We're also testing disinfectants readily available. We've tested bleach, we've tested isopropyl alcohol on the virus,' Mr Bryan said. 'And I can tell you that bleach will kill the virus in five minutes, isopropyl alcohol will kill the virus in thirty seconds, and that's with no manipulation, no rubbing, just spraying it on and letting it go.'

It was music to Donald Trump's ears. A quick-fix miracle cure that would make this whole nightmare go away. As quick as getting a property deal approved, as quick as declaring bankruptcy and walking away from a bust casino, as quick as dismissing political opponents with insulting nicknames and chants from supporters. Ultraviolet light and disinfectants? Bill Bryan was speaking Donald Trump's language.

'So, I asked Bill a question that probably some of you are thinking of, if you're totally into that world, which I find to be very interesting,' the President mused aloud. 'So, supposing we hit the body with a tremendous, whether it's ultraviolet or just very powerful, light, and I think you said that that hasn't been checked, but you're going to test it. And then I said, supposing you brought the light inside the body, which you can do either through the skin or in some other way, and I think you said you're going to test that too. It sounds interesting,' he said, turning to his scientific expert.

'We'll get that to the right folks,' Mr Bryan replied, probably hoping that the President would move on, but worse was to come.

'And then I see the disinfectant, where it knocks it out in a minute. One minute. And is there a way we can do something like that, by injection inside or almost a cleaning? Because you see it gets in the lungs and it does a tremendous number on the lungs. So it would be interesting to check that,' he said. By now, the White House Coronavirus Response Coordinator, Dr Deborah Birx, who was sitting close by, was staring at the floor and squirming in her seat. It was no surprise that she looked uncomfortable. The President of the United States had just wondered aloud, on live television, if it would be possible to inject disinfectants into people's bodies.

The following day, the company that makes Dettol and Lysol issued a statement urging its customers not to ingest its products: 'As a global leader in health and hygiene products, we must be clear that under no circumstance should our disinfectant products be administered into the human body (through injection, ingestion or any other route).' Joe Biden tweeted: 'I can't believe I have to say this, but please don't drink bleach.'

Emergency hotlines and poison control centres across the US recorded a spike in calls in the days following the President's comments. 'I can't imagine why,' Donald Trump replied when asked about it by reporters. He insisted he was just being 'sarcastic'. The White House, unsurprisingly, blamed the media for the controversy. 'President Trump has repeatedly said that Americans should consult with medical doctors regarding coronavirus treatment,' the White House Press Secretary Kayleigh McEnany said in a statement. 'Leave it to the media to irresponsibly take President Trump out of context and run with negative headlines.'

It was a new low in the President's handling of the coronavirus crisis and it marked the end of his nightly press briefings. They may have been generating big TV ratings, but they were also generating controversy and criticism for a leader who was failing to bring the virus under control. Of course, every region in the world was battling the same pandemic, but the US quickly became the worst affected country. Although America has 4 per cent of the world's population, it had 20 per cent of the world's coronavirus deaths. It would not be fair to blame all of this on Donald Trump, but leadership comes from the top and Mr Trump failed to set an example. He flip-flopped on mask-wearing and criticized lockdowns in a desperate attempt to reopen the country and salvage an economy that was falling off a cliff. He saw this as his best way of retaining the White House after the 2020 election. The federal system that exists in the US meant it was up to individual governors and mayors to issue lockdown orders, mask mandates and public health advisories. This led to a patchwork approach that saw some states enforce far more rigorous restrictions than others.

In Washington DC, schools were shut in March 2020 and did not begin to reopen again for almost a year. My two daughters had to get used to virtual learning and home-schooling. We are fortunate that my wife is a primary school teacher and was able to help the girls with their studies, but there were still lots of frustrations, like weak Internet signals and missing iPad chargers. It was a constant battle with our bored seven-year-old to convince her to stay in front of the computer while her teacher tried to conduct a lesson over Zoom, and another constant battle with our ten-year-old to ensure she was watching her virtual classroom and not surfing the Internet.

In February 2021, eleven months after they were closed, the DC schools finally started to reopen on a phased basis. There were only a handful of places available in each grade and names were chosen at random. Neither of our girls was picked in the first round of offers and we were bitterly disappointed, particularly for our younger daughter, who was really struggling with virtual learning. 'You can't take this lying down,' our neighbour Emily told us. 'Stop being polite Irish people and start behaving like pushy Americans!' She said we should demand a place for our daughter. 'You can be sure that's what all the other parents are doing.'

We sent the principal an email expressing our disappointment, outlining the difficulties Erin was having and saying we would be very interested in a place should one become available. Not quite 'pushy American' but a notch above 'pushover Irish'. It worked. Erin got a place.

While schools were closed in Washington for a year, many businesses remained open throughout the pandemic. Maskwearing was enforced initially inside buildings and on public transport, and then on the streets. Those who didn't comply could be subject to a fine, but also to public mask-shaming. I experienced this at the beginning of Washington's mask mandate. It wasn't compulsory to wear a face covering while undergoing vigorous exercise and, while it may have been a stretch to call my daily jogs 'vigorous', I knew I wasn't technically breaking the rules by leaving my face uncovered while out running. Not everyone agreed. As I crossed a street close to my home, a woman pulled down her own mask to scream in my face: 'Wear a damn mask!' Thank you for projecting into my face, I thought as I jogged on, but after that it was easier to wear a face covering while running than risk incurring the wrath of angry Americans. Being in the 'pushover Irish' camp can be hard to overcome.

With the issuing of 'stay-at-home' orders by the mayor, downtown Washington became a ghost town and many businesses boarded up their windows and doors. I started working from home, but this meant I had to gather the equipment that I would need from the RTÉ office, which meant a trip downtown. I found the building was as quiet as the surrounding streets. The few people I met on my floor were doing the same as me, carrying boxes and wheeling cases into the lifts so they could set up operations in their homes.

I had arranged to meet Murray there and we grabbed tripods, lights, a computer, a printer and various cables and accessories. He went ahead with half the load and I stayed behind to lock up. I surveyed the room to see if there was anything I was forgetting and paused to look at the two maps hanging on the wall. One was of the US, covered in those red pins I had used to mark the cities and states I had visited. The other was a map of Ireland. It filled me with a sense of uncertainty about the future as the world shut down and travel ceased. Would I be adding any more red pins to the map of America? When would I see Ireland again? It felt strange, as I turned off the lights and closed the door on the RTÉ Washington bureau, not knowing when I would see the inside of the office again.

Live TV reports from my front yard sparked lots of chatter on our quiet residential street. Neighbours got to know the timings of the *Six One* and *Nine O'Clock News* bulletins. Some would avoid passing our house at those times, others relished the prospect of being seen on Irish TV. The people who lived directly across the street from us had good friends in Ireland who got a great kick out of seeing their house in the background of my reports. While I was broadcasting outside, my wife was inside guarding the door, warning our two girls not to run out and turn Dad into the latest viral sensation by ambushing me while I was live on-air.

Working from home posed other challenges. I didn't realize how strong the office Internet connection was until the first time I tried to send a TV report from my basement back to Dublin for the *Six One News*. These packages usually transferred in a minute or two, so it was no big deal if I was editing an item and putting the finishing touches to it until close to my deadline. When I sent a report, our transfer system would tell me how long it was going to take to arrive back at base. I was used to seeing estimated times of two or maybe three minutes. The first time I sent a piece from home, it informed me that it would take twenty minutes. I looked on in horror. It was 12.55 p.m. Eastern Time, which meant it was 5.55 p.m. Irish time. The news would be half over by the time the report arrived. In a panic, and in the hope of boosting the broadband signal, I asked everyone in the house to turn off their devices and disconnect from the Internet, including the girls, who were in the middle of virtual school. It made no difference. My story had to be dropped to the end of the bulletin and even at that it barely made it. It was a baptism of fire as I, like the rest of the world, had to get used to the challenges and pitfalls of working from home.

Many of the coronavirus stories I covered related to New York, the epicentre of the outbreak in the US. A military hospital ship had to be deployed to deal with overwhelmed wards. Bodies were piled up inside refrigerated trucks that were parked outside overcrowded morgues. Central Park had been turned into a field hospital. The images that struck me the hardest, and that have stayed with me to this day, were pictures of Hart Island. It sits off the east shore of New York City's Bronx borough. The island has been used since the nineteenth century to bury New Yorkers with no known next-of-kin or whose families couldn't afford a funeral. Drone footage showed workers digging mass graves to bury those killed by the coronavirus. The numbers of bodies being brought to the island had jumped and contract labourers had been hired to carry out the burials. Some of those interred would eventually be moved when the crisis eased, but while the resting places may have been temporary, the scale of the loss and devastation in New York would never be forgotten.

I spoke to some of the Irish people working on the frontlines in New York, interviewing them over Skype and Zoom as I could not meet them in person. Clive Anderson was originally from Cork and worked as a funeral director in Westchester County, about a thirty-minute drive from Manhattan. The funeral homes in the area had become completely overwhelmed by the scale of deaths. 'People were hailing hearses instead of taxis,' Clive recalled. He usually dealt with 120 funerals in a normal year, but in April 2020 alone he organized sixty-five and described that time in New York as 'mayhem'. With families prevented from gathering and mourning in the traditional way, Clive often found himself offering counselling, comfort and support to those who had lost loved ones. 'It's nearly like I'm becoming Father Clive. I'm a funeral director and I'm trying to be there and help them as much as I can and try and have some kind of a service. Even though I'm not an ordained clergyman, I'm trying to do something because right now these people have absolutely nothing,' he said.

By June 2020, some of the restrictions had been eased and Murray and I were able to travel to the Woodlawn area of the Bronx, one of New York's most Irish neighbourhoods. Tricolours and oversized shamrocks hung from the pubs and shops that lined the main street. Many members of the community were struggling because of New York's coronavirus shutdowns, particularly undocumented migrants who typically work in industries such as construction, retail and hospitality, which had all been hit hard. We were filming on the street outside the Emerald Isle Immigration Center when we were approached by a man in his forties. Let's call him Jim, which was not his real name.

Jim told me that he was an undocumented Irish immigrant who had been living illegally in the US for twenty years. He worked in construction in New York but had lost his job three months previously when the COVID-19 restrictions began. 'It's been really hard. On 15 March everything shut down, there were no jobs. It is very difficult for me now to make ends meet. Even though I'm surrounded by a wonderful Irish community here in Woodlawn, they don't have the work to give me.' While additional financial supports were put in place to help Americans who had lost their jobs as a result of the pandemic, Jim could not avail himself of them. 'It's heart-breaking when you are undocumented. You can't pay the rent and you can't turn to the government for help, you can't ask for a handout. I'm going to be struggling for a while, but I'll get back on my feet, that's what Irish people do, we will always fight to get back on our feet.'

Even before the coronavirus outbreak, things had become a lot harder for undocumented immigrants living in the US under the Trump administration. Amid a clampdown on illegal immigration, there were increasing numbers of raids being carried out by the Immigration and Customs Enforcement agency (ICE). 'I have been afraid of ICE over the last few years,' Jim told me. 'That's the way the country has gone. I'm undocumented and so are so many of my friends, Hispanic, Mexican. We all work together and we all have the same fears. Where has the American Dream gone? I want that back, where any immigrant can come to America, do their best, work hard and stay out of trouble. That's becoming a lot harder right now.'

Jim, like many other undocumented people living in New York, had turned to Irish immigrant support centres for help with paying bills since losing his job. A group of Irish organizations had come together to set up an initiative called Sláinte 2020. It helped immigrants who were struggling amid the coronavirus lockdowns by offering grants, food and advice. Siobhan Dennehy, the Executive Director of the Emerald Isle Immigration Center, told me that they knew the undocumented Irish were out there but, because of the pandemic, they had started engaging with them and supporting them in ways they had not done before. 'They did come out of the shadows and they did ask for help and that can be a very difficult thing to do. Some of the applications for aid were very hard to read as people described the dire situations they were in,' Siobhan said.

A thirty-minute drive from the Bronx is downtown Manhattan. For three months the city that never sleeps had been comatose and the normally packed streets were empty. By June 2020, the traffic had started to build again and there were people out and about once more. They bustled around with typical New York haste, but all the while wearing face masks and keeping their distance.

The easing of restrictions had been a long time coming for businesses like the Irish-owned Fitzpatrick Hotels, but reopening meant taking extra precautions. A scanner at the door of Fitzpatrick Grand Central took customers' temperatures as they walked into the reception area. Staff worked behind screens and face masks. The deserted Manhattan streets, closed businesses and strange atmosphere reminded hotelier John Fitzpatrick of the aftermath of the terrorist attacks in 2001.

'It is similar to 9/11 in some ways, but also different. September eleventh was such a terrible disaster for New York, but the rest of the world carried on. This time, the whole world was hit. During 9/11, local New Yorkers could still come out a few weeks later and meet each other. It was so important to talk, mix and communicate. That's the kind of people we are, we like to talk about issues, it's like going to a psychiatrist,' he said. But there could be no therapy sessions over dinners or glasses of wine in 2020. John Fitzpatrick thought he had seen it all in his years as a hotelier, but he could never have predicted the fallout from the coronavirus. 'After 9/11, I remember saying to my team, thank God it's over and I don't think in our lifetime we'll ever see anything like that again. Did I ever think I'd be sitting here, waiting for a governor or a mayor to tell me that I can open my hotels again?'

By mid-2020, most parts of the US had started to ease coronavirus restrictions, but different states were reopening at different times. It led to an uneven approach that sparked anger, division and even protests. Anti-lockdown demonstrations were held in many parts of the country, and I attended one such rally in Annapolis, Maryland.

Annapolis is a beautiful city that sits on the shores of the Chesapeake Bay and is home to the US Naval Academy, where each year thousands of young Americans begin their military careers. All roads appear to lead to the Maryland State House, in the centre of Annapolis, which is surrounded by green lawns and tall trees. It is an impressive building with its distinctive dome dominating the skyline. It also has major historical significance as the oldest US state capitol in continuous use and the only state house ever to have served as the nation's Capitol Building, the seat of the US government, between November 1783 and August 1784. Today, it is where the Governor of Maryland is based and that is why, in May 2020, protesters gathered outside the building, demanding that the state be reopened and coronavirus restrictions be eased.

One of the demonstrators, Samantha Stephens, told me that if people were afraid of the virus, they should stay indoors and allow the country to reopen. 'If you're not comfortable, I ain't mad at ya, just stay in and protect yourself, but don't have your fear cause us to lose our freedom,' she said. Another protester, Jill Smith, said she did not believe the warnings from doctors and scientists who said it was too early to reopen the economy. 'They're lying to us and the mainstream media [she gestured to me] is lying to us, but people are finally starting to wake up,' she told me. There were no masks or social distancing at the rally, but there were lots of flags and placards with slogans such as 'Let the healthy get back to work' and 'Shutdown the shutdown'. Shari Carson said she wasn't concerned that the virus could be spread by those gathering at the demonstration. 'I'm not scared. I don't need to be tested, I'm fine and I've been working everyday throughout this,' she said.

David Frye was carrying a placard calling for churches to be allowed to reopen because religious services were essential. 'We have a large church where we can practise safe social separation. The people who are sick can stay at home and the people who are healthy can come and worship the Lord,' he said. Another protester, Kimberly, told me that shutting down businesses was an overreaction: 'Fear tactics are being used to keep us from living. We could go out on the street and get hit by a car but we don't stop cars from functioning on the roads.'

While the protest was getting underway in Annapolis, 30 miles away, back in Washington, President Donald Trump was in the White House Rose Garden unveiling Operation Warp Speed, his plan for the accelerated development and rollout of COVID-19 vaccines. 'It means big and it means fast,' he said. 'A massive scientific, industrial and logistical endeavour unlike anything our country has seen since the Manhattan Project. Nobody has seen anything like we're doing now, within our country, since the Second World War. Incredible.' The speech was filled with the President's usual superlatives and hyperbole as he predicted vaccines by the end of the year. His timeline ended up being correct, but he also went on to talk about 'breakthrough therapies'.

Three days later, at a meeting with restaurant executives in the White House, the President revealed that he himself was taking one of those experimental 'breakthrough therapies', the anti-malaria drug hydroxychloroquine. He dropped this bombshell while taking questions from reporters about the medicine. 'You'd be surprised at how many people are taking it, especially the frontline workers, before you catch it. I happen to be taking it.' It took the journalists who were covering the event by surprise and the follow-up questions came thick and fast. 'A couple of weeks ago, I started taking it,' he explained. 'Because I think it's good. I've heard a lot of good stories. And if it's not good, I'll tell you right, you know, I'm not going to get hurt by it. It's been around for forty years for malaria, for lupus, for other things.'

The President's attitude was, what harm will it do and what have you got to lose? The Food and Drug Administration (FDA) disagreed, however, and a few days later issued a warning about hydroxychloroquine amid fears of serious side-effects. 'The FDA has said hydroxychloroquine should not be used outside of a hospital setting or outside of a research study,' a reporter said to the President. 'No, that's not what I was told. No. There was a false study done where they gave it to very sick people, extremely sick people, people that were ready to die,' he claimed.

It was not as serious as his disinfectant suggestion, but Donald Trump's promotion of an unproven treatment did have dangerous consequences. A man in Arizona died after ingesting chloroquine phosphate, confusing it with the drug the President had been touting. The man's wife said that after watching Donald Trump on TV, the name 'chloroquine' resonated with them. She found some medicine that she had used as a parasite treatment for her pet fish. They both took it, leaving the woman in a critical condition and causing her husband's death.

In late May 2020, the President was asked by reporters how long he was planning to continue taking hydroxychloroquine. 'I had a two-week regimen and I'm still here. I tested very positively, in another sense.' Wait, did the President just say he tested positive? 'Do you mean negative?' came the confused follow-up question. 'Yeah. I tested positively toward negative, right? So, no, I tested perfectly this morning, meaning I tested negative. But that's a way of saying it: positively toward the negative.' It was the perfect metaphor for the President's handling of the virus – confusing, mixed messaging amid an unrelenting desire to find miracle cures and magic potions. Donald Trump had weathered countless storms and survived controversies that would have destroyed other politicians. He used similar tactics now. This typically involved portraying himself as the victim or the martyr and then attacking those who were attacking him, often through use of a nickname – 'Crooked Hillary', 'Lyin' Ted', 'Crazy Bernie', 'Sleepy Joe'. He used terms like the 'kung 'flu' and 'China virus' for COVID-19, but it wasn't enough to vanquish the enemy. This was a foe he could not defeat with insults nor would it just magically disappear, as he had suggested so often.

However, Donald Trump did manage to politicize the virus and use it to attack opponents. He embraced protest movements, like the one I had witnessed in Annapolis, where demonstrators called for lockdowns to be lifted. In April 2020, Mr Trump tweeted, 'LIBERATE MINNESOTA!' 'LIBERATE MICHIGAN!' 'LIBERATE VIRGINIA!' The tweets were in response to protests against stay-at-home orders in those states. It was no coincidence that Minnesota, Michigan and Virginia all had Democratic governors. A few weeks after the tweets, the anti-lockdown movement in Michigan took a particularly sinister turn when armed protesters entered the State Capitol Building in Lansing. Wearing bulletproof vests and with rifles hanging from their shoulders they stood face-to-face with security guards, angrily chanting 'Let us in' and 'Tyranny'. There were many more protesters outside the building and some of their chants and placards were aimed directly at the state's Governor, Gretchen Whitmer, with slogans like 'Heil Whitmer' and 'Lock her up'.

Whitmer was seen as a rising star within the Democratic Party and had delivered the official rebuttal to Donald

Trump's State of the Union address in February 2020. She was viewed as a possible running mate for Joe Biden. Donald Trump did not like her and infamously referred to her as 'that woman from Michigan'. Governor Whitmer jokingly embraced the title and it even started to appear on commemorative T-shirts. In October 2020, the FBI arrested seven men who had plotted to kidnap the governor. The suspects were linked to a militia group that had previously attended the armed protest at the State Capitol Building.

Throughout the pandemic, Donald Trump clashed with other governors. The entire federal system seemed to frustrate him. He was annoyed by the fact that individual states controlled their own lockdowns and restrictions, not the White House. Mr Trump would threaten to override these measures, but he had no authority to do so. In a direct appeal to his conservative, Christian base he said he wanted to see churches reopened for Easter services. 'Wouldn't it be great to have all the churches full?' he asked during a Fox News interview in April 2020. 'You'll have packed churches all over our country. I think it'll be a beautiful time.' Health experts were horrified at the suggestion and most churches remained closed that Easter, except for a small number that insisted on opening throughout the pandemic in defiance of local rules. A month later, during a White House press briefing, he demanded once again that the churches open and claimed he would intervene if governors refused, although he did not have that power. He said it was an 'injustice' that some state leaders had allowed 'liquor stores and abortion clinics' to stay open while closing houses of worship. 'I'm calling houses of worship essential. If there's any question, they're going to have to call me, but they're not going to be successful in that call,' he said.

In reality, Donald Trump couldn't tell governors what to do. He could make suggestions and apply pressure, but that didn't always work given that some of his messages were confusing and inconsistent, such as when it came to mask-wearing. At first, he downplayed the need for face coverings and was rarely seen wearing one. In July 2020, while visiting wounded soldiers at the Walter Reed Medical Center outside Washington, Mr Trump wore a mask for the first time in public. 'I think when you're in a hospital, especially in that particular setting, where you're talking to a lot of soldiers and people that, in some cases, just got off the operating tables, I think it's a great thing to wear a mask,' he said at the time and later tweeted a picture of his masked face, describing it as 'patriotic'. It was seen as a major shift, and many believed he was finally embracing the concept of masks, but, like many Donald Trump U-turns, it didn't last long.

The whole concept of mask-wearing had become mired in politics and geography. I was far more likely to see covered faces in Democrat-controlled cities and states than in rural parts of the Deep South. 'Why are you wearing that mask?' I would get asked at Donald Trump rallies. 'There's no need for it!' The opposite was the case in Washington, where I had been berated for not covering my face while jogging. Anger on both sides, over something as simple as a mask.

12. The Weeping Time

I have always been fascinated by how Americans think nothing of driving vast distances in one day. It is commonplace to embark on a road trip lasting ten or twelve hours, overnight in a roadside motel, and then wake up and do it all again the following day. My family and I undertook one such journey in late May 2020. With lockdown measures beginning to ease, we decided to take an early summer break before the beaches and tourist destinations became too crowded. We drove ten hours to Savannah, Georgia. To mitigate risk, we brought packed lunches so we would have to stop only for petrol and bathroom breaks. We left behind closed businesses and almost universal mask-wearing in Washington. When we arrived in Georgia, it was like another world. A world where it appeared as if the coronavirus did not exist. Shops and restaurants were open and while we wore our face masks in public, we were in the minority.

The Republican Governor of Georgia, Brian Kemp, who was a Donald Trump ally, had announced some of the lightest lockdown measures of any US state and was among the first to lift them. By late April 2020, hair salons, gyms, bowling alleys and even tattoo parlours had reopened. We didn't get tattoos, but we did spend a very enjoyable few days in what is one of America's most beautiful and historic cities, a place that had been on our must-see list of destinations ever since watching *Midnight in the Garden of Good and Evil*, which was filmed there.

Savannah is known for its lavish mansions, shaded parks and giant oak trees draped in Spanish moss. The moss looks soft and fluffy but 'Do not touch it', a tour guide warned us. It can be filled with biting insects known as chiggers. It was a metaphor for our trip to the South during the pandemic – look, but don't touch, admire, but don't get too close.

On our first walk through Savannah, there was music playing in a city-centre park. Crowds were sitting on the grass surrounding a fountain, enjoying the sunshine. It looked normal, like a time before the world had gone into lockdown. Beers were being chugged, plastic champagne flutes were sipped, a delicious aroma of barbecued food hung in the air and there were shrieks and screams of unadulterated joy from the children in the playgrounds. Did Georgians know better than the rest of us? Had they figured out that business closures, maskwearing and social distancing were not needed after all? Of course not. Georgia's coronavirus cases and death rates were among the highest in the US in mid-2020 and surged in the weeks that followed the easing of restrictions.

Despite this, Governor Brian Kemp pressed ahead with his aggressive reopening plans. He even issued an order banning cities in his state from implementing mask-wearing mandates. The Republican governor took legal action against the Democratic mayor of Georgia's largest city, Atlanta, to prevent her from introducing COVID-19 restrictions. 'As the Mayor of the City of Atlanta, Mayor Bottoms does not have the legal authority to modify, change or ignore Governor Kemp's executive orders,' the lawsuit stated. It was another example of the divides within the US that were highlighted by the pandemic. The virus did not care which state people lived in or which political party they supported, and the death toll across America continued to rise.

Much of the allure of Savannah, Georgia, is, rather macabrely, linked to death. Tourists are told tales of ghosts and haunted mansions and Bonaventure Cemetery, on the outskirts of the city, is a must-see for visitors. There are also strong historical links to Ireland. The Irish were among the first settlers to arrive in Georgia, in 1734, in what was then a new colony. There was a further influx from Ireland in the 1830s, with labourers flocking to build the railways and canals needed to serve a booming Georgia. Another wave of Irish followed the Great Famine in the 1840s. As we strolled through Savannah, there were reminders of home at every turn. Tricolours hanging from buildings, Irish-themed bars and shops, and Emmet Park, named after Irish patriot Robert Emmet, which houses the Celtic Cross Monument that honours all citizens of Savannah who are of Irish descent. With this strong Irish influence, it is no surprise that Savannah hosts one of America's largest St Patrick's Day parades each year, but not in 2020. That year, just as in cities and towns across the world, parades and events were cancelled, and there were constant reminders of the reason why.

On 24 May 2020, *The New York Times* published a stark front page. To mark the US coronavirus death toll approaching 100,000 it ran the headline 'An Incalculable Loss', and listed the names and biographical details of 1,000 COVID-19 victims. However, the following day, 25 May, an event occurred that would replace the coronavirus on the front pages, at least for a while.

Police were called to Cup Foods, a convenience store in Minneapolis. A 46-year-old African American man named George Floyd was suspected of using a fake $20 bill to buy cigarettes in the store and the staff called 911. During his arrest, Mr Floyd was restrained on the ground and police officer Derek Chauvin pressed his knee to the man's neck for nine minutes and twenty-nine seconds. Seventeen-year-old Darnella Frazier had come to the convenience store that day with her nine-year-old cousin. They happened upon the arrest of George Floyd. Frazier filmed it on her phone and the video subsequently went viral. George Floyd could be heard uttering his dying words, 'I can't breathe.' It would become the rallying cry for a massive protest movement.

Studies suggest that between 15 and 26 million people in the United States participated in the demonstrations, making it the largest movement in US history. Marches were held in cities and towns across America and around the world. There were even protests in the seaside tourist town of Myrtle Beach, South Carolina. We had made the four-hour journey there from Savannah for the final days of our summer holiday. Under glorious sunshine the children splashed in the sparkling Atlantic Ocean at Myrtle Beach. It was our first time swimming in the sea since taking a dip in the similarly named Myrtleville, in Cork, twelve months previously.

The Black Lives Matter (BLM) protests were growing in size. While the vast majority of the demonstrations were peaceful, some descended into violence, vandalism, rioting and looting. Donald Trump did nothing to ease the tensions, issuing threats and warnings rather than calling for unity and calm. 'These THUGS are dishonoring the memory of George Floyd, and I won't let that happen,' he tweeted on 29 May. 'Just spoke to Governor Tim Walz and told him that the Military is with him all the way. Any difficulty and we will assume control but, when the looting starts, the shooting starts. Thank you!' he wrote.

Twitter flagged the tweet with a warning message, noting it had violated its rules on glorifying violence. It was one of the first times the social media company had done that to a Donald Trump tweet, but it would not be the last. His Twitter feed would become littered with disputed labels and advisories in the aftermath of his election loss.

The phrase 'when the looting starts, the shooting starts' was a controversial choice of words. It had been used in 1967 by the police chief of Miami, Walter Headley. He was speaking during a hearing about crime in his city. His comments sparked an angry reaction from civil rights leaders and are thought to have fuelled the intensified race riots that followed. Segregationist presidential candidate George Wallace also used the expression during his 1968 campaign. Donald Trump's tweeting of the words, more than fifty years later, sparked outrage and he sought to clarify the comment by saying it was not a threat of violence. 'It was spoken as a fact, not as a statement. It's very simple, nobody should have any problem with this other than the haters, and those looking to cause trouble on social media,' he wrote.

Donald Trump was asked about it by reporters later that day. 'I've heard that phrase for a long time. I don't know where it came from or where it originated,' Mr Trump said. 'Frankly, it means when there's looting, people get shot and they die. And if you look at what happened last night and the night before, you see that, it's very common. And that's the way that's meant.' Donald Trump's attempted clarification did nothing to reduce tensions. The protests and unrest continued to spread.

It was a huge news story and my summer vacation would have to be cut short. Technology allows for TV and radio reports to be filed from almost anywhere, including holiday apartments by the sea. I was keen to ensure that my live broadcasts did not have a beach backdrop, choosing the side of the apartment building that faced the nondescript car park as opposed to the Atlantic Ocean. While it may have looked like a generic background for the viewers at home in Ireland, it raised a few eyebrows at the Ocean Pier Apartment Complex.

Experience has taught me to always pack a suit, even on holidays to the beach, in case there is a breaking news story that requires on-camera reporting. It was 35°C under the South Carolina sun and, as my legs would not be in shot, my blazer, shirt and tie were accompanied by shorts and sandals. Joanna was at the swimming pool with our daughters when she overheard some fellow guests expressing concerns about a man behaving strangely on the third-floor landing. 'He's holding a microphone, doing some kind of news report, but he's wearing shorts!' a woman exclaimed. 'I wonder if something has happened in the apartment complex?' her husband asked, then said he would go and check it out.

Joanna texted to warn me that I would soon have company, but by then I was already midway through a live report into the *Six One News*. Out of the corner of my eye I could see a man watching me. He returned to the pool to inform his family that I was reporting on the racial unrest gripping the country. 'It looks like someone who was on vacation but had to work,' he said.

We checked out of our accommodation early the next morning. The clock was ticking, I needed to be outside the White House for a live report into the *Nine O'Clock News* that evening, 4.00 p.m. Eastern Time. Joanna drove as I filed stories and recorded radio reports from the passenger seat.

I was receiving regular updates on the scale of the damage following another night of protests, looting and vandalism. One email was from the building management company that looks after the RTÉ office in downtown Washington DC and it referred to a fire, broken glass and graffiti. A pharmacy on the ground floor had been broken into, looted and set on fire following a BLM protest outside the White House, just a few blocks away. I was sent a photo of the boarded-up building by a colleague and was told that, apart from a smell of smoke, the RTÉ studio was unharmed. I was relying on second-hand information as I was still more than 400 miles away.

We drove for hours along Interstate 95, better known as the I-95. It is a massive highway, more than 1,864 miles long, stretching the entire east coast from the Canadian border all the way down to Miami, Florida. There were constant reminders that we were on the section of the highway that runs through the southern states, with Trump–Pence posters along the roadside and lots of signposts for places of historical interest, such as Civil War battlefields and plantation houses. Memorials from America's shameful past when slaves worked the surrounding fields. Hundreds of years after the first captured men and women were brought in chains to the US from Africa, that legacy of injustice still lived on. As I rushed north to cover a wave of protests calling for change, we were making our way through the very lands where the inequality was born.

One of the best sources of radio news in the US is NPR, National Public Radio. Each state has its own station and as we crossed over state lines from South Carolina, into North Carolina and on into Virginia, the radio crackled and hissed and had to be tuned to the local frequency. Our 2007 Kia Optima did not have CarPlay or a Bluetooth-enabled sound system, but it served us well on our many road trips across the US. On that day, the message coming from the car's radio was the same on every station: there had been another night of unrest in cities across the US and Donald Trump was planning to deliver an address to the nation that night.

As we arrived in Washington DC, we were greeted by boarded-up shopfronts, broken glass and damaged buildings, some of them on a street close to our home. My eldest daughter, Lucy, got upset and asked me if we should be scared. 'What if they come to the houses?' she said. We reassured her that there was nothing to be worried about and that she would be safe.

A few hours later, Murray and I were in front of the White House covering a massive BLM protest. For more than two months I had been busy reporting on the coronavirus and the devastating impact it was having on the US. Much of this work was done from home, using footage gathered from wire services and pool feeds. Now, for the first time in weeks, there was a massive story on our doorstep that was not directly linked to the virus. But the pandemic had not gone away. We had to take precautions while interviewing protesters, using a long boom pole for our microphone to maintain social distancing. We wore face coverings and were relieved to see that the vast majority of the demonstrators were also wearing masks, many of them emblazoned with the dying words of George Floyd: *I can't breathe.*

Subsequent studies have shown that the level of virus spread during the Black Lives Matter protests in the summer of 2020 was minimal, mainly due to the wearing of face coverings. The mask became part of the protest uniform, carrying messages of defiance and hope, and calls for change. Slogans such as 'No Justice No Peace' and 'Black Lives Matter' were also visible on the signs carried by the thousands who had gathered. Some of the placards had been hastily constructed from cardboard boxes and sheets of paper, the messages written in thick, black marker.

The protesters and their chants filled the section of 16th Street that leads to Lafayette Square in front of the White House, an area that was subsequently renamed Black Lives Matter Plaza. On the evening of 1 June, construction workers were busy boarding up the windows and doors of the businesses close to the White House amid fears of more looting and vandalism. From a cart, a man was selling Black Lives Matter T-shirts and face masks. It was a hot summer evening but, mercifully, the usually oppressive Washington DC humidity was low.

As the chants of protesters got louder, phones started to ping simultaneously with an alert from the mayor warning people that, because of the unrest on the streets, a curfew would be enforced at 7.00 p.m., after which time everyone would have to remain indoors. The message did not dampen the enthusiasm of the crowd.

A young African American named Walter Emanuel told me that he had joined the protest because he was tired of the cycle of injustice. 'My parents went through this when they were children. I hope future generations won't have to go through it too. We need to be heard,' he said. Lots of the protesters I spoke to made references to their parents and grandparents going through similar struggles, speaking about the civil rights marches of the 1960s and the riots that followed the assassination of Dr Martin Luther King Jr in 1968. 'We have to come together in a peaceful manner to express ourselves. It is my American right because I am American too,' Walter told me. He described the vandalism and looting that had followed some of the protests as a distraction that was taking away from the cause. 'I'm not here for violence.

I'm here to peacefully protest and express myself. I'm not here to vandalize and I think when you do that, you distract from the mission.'

The former US President Barack Obama spoke at the time about how he felt this protest movement was different, bigger, more significant and more inclusive. 'I know enough about that history to say there is something different here. You look at those protests, and that was a far more representative cross-section of America out on the streets, peacefully protesting, who felt moved to do something because of the injustices that they have seen. That didn't exist back in the 1960s, that kind of broad coalition. There is a change in mindset that's taking place, a greater recognition that we can do better,' Mr Obama said.

I witnessed that broad coalition of support first-hand on the protest lines. While African Americans may have marched alone in the 1960s, this time around people of all races were out in force. People like Jestelle Hanrahan, a white woman who had joined the protest outside the White House on that warm June evening. She was holding a sign made from a piece of cardboard, and in red marker she had written the words 'Police brutality is criminal, accountability is justice'. She told me, 'I came out to support the black community. I certainly don't want to speak for the black community, I am here to listen and show solidarity. Police violence in this country is now being documented for the first time, it's been going on for years, but now it is being filmed. It is our job as people with privilege to stand with our community and say enough is enough.'

I asked her about the negative side of the protest movement, the looting and the vandalism. 'I think there is a lot of rage and I understand that. But I think we need to differentiate between people who are expressing centuries of rage and the people who are taking advantage. I think there are two very distinct groups and the people here today are peaceful and are here to make a statement,' she told me. Jestelle was protesting alongside her friend Stephanie Krenrich. 'I think this is one of those times in history when it is going to make a difference. Maybe it's a combination of people being home from work and school, people are awake, and this is a good sign,' she said. There is no doubt that the pandemic had added to the scale of the protests. People were at home, many with nothing to do. With no work or school, it was easier to grab a square of cardboard and a marker and join the local protest, wherever it might be.

The pandemic also added to the levels of anger and frustration. The African American community was disproportionately affected by the coronavirus. The economic downturn hit the poorest hardest. Greater numbers of black people tended to be employed in jobs deemed frontline or essential and were unable to work from home. Those who got sick often fell victim to the healthcare inequalities that continue to bedevil the US. Another protester I spoke to, an African American man named Leroy, told me that he understood why people were looting. He pulled down the black bandana that covered his mouth to make his point. 'We're in a recession. There are millions of unemployed people, some can't feed their families. You are damn right they are going to go into Walgreens, they are going to go into Target, some people can't even clothe their kids, you are damn right they are going to go into these stores and get what I feel is what is due to them, what they are owed. There are also two sides to things, there will be people out protesting just to cause trouble, but when it comes to taking stuff, I feel like we are owed that anyway.'

While it was the death of George Floyd that had sparked the protests, the names of other African Americans who had died violently were also chanted by demonstrators. People like Breonna Taylor, a 26-year-old emergency medical technician who was shot eight times when police raided her apartment in Louisville, Kentucky, in March 2020. Ahmaud Arbery had not died at the hands of police but his killing was no less shocking. The African American man was shot by a white father and son while he was out jogging in Georgia in February 2020. The racial unrest was reignited in August that year with a series of protests following the police shooting of Jacob Blake. The 29-year-old man was left paralysed after being shot in the back by police officer Rusten Sheskey in Kenosha, Wisconsin.

Given that Wisconsin is a key swing state, and with the election just weeks away, it was no surprise that both Donald Trump and Joe Biden travelled to Kenosha. The candidates' visits to the city were just two days apart, but their trips were very different and highlighted the contrasts between the two men when it came to their approach to the Black Lives Matter movement. Donald Trump visited burnt-out buildings to assess the damage caused by days of rioting. He pushed his message of law and order and vowed to clamp down on the unrest. 'These are not acts of peaceful protest but, really, domestic terror,' he said. He met with business owners whose premises had been vandalized and held talks with local law enforcement. He did not meet with the family of Jacob Blake, the black man whose shooting had sparked the protests.

Joe Biden did meet with the Blake family and then held a town-hall meeting with community leaders in a church where he vowed to tackle the issue of criminal justice reform if elected. 'I'm going to go down fighting for racial equality, equity across the board,' he said.

Although African Americans make up less than 14 per cent of the US population, in 2019 they accounted for more than 23 per cent of the just over 1,000 fatal police shootings. Black people are also statistically more likely to end up in prison and in 2018 represented almost a third of the country's incarcerated population. African Americans are imprisoned at five times the rate of white Americans and at almost twice the rate of Hispanic Americans, according to the latest data. A 2020 analysis by ABC News revealed that in 250 jurisdictions, black people were ten times more likely to be arrested than their white counterparts.

The 2020 racial unrest erupted while I was in Savannah, Georgia. The city's lavish mansions and ornate squares were hiding a shameful past, a history of wealth and luxury built on the backs of slaves. Fertile soil and a favourable climate saw cotton plantations spring up around Savannah and its port became a hub for the transatlantic slave trade. A short distance outside the city there is a memorial to the largest slave auction ever held in US history. In March 1859, 436 men, women and children were sold at a racetrack. The auction became known as 'The Weeping Time', following reports that it rained incessantly throughout, the weather mirroring the tears being shed by the slaves. From a city known for ghost stories, it is another grim chapter in US history which still haunts the country to this day.

13. What's the milk for?

While speaking to the BLM demonstrators outside the White House on 1 June, I noticed several cartons of milk had been left on street corners and along the footpaths where the protesters were gathering. 'What are they for?' I asked one of my interviewees. 'If you get tear gas or pepper spray in your eyes, milk helps,' came the reply. Hopefully it won't come to that this evening, I thought, as Murray and I got ready to pack up, but I was aware that in recent days the authorities had been heavy-handed with both the protesters and the media covering the demonstrations.

Suddenly, there were loud bangs and shouts. Smoke filled the air and people started running. There was a sense of sheer panic. We had no choice but to run, too, pushed along by the rush of the crowd. The police had begun the process of clearing protesters. Chemicals and smoke were used, projectiles were fired. Some officers carried shields and batons, others were on horseback. It was a controversial action that would spark outrage and widespread condemnation.

'No tear gas was used, and no rubber bullets were used,' the White House Press Secretary Kayleigh McEnany told reporters in the days that followed, echoing similar claims from police. But it was a matter of semantics. While the chemicals deployed and the projectiles fired were not technically labelled as tear gas and rubber bullets, the use of force had been excessive. The images that played on TV screens around the world were reminiscent of protesters being targeted under authoritarian regimes, not the USA. Whatever weapons and tactics were used by the police, it had the desired effect and the thousands of protesters who had gathered outside the White House that evening fled, and so did we. We ran for a few blocks before stopping to catch our breath. I checked my watch. It was only 6.30 p.m., still thirty minutes before the city-wide curfew. Why had they cleared the protesters half-an-hour early? This hadn't happened on previous evenings.

Soon it would become clear what was going on, but for now I had to concentrate on the next part of what had already been a crazy day – Donald Trump's address to the nation. At 6.43 p.m. Eastern Time, he began delivering his speech from the White House Rose Garden. I was standing on a nearby street corner, still out of breath from our panicked run a few minutes earlier, hoping that my battery and 4G signal would last as I watched the President's address on my phone.

'My fellow Americans, my first and highest duty as President is to defend our great country and the American people. I swore an oath to uphold the laws of our nation, and that is exactly what I will do,' the address began. Mr Trump went on to describe how the country had been rightly sickened and revolted by the brutal death of George Floyd and he vowed that justice would be served.

'He will not have died in vain. But we cannot allow the righteous cries and peaceful protesters to be drowned out by an angry mob,' he said before going on to utter the words that would dominate much of his election campaign message for the following months: 'I am your President of law and order.' As with his 'Make America Great Again' slogan, which had been used by Ronald Reagan in the 1980s, Donald Trump was borrowing another campaign message from one of his Republican predecessors. Richard Nixon had vowed to be a president of 'law and order' when running for office in 1968. It came at a time of racial unrest and massive protests following the assassination of Dr Martin Luther King Jr. It was a powerful message and it helped get Nixon elected.

Donald Trump continued to channel his inner Nixon. 'In recent days, our nation has been gripped by professional anarchists, violent mobs, arsonists, looters, criminals, rioters, Antifa, and others.' For the US President, Antifa had become the enemy. As the name suggests, it means 'anti-fascist' and Mr Trump had gone so far as to designate the group as a terrorist organization. The problem, however, is that it doesn't have a defined structure or leader, but rather is a loosely affiliated group of far-left, anti-fascism activists. But for Donald Trump, there had to be an enemy, an 'us versus them' scenario that would allow him to rally his base and continue with his politics of division. 'Antifa' would be the bogeymen of this protest movement, the radical left mobs that were burning buildings and trying to tear down Confederate statues and monuments.

'Here in the nation's capital, the Lincoln Memorial and the World War Two Memorial have been vandalized,' he went on. 'One of our most historic churches was set ablaze. A federal officer in California, an African American enforcement hero, was shot and killed. These are not acts of peaceful protest. These are acts of domestic terror. The destruction of innocent life and the spilling of innocent blood is an offence to humanity and a crime against God.' The references to God were undoubtedly included to appeal to Donald Trump's base, and there was more to follow.

'That is why I am taking immediate presidential action to stop the violence and restore security and safety in America. I am mobilizing all available federal resources, civilian and military, to stop the rioting and looting, to end the destruction and arson, and to protect the rights of law-abiding Americans, including your Second Amendment rights,' he said in another shout-out to his base. The Second Amendment to the US Constitution protects the right to bear arms and was passed by the US Congress on 25 September 1789. During a speech on restoring law and order, Mr Trump had decided to insert a line to keep his gun-owning supporters happy.

He then went on to call on governors and mayors to 'dominate the streets' with 'an overwhelming law enforcement presence until the violence has been quelled'. He even threatened to use US troops to restore order. 'If a city or a state refuses to take the actions that are necessary to defend the life and property of their residents, then I will deploy the United States military and quickly solve the problem for them.' He vowed to take swift action to protect Washington DC, describing the previous night's rioting and looting in the city as a 'total disgrace'. He added: 'As we speak, I am dispatching thousands and thousands of heavily armed soldiers, military personnel, and law enforcement officers to stop the rioting, looting, vandalism, assaults, and the wanton destruction of property. We are putting everybody on warning: our seven o'clock curfew will be strictly enforced.'

No shit, Sherlock, I thought, my heart still pounding following our dash from the White House just minutes before. Donald Trump concluded his remarks with a cryptic reference to what was to come next. 'And now I'm going to pay my respects to a very, very special place. Thank you very much.' Flanked by members of his staff, he then marched from the White House, through Lafayette Park, and across the street to St John's Episcopal Church.

It is known as the Church of the Presidents because every US Commander in Chief since James Madison (1809–1817) has attended services at St John's. Donald Trump, who is not particularly religious, had only been there on a handful of occasions in the past, but now he was standing in front of the building holding a Bible aloft. The church had been vandalized during recent protests, with a fire being set in the basement of the parish house. 'Is that your Bible?' a reporter asked. 'It's a Bible,' came the reply from the President. 'We have the greatest country in the world, we're going to keep it nice and safe.' He then returned to the White House and it was all over.

But the controversy was just beginning. The President of the United States was being accused of ordering the removal of peaceful protesters from in front of the White House so he could pose for a photo opportunity. Donald Trump had tried to seek cover behind two central pillars of American society: God, and the military. He had delivered a speech threatening to use US troops to restore order and then, angered by news reports that he had spent time in an underground bunker as protesters gathered, he had crossed the street to pose for photos in front of a church. The bishop of the Episcopal Diocese of Washington DC was not happy.

'He used violent means to ask to be escorted across the park into the courtyard of the church,' Bishop Mariann Edgar Budde told NPR. 'He held up his Bible after speaking an inflammatory militarized approach to the wounds of our nation. He did not pray.' She said Mr Trump had held up the Bible 'as if it were a prop or an extension of his military and authoritarian position. I was outraged that he felt that he had the licence to do that, and that he would abuse our sacred symbols and our sacred space in that way.'

There was a visit to another holy place the following day when the President and the First Lady paid their respects at a shrine to Saint John Paul II. That, too, was met with criticism from Church leaders. The Catholic Archbishop of Washington, Wilton Gregory, said he opposed letting the President visit the site: 'I find it baffling and reprehensible that any Catholic facility would allow itself to be so egregiously misused and manipulated in a fashion that violates our religious principles.'

When Donald Trump returned to the White House after that visit, he signed an executive order on religious freedoms. Lots of people turn to religion at times of crisis and the President knew that this stance would appeal to the conservative Christian voters who had helped him win the presidency in 2016. In early June 2020, with the election just five months away, he needed their support once again, but his blatant actions had attracted the ire of US religious leaders.

Next, we come to that second pillar of American society that Donald Trump turned to in his hour of need: the military. Here again, his efforts backfired. Military leaders past and present criticized his handling of the protests and unrest. There was stinging condemnation from his former Defense Secretary James Mattis. Writing in *The Atlantic*, Mr Mattis described the President as a threat to the Constitution: 'Donald Trump is the first president in my lifetime who does not try to unite the American people, does not even pretend to try. Instead, he tries to divide us.'

The man who succeeded Mattis as Defense Secretary, Mark Esper, also distanced himself from the President when he said that he would not support the use of the Insurrection Act to deploy US troops to restore order. 'The option to use active-duty forces in a law enforcement role should only be used as a matter of last resort, and only in the most urgent and dire of situations. We are not in one of those situations now. I do not support invoking the Insurrection Act,' Mr Esper said. Donald Trump was furious at the intervention and never forgave his Defense Secretary. Mr Esper was sacked five months later, in the days after Mr Trump's election defeat.

America's top general said he regretted his role in the controversial photo opportunity outside St John's Church. The Chairman of the Joint Chiefs of Staff, General Mark Milley, had accompanied Mr Trump, dressed in his camouflage combat uniform, as he walked from the White House to the vandalized church. 'I should not have been there. My presence in that moment and in that environment created a perception of military involvement in domestic politics.'

Throughout the summer, calls for equality swept across America as the Black Lives Matter movement gained a new impetus that had not been seen before. Our daughters embraced it, joining their friends and neighbours by putting drawings in our windows calling for an end to injustice. 'Where are you going?' I asked my eleven-year-old, Lucy, as she and her friend Blake tucked posters under their arms and grabbed a box of chalk. 'We're going to the protest,' she replied, informing me that there was a local Black Lives Matter rally close to their school, which is just a short distance from our home. After about thirty minutes, I decided to see how the protest was going.

As I approached the area, I found it odd that I couldn't hear any chanting. There was no noise at all, in fact, except for the sporadic beeping of car horns. When I rounded the corner, I found Lucy and Blake. They had written messages of hope and equality on the street in chalk and were standing on the footpath waving their Black Lives Matter posters at passing cars. They were the only people there. 'Oh no,' I said as I approached them, 'did nobody turn up for the protest?' They then informed me that this was 'our protest'. There was no organized event, they had decided to do this on their own. It was a reminder of the impact of the BLM movement, an indication of just how much momentum was behind the protests. The injustice of George Floyd's death had resonated with people of every background. There was a genuine and widespread hunger for change.

There were demonstrations big and small over the following months and the fence surrounding the White House became a monument to the Black Lives Matter campaign. The railings were covered with messages of support and tributes to those who had lost their lives at the hands of police. Visitors, many of them African Americans, came to take pictures and read the posters and signs.

'No matter where we go, we're going to get judged,' Trey Morgan told me. He was there with his heavily pregnant girlfriend, Deshawn Collington. The couple were expecting their first child a month later and had come to the White House to take photos to show their son when he is older, in the hope that his experiences will be different from their own. 'I've gone into different stores and locations where I get stereotyped as soon as I get there. It's the way I dress or my hair, or especially my skin colour,' Trey said.

For mother and daughter Angela and Dahra Johnson, their visit to the White House also led them to recall their own experiences of racism and inequality. 'I've encountered the issues that most of us black Americans have lived with, like going into a store and being followed. Once, when my hair was cut short, I was pulled over by a police officer just because he thought I was a guy,' Angela said. 'Unfortunately, you have to navigate through things like that in the US and I've been navigating through it my whole life.'

It is something Angela's daughter, Dahra, also had to deal with: 'I went to a majority white elementary school and the teachers there didn't believe I lived in the neighbourhood. They used to pull me aside to ask me questions like, "Where do you really live, how did you get here, how do you get home?" Growing up, I experienced a lot of micro-aggressions like that.'

I met Jerome Chase buying a Black Lives Matter T-shirt from a street vendor outside the White House. 'I went to prison for a crime I never committed in the eighties. There are a lot of black people who are accused of things and targeted for things they didn't do. In the last five years I've come to learn that not all police officers are bad, but police departments have to pull out the bad apples,' he said.

A twenty-minute drive from the White House is the Southeast district of Washington DC, where there are many predominantly African American communities and some of the poorest neighbourhoods in the US. Yaida Ford worked as a lawyer and community activist in Washington's Ward 8, the city's most disadvantaged area. 'Systemic racism drives where we put our money. There's a lot of talk of supporting communities of colour and men and women of colour but not a lot of walk, lots of talk but not a lot of walk,' Yaida said. 'There are underlying health conditions that African Americans experience disproportionately more than white people, for example stress-related conditions and high blood pressure. There are also food access issues that create health problems.'

For many, the President embodied a lot of the attitudes

that allowed inequality to continue to prevail, highlighting how there would have to be top-down fundamental change if real progress were to be made towards achieving a just society. Aside from his handling of the racial unrest, there were now wider, more troubling questions about Donald Trump. Was the President of the United States racist? He would dismiss such suggestions, of course. He has repeatedly claimed to be the 'least racist person that you've ever met'. But over the years there has been evidence to the contrary.

In 1973, the US Department of Justice sued the Trump Management Corporation for violating the Fair Housing Act. Federal officials accused Donald Trump of refusing to rent apartments to black tenants and of lying to black applicants about the availability of apartments. The case resulted in Mr Trump signing an agreement committing not to discriminate against tenants of colour.

The Fair Housing Act had been introduced in 1968 to make it illegal for anyone to be discriminated against when renting or buying a home. Prior to the passing of this civil rights legislation, black families were locked out of the opportunity to create generational wealth by purchasing a home and passing it down to their children. They were denied mortgages and access to certain neighbourhoods because of their skin colour. This was known as 'redlining' and involved federal agencies and banks literally drawing a red line on a map around African American neighbourhoods. Within these areas, home loans would not be granted. Neighbourhoods in more affluent, typically white areas, where banks would provide home loans, were outlined in green, giving rise to the term 'greenlining'.

Although the practice of 'redlining' has been outlawed for

decades, it has created a wealth gap that exists to this day and has had a long-lasting impact on homeownership among African Americans. In 2020, black homeownership rates stood at 47 per cent, the lowest rate of any racial group. White Americans have a homeownership rate of 76 per cent. It is just one of many economic indicators that see black communities on the bottom rung of the ladder. According to 2018 census data, the mean annual income for African American households was $58,985, compared to a figure of $89,632 for white households.

Accusations of racism were also levelled against Donald Trump over his involvement in the case of the so-called Central Park Five. In 1989 four black teenagers and one Latino teenager were wrongly convicted of attacking and raping a white female jogger in New York City. Mr Trump led the charge against the accused men and even took out newspaper ads demanding: 'BRING BACK THE DEATH PENALTY. BRING BACK OUR POLICE!' The teens spent years in prison before having their convictions quashed after being cleared by DNA evidence. New York City paid $41 million in 2014 to settle the men's civil rights lawsuit, but Donald Trump said in October 2016 that he still believed they were guilty. He also refused to apologize for calling for the death penalty.

In his tell-all memoir, Mr Trump's lawyer Michael Cohen described his former boss as a racist who spoke disparagingly about African Americans and had a 'low opinion of all black folks'. He claimed Mr Trump said: 'Tell me one country run by a black person that isn't a shithole. They are all complete fucking toilets!' According to the memoir, Mr Trump praised apartheid-era South Africa and criticized Nelson Mandela.

Donald Trump began his political career by promoting the 'birther' conspiracy theory that falsely claimed Barack Obama was not born in the US. During his 2016 election campaign, Mr Trump called Mexican immigrants criminals and rapists and vowed to ban Muslims from entering the US. While in office, in August 2017, he said there were 'very fine people on both sides' of clashes at a white supremacist rally in Charlottesville, Virginia. Throughout the pandemic he repeatedly referred to the coronavirus as the 'Chinese virus' and the 'kung 'flu'. In June 2020, he retweeted a video of one of his supporters yelling, 'White power!' During the first presidential debate against Joe Biden, he told the far-right extremist group known as the Proud Boys to 'stand back and stand by', comments that were celebrated by the organization.

So, was Donald Trump a racist president? It is a question I put to Martin Luther King III in the summer of 2020, at the height of the Black Lives Matter movement.

'Everything he is doing has a racial tone,' he told me. Dr Martin Luther King Jr's eldest son pointed to the Trump administration's policies in areas such as education and housing. 'There are a few positive things he has done, like supporting Historically Black Colleges and criminal justice reforms. But many of the things he has done have hurt the African American community, like removing diversity and sensitivity training from government operations, basically saying that insensitivity doesn't exist.

'I consider the implications of what he has done are certainly racist, with overtones of constant racism. I don't know if we've seen this since the 1960s. The Confederate monuments are another example. The Confederacy in the Civil War fought to preserve slavery. Those monuments may go in a museum, but they should never be in a place of honour. For him to say they're taking down our monuments means this man clearly has some racist blood.'

I was at the Lincoln Memorial in Washington DC to hear Martin Luther King III speak in August 2020. He delivered an address from the same spot where his father had made his iconic 'I Have a Dream' speech in 1963. 'I have a dream that my four children will one day live in a nation where they will not be judged by the colour of their skin, but by the content of their character.' Those famous words were heard by the thousands who had gathered for the March on Washington. Fifty-seven years later, another March on Washington was held to once again call for racial justice and equality in the aftermath of George Floyd's killing.

'There's a knee upon the neck of democracy, and our nation can only live so long without the oxygen of freedom,' Martin Luther King III told the crowd. His daughter, twelve-year-old Yolanda Renee King, also spoke at the rally: 'Less than a year before he was assassinated, my grandfather predicted this very moment. He said that we were moving into a new phase of the struggle. The first phase was for civil rights, and the new phase is a struggle for genuine equality.' Loud cheers rose from the crowds that lined the reflecting pool between the Lincoln Memorial and the Washington Monument.

A very different address had been delivered a short distance from there, less than twenty-four hours earlier. It was Donald Trump's acceptance speech, marking the end of the Republican National Convention. He spoke from the South Lawn of the White House and focused on the negative aspects of the Black Lives Matter movement – the rioting and looting that had followed some of the demonstrations. 'Your vote will decide whether we protect law-abiding Americans or whether we give free rein to violent anarchists and agitators and criminals who threaten our citizens,' he told cheering supporters. 'Make no mistake, if you give power to Joe Biden, the radical left will defund police departments all across America. They will pass federal legislation to reduce law enforcement nationwide. They will make every city look like Democrat-run Portland, Oregon.'

Donald Trump repeatedly accused Joe Biden of wanting to 'defund police departments'. It wasn't true, but it was an effective campaign tactic and something that featured regularly in attack ads targeting the Democratic candidate. Mr Biden himself acknowledged that the calls by some protesters to defund the police were problematic and had damaged the campaigns of Democrats in other, down-ballot races. 'That's how they beat the living hell out of us across the country, saying that we're talking about defunding the police. We're not. We're talking about holding them accountable,' Joe Biden was heard saying in a leaked recording from a meeting with civil rights leaders shortly after Election Day.

Donald Trump's politics of fear and division found a new voice amid the racial unrest of 2020. As part of his strategy of 'divide and conquer', he was always quick to highlight that some of the biggest protests were happening in states and cities with Democratic governors and mayors. 'In the strongest possible terms, the Republican Party condemns the rioting, looting, arson, and violence we have seen in Democrat-run cities, like Kenosha, Minneapolis, Portland, Chicago, and New York,' he told his party's National Convention. He then reached out directly to black voters. 'Last year, over one thousand African Americans were murdered as a result of violent crime in just four Democrat-run cities. The top ten most dangerous cities in the country are run by Democrats and have been for many decades. Thousands more African Americans are victims of violent crime in these communities. Joe Biden and the left ignore these American victims. I never will,' he said.

Martin Luther King III was ten years old when his father was assassinated in 1968. He told me that if his parents were alive today, he believes they would be disappointed and saddened to learn that the US has become more divided than ever. 'President Trump is not a unifier, he is intentionally a divider. I have to assume that the main reason he is that way, beyond the fact that he has no moral compass, is because he thinks this is the way he wins. He was able to win the first time because he divided people and he thinks that is his formula for winning, so he continues to divide.'

I spoke to Martin Luther King III with my RTÉ colleague Jackie Fox for a podcast we hosted called *States of Mind*. It was a series about the US election but became dominated by the Black Lives Matter movement in the summer of 2020. Not all of the guests were critical of Donald Trump's handling of the unrest and some insisted that the US President had done a lot of good for the African American community. People like Immanuel Jarvis, the Chairman of the Durham County Republican Party in North Carolina. He spoke about what it was like to be a black Donald Trump supporter: 'I akin it to probably being a homosexual black man in a southern US state in the 1970s. To some degree, you have to be careful who knows what you are and what you believe. You are happy to find others who share your ideological views. And when you find others who do, you meet together, socialize together and they become your friends.'

Immanuel Jarvis believes that many black Republicans share his story: growing up in predominantly Democratic households and listening to their preachers in church every

Sunday. 'They went to public schools where they were taught a liberal ideology. They didn't realize until later in life that what they were being told was incomplete and biased,' he said. He switched from Democrat to Republican when he was in his early twenties. He was living in Virginia Beach and working in sales. There was a hurricane coming from the Atlantic and he wanted to find information about the path of the storm. 'I knew AM radio stations carried more news and I came across a conservative talk radio station. I thought, this is dumb, who listens to this trash, but decided I would stomach it and wait until the news at the top of the hour,' he recalls.

Over the course of the next two or three days, as the storm was approaching, he got more interested in the radio station and found himself agreeing with the conservative commentators. 'I then started reading about black history, I started looking at articles about Frederick Douglass, about Booker T. Washington, and I started to realize that our black history comes from Republican roots. By the age of twenty-two or twenty-three I realized, I'm not a Democrat, I'm a Republican, because this is my history. I see people who live with conservative ideologies and to me they tend to be happier, they tend to be more prosperous, even if they are not rich, their children end up being better off.'

On 2 June 2020, Donald Trump tweeted that his administration had done more for the black community than any president since Abraham Lincoln. 'That's pretty close, man,' Immanuel Jarvis told me. 'You might have your jaw on the floor right now, but my daughter is a recipient of increased funding for Historically Black Colleges and Universities. We keep saying education is the key, well, Donald Trump has gone to the locksmith and made copies of the keys and handed them to African Americans.' He also pointed to Mr Trump's famous wall along the Mexican border and claimed that of any racial group, black people are the greatest beneficiaries of enhanced border security. 'When illegal immigrants come, they typically gravitate towards inner cities because that is where the resources are. African Americans typically tend to live in inner cities. They came here in chains and by literally shedding blood, sweat and tears for the last four hundred years, we reached a point where we can avail of some social services to help our people, and so when we are competing with illegal immigrants in these cities, it is taking away resources that we desperately need and have desperately worked for and is owed to us.'

Immanuel Jarvis is clearly annoyed that the vast majority of black people tend to vote Democrat. 'Sadly, if they had a cardboard box running for president, 85 per cent of the African American community would vote for the box. We've put all our weight on one side and then wonder why politics doesn't work for us. It doesn't work for us because we are not balanced.' He sees the Republican Party as a source of common-sense, conservative principles that will lift people up out of poverty, whereas the Democratic Party is about sticking with the status quo and accepting poverty. 'What I see with the black community here in the US, even though there is more opportunity in this nation than ever, is that we are suffering and that it is getting worse and worse, not because the lifelines aren't there but because we refuse to grab onto those lifelines as a result of indoctrination and what we have been taught.'

Despite months of racial unrest before the 2020 election, Donald Trump actually increased his share of support from black voters compared to the previous election. He attracted 8 per cent of the African American vote, a 2 percentage-point gain on his 2016 result. In an interview for Bob Woodward's book *Rage*, Donald Trump complained that he wasn't receiving more support from African American voters. 'I've done a tremendous amount for the black community and, honestly, I'm not feeling any love.' In the same book, he did acknowledge that there was systemic racism in the US, but downplayed the significance of it: 'Well, I think there is everywhere. I think probably less here than most places. Or less here than many places.'

The Democratic Congressman James Clyburn believes that the systemic racism that still exists in the US can be traced all the way back to the arrival of the first enslaved people from Africa five hundred years ago. 'African Americans did not come here escaping from bondage, we came here to be bound. Our history in this country is the opposite to white Americans, people running away from poverty or fleeing one form of government or another, coming to this country seeking freedom. Black folks were brought to this country to be enslaved and that sets out the foundation on which this whole country was built; white people to be free and black people to be enslaved.'

James Clyburn is the most senior African American representative in Congress and his endorsement of Joe Biden helped rescue the former Vice President's struggling campaign during the 2020 Democratic primaries. He grew up in segregated South Carolina and was a prominent activist in the civil rights movement of the 1960s.

'I always felt that we were doing things so our children and grandchildren would not have to do them but here we are, lo and behold, and my children and grandchildren seem to be having to live the same things that I lived,' he told me. 'Everything has been structured to maintain white superiority and some people take it as far as white supremacy. Our judicial system, healthcare system and education system all have to be restructured. They've all been set up to be against black folks.'

James Clyburn believes that what makes America great is that it has always been able to repair its faults. Abraham Lincoln's Emancipation Proclamation ended slavery, a fault that had to be repaired. Other examples would follow over the decades, like the Brown v. Board of Education (1954) Supreme Court decision which ruled that racial segregation of children in public schools was unconstitutional, like the Great Society programmes of Lyndon B. Johnson, which tackled poverty and racial injustice through funding for education and medical care, like the Voting Rights Act, the Civil Rights Act and the Higher Education Act.

'The first thing we've got to do is admit we have a problem we have to solve. For the last twenty years in this country, we've been pretending we didn't have a problem, pretending that all we had to do was elect an African American president and that would take us beyond race in this country. That is a pretence for other things that people are beginning to see now. We've got to admit that there's a structural problem when it comes to race in this country.'

Back at the White House, where the protesters were trying to be heard, trying to force that admission Clyburn described, the fences and barricades were eventually taken down. But the barriers to equality felt by many who had gathered there will be much harder to remove.

14. Unconventional conventions

By August 2020, the racial unrest and the protests had started to ease and the focus began to shift to November's presidential election. Murray and I travelled to Wilmington, Delaware, Joe Biden's hometown, to cover the Democratic National Convention. We took the train and filmed a TV report on board as this was the same route travelled by Mr Biden every day for almost forty years. Each morning, the then US senator would take the ninety-minute Amtrak train ride from Wilmington to Washington, and back again each evening, earning him the nickname 'Amtrak Joe'.

It is a part of Joe Biden's life that has frequently been used in his campaign ads to promote his image as someone who is in touch with the common man, but it is also a part of his life that stemmed from unimaginable tragedy. His first wife and his baby daughter were killed in a car crash in 1972, leaving him a widower with two young sons. He was determined to be home every night to look after his boys. More heartbreak was to follow in 2015, when Joe Biden lost his son Beau to brain cancer.

It is estimated that over the course of more than three decades, Joe Biden travelled around 2 million miles and spent four years of his life commuting by train to work. The journey looked very different in the era of COVID-19, with social distancing, near-empty carriages and masked passengers. We spoke to those on board to ask what they thought of Joe Biden as a candidate. Cole Cooper told me that anybody would be an improvement on Donald Trump: 'As a candidate, Joe Biden's fine, but overall we just need a return to some sort of logic in American politics.'

Another passenger, Georgina Scoville, also said she would be backing Joe Biden, but added that he was not her first choice during the Democratic primaries. 'I'm twenty and this is my first election. I'm pretty disappointed that the candidate is an old white man, but it is what it is, and I will be voting for him,' she said.

There was a sense from many of the train passengers that while they would be voting for Joe Biden, they did not see him as the perfect candidate. He could be gaffe-prone and had been accused of exaggerating and fabricating stories. Claims of plagiarism helped scupper a previous presidential run in 1987. He had to address allegations of inappropriate touching and was criticized for opposing court-ordered busing as a method of desegregation in public schools. It was an issue that saw him come under attack from Kamala Harris during the Democratic primaries, but the pair were clearly able to put their differences behind them, with Harris joining him as his running mate.

When we arrived in Wilmington the train station was, appropriately enough, named after Joe Biden – the Joseph R. Biden Jr. Railway Station. The journey to the top of US politics had been a long one for 'Amtrak Joe', but it was a route that would take him all the way to the White House.

His opponent was struggling to deal with the realities of the pandemic, which threatened to completely upend his campaign strategy of holding big rallies. The President continued to try to pack arenas and venues, in defiance of local health advisories, and these gatherings were frequently criticized for being 'super-spreader' events. A study by Stanford

University looked at eighteen Trump rallies between June and September 2020 and found that they had led to more than 30,000 coronavirus cases. The research involved comparing the counties where the rallies were held to other counties with similar COVID-19 case numbers prior to the events taking place.

'Our estimate of the average treatment effect across the eighteen events implies that they increased subsequent confirmed cases of COVID-19 by more than 250 per 100,000 residents. Extrapolating this figure to the entire sample, we conclude that these eighteen rallies ultimately resulted in more than 30,000 incremental confirmed cases of COVID-19,' the study found. Researchers also concluded that the rallies likely led to more than seven hundred deaths, though not necessarily among attendees.

The first rally that Donald Trump held during the coronavirus lockdown was in June 2020 in Tulsa, Oklahoma. Attendees had to a sign a legal waiver promising not to sue the Trump campaign if they got sick. President Trump claimed that one million people had requested tickets. An overflow area was put in place in anticipation of the massive crowds, but when the night arrived, the arena was only one-third full. The Bank of Oklahoma Center in Tulsa holds 19,000 people, but the local fire department said only 6,000 people were in attendance. Images of rows of empty seats dominated the coverage of the rally and the overflow area was, needless to say, not required. It turned out that in the days leading up to the rally, activists had used TikTok to encourage people to register for a free ticket and then not show up. The Trump campaign denied that this was the reason for the poor turnout and instead blamed negative media coverage and protests. Maybe people were just worried about attending a packed, indoor event at the height of the pandemic? Whatever the reason, it was an embarrassing return to the rally stage for a man who was obsessed with crowd size.

The next Trump rally was scheduled to take place in Portsmouth, New Hampshire, but it was cancelled. Organizers claimed this was due to an incoming storm, although forecasters were predicting that the bad weather would have passed by the time the event was due to begin. There was a strong suspicion that the rally was scrapped amid fears of another poor turnout. Despite these setbacks, Donald Trump was determined to have a traditional, in-person Republican Convention. It was originally due to take place in Charlotte, North Carolina, but the state's governor said he could not allow the packed, mask-less gathering that the President was insisting on. It led to a big public row and Donald Trump decided to take his business elsewhere, announcing that the event would be moved to Jacksonville, Florida, where less stringent public safety rules would allow for a gathering that would at least resemble a traditional convention. The plan would see Republican delegates meeting in Charlotte for the formal business of the convention while Donald Trump's big acceptance speech would take place in Florida. But just a few weeks later, that too had to be scrapped.

President Trump made the surprise announcement at one of his daily coronavirus briefings: 'I looked at my team and I said the timing for this event is not right. It's just not right with what's been happening. I said there's nothing more important in our country than keeping our people safe, whether it's from the China virus or the radical left mob,' he said. The President insisted that he had not been asked to cancel the event by officials in Florida, but the local sheriff had warned that his officers would be unable to provide security for the gathering because of poor planning and a lack of funding. A majority of Florida voters also viewed the holding of the convention as unsafe, according to opinion polls that were carried out at the time. Donald Trump eventually had to bow to the inevitable and hold a mainly virtual convention, just like the Democrats.

The keynote address at the Democratic Convention was delivered by seventeen 'rising stars' from within the party, who each read a section of the same speech. Congressman Brendan Boyle was one of those who spoke. 'I was honoured to be asked to be one of the keynote speakers. My segment made sense for me and spoke to some of the issues I've been active on and it fit in with the wider speech. You couldn't have done that with a traditional convention. I did miss the usual hoopla if we had been there in person, but this convention got high praise because it was better for television and better for viewers than an in-person convention. So, I think, moving forward, you're permanently going to see elements like we saw in 2020.'

The convention also saw history being made as Kamala Harris became the first woman of colour to be nominated for the role of Vice President. In her acceptance speech, she paid tribute to her mother, Shyamala: 'Oh, how I wish she were here tonight, but I know she's looking down on me from above. She probably could have never imagined that I would be standing before you now, speaking these words: I accept your nomination for Vice President of the United States of America.'

There were harsh attacks against Donald Trump, with his predecessor, Barack Obama, describing him as a self-absorbed and self-serving president who 'hasn't grown into the job because he can't' and as someone with 'no interest in treating the presidency as anything but one more reality show that he can use to get the attention he craves. I did hope, for the sake of our country, that Donald Trump might show some interest in taking the job seriously, that he might come to feel the weight of the office and discover some reverence for the democracy that had been placed in his care. But he never did. He's shown no interest in putting in the work, no interest in finding common ground, no interest in using the awesome power of his office to help anyone but himself and his friends.'

Despite all the big names who addressed the convention, it was a thirteen-year-old boy who became the star of the show. Brayden Harrington spoke about how Joe Biden had helped him overcome a stammer. 'Without Joe Biden, I wouldn't be talking to you today. About a few months ago, I met him in New Hampshire. He told me that we were members of the same club. We stutter.'

Mr Biden had a debilitating stammer as a child and would read from books of Irish poetry in front of a mirror to practise his diction. These were tips that he passed on to young Brayden. 'I'm just a regular kid and in a short amount of time, Joe Biden made me more confident about something that's bothered me my whole life. Joe Biden cared. Imagine what he could do for all of us.'

Joe Biden's love of Irish poetry has continued to this day and, as expected, his acceptance speech ended with a quote from *The Cure at Troy* by Seamus Heaney. 'This is our moment to make hope and history rhyme,' he said.

Joe Biden didn't hold big, in-person campaign events. Instead, he chose to address drive-in rallies. Supporters remained in their cars and honked their horns as the candidate arrived on stage. He had a tendency to run onto the stage at these events, perhaps to dispel any worries that a 77-year-old candidate wasn't up to the rigours of the campaign trail. My seven-year-old daughter, Erin, was fascinated by the fact that every evening on the news she would see the Democratic candidate sprinting from a car or up a flight of stairs. She would dash around the house singing, 'Joe Biden runs, Joe Biden runs'. It became a nightly ritual.

While the candidate was running, his supporters were cycling. 'Ridin' with Biden' saw groups of cyclists getting together wearing their Joe Biden T-shirts and riding their bikes to show their support for the Democratic hopeful. There were plenty of online events too, including several 'Irish Americans for Biden' virtual rallies. They involved prominent Irish American Democrats delivering glowing endorsements of the candidate while performers played traditional Irish music. A recurring song at these events was 'Cast a vote for Biden', which was sung to the same tune as 'The Waxies' Dargle':

> Says my aul' wan to your aul' wan
> Do you remember
> Come this fall
> One and all, we'll be voting in November
> We have a voice, make a choice
> For our country and our children
> Clear the way for a better day
> Cast a vote for Biden!

It wasn't exactly *The Cure at Troy*, but it certainly was catchy.

Joe Biden's acceptance speech was delivered at the Chase Convention Center in Wilmington, Delaware. I was there to cover it, and I was struck by the massive security operation that was in place. The building was like a fortress. A high steel fence surrounded the entire complex, with Secret Service agents and police patrolling the perimeter. Joe Biden was going to be delivering a speech in an empty room, thanks to social distancing. So how do you drum up enthusiasm at a virtual convention during a pandemic? The Democratic Party decided to set up an invite-only, drive-in watch party in the car park. Party officials and Biden family and friends were among those who watched the address on big screens in a scene that resembled a drive-in movie theatre.

Supporters were glued to Joe Biden's speech as if it were the latest Hollywood blockbuster, but there was also plenty of drama on the street outside. A group of Trump supporters had gathered to protest against the Democratic nominee. They wore 'Make America Great Again' hats and T-shirts and waved Trump flags. Chants included 'Four more years', 'U-S-A' and 'Sleepy Joe has got to go!'

Bruce Wilmoth had come to the Democratic Convention holding a large Trump flag. I asked him why he was there. 'We love our president and we do not like Joe Biden. He has been in this state for many, many years and he has done nothing for Delaware,' he told me. Sam Chick was at the protest in his role as the chair of Delaware Young Republicans. 'Donald Trump represents what this country is all about, which is freedom. People should be able to make their own choices without the government getting involved, that's why we need to keep Joe Biden away from the levers of power.'

Vicki Santoro was also a Trump supporter and told me she was not concerned by the big lead that Joe Biden had in the opinion polls at that time. 'It was the same four years ago, they kept saying Donald Trump was behind, but he won. I think it will be the same this time. There are more silent Trump voters out there than we can imagine,' she said.

The Biden voters certainly were not silent as their candidate wrapped up his acceptance speech. They cheered and beeped car horns as the nominee appeared on a stage outside the venue to view a fireworks display. The virtual Democratic Convention had been a success. The following week, it was the turn of the Republicans.

As the ultimate TV president, Donald Trump understood the medium and drafted in some of his television producer friends to help with the convention. It all looked very professional, with slickly produced campaign-style videos accompanied by dramatic music and patriotic images of American flags and well-known US monuments. The speakers delivered passionate addresses outlining Donald Trump's achievements in office and urging voters to re-elect him. One of the stand-out moments came when Kimberly Guilfoyle took to the podium. She was a senior Trump campaign adviser and girlfriend of Donald Trump Jr. A former TV host, she delivered a rousing, dramatic speech that got louder and louder as she went along. In a packed auditorium it would have been met with cheers and applause, but in an empty room it just sounded like she was shouting as she delivered her closing line: 'The best is yet to come!' Kimberly Guilfoyle's father had emigrated from county Clare, so perhaps her thunderous delivery was a nod to 'The Banner Roar'.

While the Republican Convention was a mainly virtual affair, delegates did gather in person in Charlotte, North Carolina, to nominate Donald Trump formally as the party's candidate for president. He was due to visit the convention to thank officials and was also planning to address a small rally in the rural town of Mills River, two hours west of Charlotte.

Murray and I arrived there early to get though security and to find a position for our camera. It was August and when the morning cloud had cleared, blazing sun shone on the open, unshaded yard of the Flavor First farm produce packaging facility where the event was taking place. Members of the media grumbled about the heat as jackets were removed and sunscreen applied, but the crowd that had gathered for the proceedings didn't care. They were there to see Donald Trump and they didn't mind that the US President was running two hours late. Earlier that day he had taken to the stage in front of Republican delegates to thank them for their nomination. He was eager to get a taste of a traditional convention at a time when COVID-19 had made it impossible to have packed arenas with balloons and confetti falling from the ceiling.

Back at the farm produce facility, the President's supporters were seated on socially distanced chairs, but they took to their feet when the presidential seal was placed on the podium on the stage, a signal that Donald Trump's address was just minutes away. The crowd erupted in cheers as he was introduced and his signature campaign rally song, 'God Bless the USA', played on the speakers. Mr Trump spoke for around twenty minutes and left. It was a long day of waiting, queuing, security screening and temperature checks for a twenty-minute speech, but for his supporters it was worth it. They loved him.

The controversies, scandals and offensive comments that shocked his critics and enraged his opponents only served to endear him further to his base. Lindi Jo Rettig had come to Mills River to hear Donald Trump speak and said she believed he had his finger on the pulse of America: 'Some people say he's a little too outspoken, but he's speaking my language. I would like to see law, order and decency restored to this country and I believe in him 100 per cent.' She also defended the President's handling of the coronavirus crisis: 'Only God can end a pandemic, not any politician, and to claim they can is foolish. We can try to control it and take precautions.' But, I asked, what about the fact that Donald Trump had arranged this crowded campaign event during a pandemic? 'People are in the street rioting and looting. If you can go riot, loot or stand in line at a Walmart, then you can come out to vote and come to support Donald Trump,' she replied.

Michael Loomis was wearing a blue Trump/Pence T-shirt and he praised the President's response to the recent wave of racial unrest and protests. 'He will keep law and order in America. We have a real crisis right now, with Democrats letting the cities burn,' he told me. Mike Lyons was wearing a 'Make America Great Again' hat signed by Donald Trump and a Republican Party face mask. He highlighted the 'America First' policy of protecting US jobs and industries. 'He believes in the strength that was and is America and he is for good and healthy trade with our neighbours,' he said.

Later that week, Donald Trump delivered his acceptance speech from the South Lawn of the White House. It led to criticism that he was using the office of the President for a party-political event. There was also criticism over the fact that 1,500 supporters were packed together to hear the speech, with little social distancing or mask-wearing on display. 'This election will decide whether we save the American Dream or whether we allow a socialist agenda to demolish our cherished destiny,' the President told the crowd.

Donald Trump always thrived in front of a live audience. When his speeches were read from autocues in empty rooms, they tended to be flat and lacking in energy. When he was at a podium surrounded by cheering crowds, it was a very different performance. His White House address clearly gave the President a taste for the campaign stage and soon afterwards he resumed holding the packed rallies that he had become known for. Murray and I attended one such event in Gastonia, North Carolina, in late October 2020, just two weeks before the election.

In a bid to reduce health risks, the Trump campaign had moved their rallies outdoors, usually to airports. Donald Trump would fly in on Air Force One, step off the plane, deliver his speech and then return to Washington or wherever the next campaign stop might be. It was an efficient system as he criss-crossed the country in the closing weeks of the campaign. As we approached Gastonia Municipal Airport, it was like going to a music festival or a football match at a time when no such gatherings were allowed. Cars had to be parked at a nearby high school and we were bused to the venue. Crowds of Trump supporters filled the approach roads, and our bus driver eventually gave up and told us to walk the final section of the route. Street vendors were selling Trump merchandise and we could hear music blaring from the speakers inside.

When we finally made it through the crowds and the security checkpoints, we were escorted into the media section. Thousands of people were packed onto the airport tarmac, many not wearing masks. Before Donald Trump took to the stage, I spoke to some of those who had gathered to hear him speak. Patti Lane said she wasn't concerned that she could be putting her health at risk by attending a rally during a pandemic. 'You have to live your life. I believe in God. I have my faith and if it's my time, it's my time, but I think this is important enough to come out here and support him,' she told me.

Many supporters said they were backing Donald Trump because of his success as a businessman. 'America is a corporation and it should be run as such, therefore he is the man for the job,' Tabatha Moses said. I asked her about recent media reports that the US President was hundreds of millions of dollars in debt and had avoided paying income tax. 'I don't care about all of that, it's what he has done for the country that matters,' Tabatha said.

Theron Suddeth dismissed reports of Donald Trump's struggling businesses and tax avoidance as lies. He was a large man with a white beard and looked like a Trump-supporting Santa Claus. 'He's the smartest man we've ever had as president. He is someone who builds skyscrapers. A man isn't going to have a plane and helicopters if he doesn't pay taxes, that's ridiculous,' he said.

When Donald Trump took to the stage, the crowd cheered. He quickly embarked on his usual tirade about how a vote for Joe Biden would be a vote for socialism and lawlessness. He pointed to us in the media section. 'Look at the fake news media back there,' he exclaimed, and the crowd responded with a chorus of boos. But it was all pantomime and theatre. Donald Trump loved the media and being on TV, he just didn't like journalists questioning his claims and calling him out on his falsehoods.

I never encountered any animosity from Trump supporters during the election campaign. That would come later when furious protesters, fuelled by unfounded claims of voter fraud, gathered to object to the election results, culminating in the storming of the Capitol Building. The Trump rally in North Carolina had reminded me of going to a football match as I arrived at the venue, and I got that sense once again as the event was wrapping up. Donald Trump had been talking for over an hour when I noticed large numbers of his supporters starting to head for the exits, even though he was still speaking. They were like sports fans who had decided to leave early and beat the traffic because they knew their team was either so far out in front that they could not be beaten, or so far behind that they could not recover.

The Trump and Biden campaigns were now in full swing and while they looked very different, there were similarities between them. Just as Democrats had gone on the attack against Donald Trump in their convention, the Republican event contained lots of warnings of the chaos that would ensue if Joe Biden were to be elected president. With America emerging from a summer of racial unrest and protests, there were claims that a Biden presidency would lead to defunded police departments as well as looting, burning and mob violence on the streets. Donald Trump, on the other hand, had vowed to be the president of 'law and order' who would protect America's suburbs. As Election Day approached, the dividing lines between the two sides were growing ever wider.

15. God and guns

While Joe Biden was claiming that four more years of Donald Trump would cause irreparable damage to the country, the incumbent was warning that a vote for his opponent would lead to socialism, greater government control and the loss of gun rights. These messages were echoed at campaign rallies and throughout the Republican Convention in August 2020. The convention was addressed by a husband and wife who had pointed guns at Black Lives Matter protesters. Mark and Patricia McCloskey, who were both lawyers, were filmed brandishing weapons as demonstrators marched past their home in St Louis, Missouri, in June 2020.

At the convention, the couple claimed that US neighbourhoods would be overrun by crime and lawlessness if Joe Biden were to win the election. 'No matter where you live, your family will not be safe in the radical Democrats' America,' Patricia McCloskey said. 'President Trump will defend the God-given right of every American to protect their homes and families,' Mark McCloskey said, a clear reference to Donald Trump's repeated promises that he would protect the Second Amendment of the US Constitution, the right to bear arms. In May 2021, Mr McCloskey announced that he was running for a seat in the US Senate. 'I've always been a Republican, but I have never been a politician,' he told Fox News. 'But you know, God came knocking on my door last summer disguised as an angry mob, and it really did wake me up.'

On our way to cover the Republican Convention in

Charlotte, North Carolina, Murray and I stopped off at a gun show in neighbouring Virginia. Amid the stalls selling rifles and pistols, the Republican Party had set up a stand to register voters. Officials held clipboards and pens as they encouraged attendees to vote early and in person, echoing the concerns expressed about postal voting by their candidate, Donald Trump.

Lance Thomas was wearing a red Trump face mask and was in his fifties. He said he had never voted before but had just registered that day in the hope of keeping the President in power. 'He speaks his mind and tells the truth. I think he'll win as long as there isn't mail-in voting, there's just too much dishonesty in this country,' he told me.

Among the rows of weapons and ammunition, 'Make America Great Again' hats and bumper stickers were also on sale. Heidi Singhas examined the merchandise while wearing a blue Trump face mask. 'I like everything about him. His policies are important to me. He doesn't care about people's feelings. He's outspoken, honest and blunt, that's why I like him,' she said.

One of the gun sellers, Paul Voska, said he would be voting for Donald Trump. 'He's a bit crass and runs his mouth, but I like that about him. I'd rather have someone saying the things that need to be said and not hold back. Donald Trump has done a lot to promote business and I also like that he bashes the media because unfortunately in America media outlets promote their own agendas and that destroys democracy.'

When we arrived at the gun show venue with our camera and equipment, I told the woman at the front desk that we were from an Irish TV station and were planning to do a news report on gun ownership in the US. 'I don't know,' came the suspicious reply. 'Are you going to make us look bad?' she asked. I explained that I had no agenda or bias and would report factually on what I saw and heard. 'Do you have guns in Ireland?' she asked. 'Not many,' I said. I explained that only hunters and some farmers had rifles and shotguns and that handguns were illegal. 'That's why Irish people are very interested in gun ownership in the US, because it is very different from what we are used to,' I told her. She thought for a moment. 'OK then,' she said and, with some reluctance, handed me two press passes. 'Wear these at all times and please don't film anyone without asking them first.'

I had had an almost identical experience the previous year at the first gun show I attended. It was in Maryland and while there was a different person at the front desk, she gave me the same sceptical, suspicious interrogation about my intentions and 'not making us look bad' before eventually granting us access. That was in March 2019 and a ban on 'bump stocks' had just come into effect in the US. These are devices that allow rifles to fire like machine guns. They were outlawed in the wake of the Las Vegas mass shooting in 2017, when fifty-eight people were killed and five hundred wounded after Stephen Paddock opened fire on an outdoor concert from a hotel-room window. He had twenty-two semiautomatic rifles with him and fourteen of the weapons were equipped with bump stocks. It was one of the few gun control measures introduced by the Trump administration and while campaigners criticized him for not going further, gun rights activists fought the bump stock ban in the courts.

The event I attended in Maryland was billed as a 'gun and hunting show'. Inside a long exhibition hall there were rows of stuffed dead animals, fishing rods, boats and clothing stalls, but there were also guns. A lot of guns. They came in a variety of shapes, sizes and colours. There were firearms for sale and weapons to be won in raffles and competitions. There were gun accessories and various pieces of merchandise, like T-shirts, mugs and posters. Written in pink letters across one shirt were the words 'Girls just wanna have guns'. You could also buy a sign that read 'I plead the 2nd', a reference to the Second Amendment.

I visited the Maryland gun show shortly after a mass shooting in New Zealand in which a gunman targeted two mosques and killed fifty-one people. Following the atrocity, the government there moved quickly to ban military-style semiautomatic weapons and assault rifles. I asked the gun show attendees if they thought similar measures would ever be introduced in America.

'I would hope not,' one man told me. 'I'm sure that the liberals will want to ban certain guns, but it's not the gun that kills people, it's people that kill people.' Another man used the same words and added: 'It's the same as blaming a pencil for misspelling a word.' Some of those I spoke to were in favour of tougher gun laws. One man told me that, as a hunter, he was an avid believer in gun ownership but added: 'I don't believe someone in the United States technically should have a fully automatic weapon.'

Another attendee said she would like to see stricter rules around the age limits for people who can buy guns. Many of those I met spoke about how the vast majority of gun owners are responsible, law-abiding citizens. One man said: 'Nobody in their right mind who owns a gun would ever walk into a school, a church or a mosque and just start shooting people.'

I have long been fascinated by the gun control debate in the US. Following each mass shooting there is a similar pattern of events. Politicians from all backgrounds extend their 'thoughts and prayers' to the victims' families, but then the divisions start to emerge. On one side, there are calls for tighter restrictions and tougher background checks. On the other side, gun rights activists will tell you that it is a mental health issue and that the answer is more guns, not less. They suggest armed security guards at businesses and churches, armed teachers to prevent school shootings.

In February 2018, seventeen people were killed when a gunman opened fire in Marjory Stoneman Douglas High School in Parkland, Florida. We travelled to Parkland to meet Irish couple Rachel and John Crean and their daughter, Anna, who had survived the school shooting. Anna was fifteen years old at the time of the attack. 'Looking back, it was obviously the worst day of my life, but I think that I've grown a lot from that day,' Anna said. She told me she wanted to move somewhere safer and was hoping to attend Trinity College in Dublin when she left high school. 'This event has definitely affected my idea of living in America. Nowhere is safe, obviously, but I think I'd feel more secure in a country that has stricter gun laws and stricter gun control.'

Anna's mother, Rachel, told me that she would never forget the text she received from her daughter on the day of the shooting. The message read: 'There's a shooter in the hallway. He shot into my classroom. This is real. I'm very scared but I'm OK.' Rachel said she then got a notification from the local news channel saying there was an active shooter at the school. 'My heart just dropped. I felt panic, confusion, disbelief. I couldn't believe this was actually happening,' she said.

Anna's father, John, recalled the moment he got home from work: 'Rachel was here with Anna and I'd never seen a child shake so much for two-and-a-half hours. It was a terrifying, horrendous, surreal day and I hate to relive it even now.' Anna and her Parkland classmates had campaigned for stricter gun controls and they had some successes. One law they did not support, however, was a controversial bill to allow teachers in Florida to carry guns in classrooms. Most school districts rejected the new legislation, but many in Florida believed arming teachers would make schools safer.

Less than an hour from Parkland we visited a gun shop and firing range in Miami, where we met former law enforcement officer Jeff Stanley. 'They say guns are killing people, but it's not guns that kill. It's people that pull the trigger,' he said, echoing an argument we heard many times. I asked him if he thought arming teachers was a good idea. 'Yes,' he replied, 'if they are trained.'

Jeff was at the firing range to get in some target practice with his pistol. The only other customers there at the time were a group of Danish flight attendants who had some time to kill between flights and decided to come to the range to fire some semiautomatic weapons. Interesting way to spend your downtime, I thought, as they agreed to let us film them while they blasted their way through several rounds of ammunition at paper targets at the end of a long, concrete-lined room. The manager had given us earmuffs for the noise and had also asked us to sign an insurance waiver. It must have been at that point that I gave him my phone number because a few days later, the text messages started to arrive.

'Specials going on now! Stop by for that last minute gift or some range time with that special someone.'

I should have unsubscribed, but I was intrigued. The volume of texts increased in the run-up to the election and some of them had an almost panicked tone, with capital letters and exclamation marks: 'STOP BY TODAY AND GET YOUR AMMO WHILE STOCKS LAST!' That year, 2020, saw record firearms sales in the US, with 40 million background checks carried out by the FBI. Uncertainty over the pandemic, lockdowns, racial unrest and the election all contributed to the surge. There were fears among many gun owners that if Joe Biden won the White House, it would threaten their 'right to bear arms'.

The text of the Second Amendment to the US Constitution reads in full: 'A well-regulated Militia, being necessary to the security of a free State, the right of the people to keep and bear Arms, shall not be infringed.' At the time it was ratified, back in 1791, the term 'militia' referred to groups of men who banded together to protect their communities, towns and states. The exact meaning of the Second Amendment has sparked years of heated debate, with one side arguing that it protects the rights of private individuals to keep and bear arms. The counter argument is that the law refers to a collective right for a 'well-regulated Militia', like an army or the National Guard.

Gun rights campaigners invoke the Second Amendment and claim their rights are under attack whenever the federal government or individual states try to introduce tougher firearms laws. In January 2020, I attended a massive pro-gun rally in Richmond, Virginia. The state legislature was traditionally controlled by the Republican Party but flipped in November 2019 after the Democrats won both the House of Delegates and the State Senate. They set about strengthening the state's gun control legislation following a mass shooting in Virginia Beach in May 2019, which had left twelve people dead.

The proposed new laws included banning magazines with more than ten rounds, blocking the purchase of more than one gun per month and allowing judges to seize weapons from people who were deemed to be dangerous. It was met with a severe backlash from gun enthusiasts. Dozens of counties and districts declared themselves 'Second Amendment sanctuaries' where local leaders said they would not enforce the new laws.

The pro-gun rally saw thousands of protesters gather outside the Virginia State Capitol Building to voice their opposition. Many were dressed in camouflage and carried their weapons with them. Handguns hung from belts. Rifles and machine guns were slung over shoulders. The groups resembled militias, like those referenced in the text of the Second Amendment they were defending. The Governor of Virginia had declared a state of emergency ahead of the demonstration amid fears of violence. Guns were banned from the main rally in front of the State Capitol Building, but activists were allowed to carry their weapons if they stayed outside the security cordon.

A woman from Texas, with a machine gun hanging from her shoulder, told me she had travelled to Virginia for the rally to show her solidarity with those opposed to the state's new laws. When it comes to tackling gun violence and mass shootings, she said, stricter laws were not the answer. 'You can take the firearms away from criminals and evil people, but they will still find a way. They'll just move on to another tool.'

I heard the same message from dozens of other pro-gun activists at the rally, many of whom had placed bright orange stickers on their weapons and bulletproof vests which read 'Guns Save Lives'. One young man had an antique pistol hanging around his neck and a rifle on his shoulder. 'If I were to hit you over the head with a stick, you wouldn't blame the stick, you would blame me. If I hit you with a car or a rock, you wouldn't try to ban cars or rocks,' he said.

It is unnerving to interview people who are armed to the teeth. My unease was not helped by the fact that my interviewee was using the words: *If I were to hit you over the head with a stick* . . . I have covered many protests over the years, some of which have turned violent with demonstrators throwing rocks and bottles. As I looked around at the vast array of weapons on display, I wondered what chaos and destruction would unfold if this rally turned nasty. Thankfully, a massive security operation was in place for the protest because authorities were worried that white supremacists and other extremist groups would try to join the demonstration. When I asked the gun activists about these fears, they dismissed it as 'fake news' and as an attempt by the governor to put people off. In the end, those fears weren't realized and the large rally ended peacefully.

It was the beginning of an election year and many of the protesters waved Donald Trump flags. The President was quick to seize upon the moment. 'The Democrat Party in the Great Commonwealth of Virginia are working hard to take away your 2nd Amendment rights. This is just the beginning. Don't let it happen, VOTE REPUBLICAN in 2020!' Mr Trump tweeted.

On the issue of gun control, the Democratic nominee and the President were poles apart. Mr Biden had a long history of working alongside gun safety advocates and supporting tighter controls. On the campaign trail later that year, Joe Biden said he was in favour of stricter background checks as well as the banning of assault weapons and high-capacity magazines. Donald Trump used this to attack his opponent, repeatedly telling supporters that the Democrats 'will take away your guns' if they win control of the White House and Congress. Mr Trump would often conflate gun rights with religious freedoms, telling a campaign event in Ohio in August 2020 that Joe Biden was following a radical left agenda that would 'take away your guns, destroy your Second Amendment, no religion, no anything, hurt the Bible, hurt God. He's against God, he's against guns.'

The following month, Mr Trump added to the list of things that Joe Biden would destroy, telling a campaign rally in Wisconsin that a Democratic victory would mean 'no guns, no religion, no energy, no oil'. There was a similar message a few weeks later, at a rally in Pittsburgh. 'My opponent is against oil, guns, and God,' Donald Trump said.

The idea that the right to bear arms is 'God-given' is not a new phenomenon. In February 2018, following the school shooting in Parkland, Florida, the Executive Vice President of the National Rifle Association (NRA), Wayne LaPierre, addressed the Conservative Political Action Conference. The NRA boss said the right to bear arms was 'not bestowed by man but granted by God to all Americans as our American birth right'.

The merging of God and guns made sense for Donald Trump, as a direct appeal to his conservative base. Whether it was holding up a Bible outside a vandalized church, demanding the resumption of religious services during the pandemic or pursuing pro-life policies, he knew his audience.

'God, Guns and Trump' was one of the many slogans emblazoned across the T-shirts and flags on sale at the gun show in Virginia that we had visited on our way to the Republican Convention. As I left the event that day, my phone beeped with a text message informing me of the latest special offers at the Miami firing range I had visited two years before. At that moment, I felt surrounded by firearms and consumed by the dominant and divisive role they play in the US. Perhaps that is the link between God and guns – at times in America, it feels like both are omnipresent.

16. The S word

As Donald Trump's rally in North Carolina drew to a close, loud music blared from the speakers on the stage. Queen's 'Bohemian Rhapsody' was playing as I spoke to Gary Seawell, who was wearing a red 'Trump 2020' baseball cap. 'Why are you supporting Donald Trump?' I shouted over Brian May's iconic guitar solo. 'Because Trump is the clear-cut choice for president, there is nobody else,' he replied. 'But what about Joe Biden as a candidate?' I asked. 'I don't want to live in a government-controlled society. I want to be able to do things that I want to do without having to ask people from the government permission in order to do so. Joe Biden is socialism.'

And there it was. The S word. For months before the election, Donald Trump had run an effective attack campaign against his Democratic opponent, branding him as a socialist and a puppet of the radical left. He had used the unrest that accompanied the Black Lives Matter protests as an example of the chaos that would engulf America if Joe Biden and his extremist ideologies were allowed to take over. For some in the US, socialism is like a bad word – not least among Latino immigrants who fled countries such as Cuba, Venezuela and Nicaragua. For many of them, Donald Trump and his capitalist-driven Republicans represented the opposite of those regimes and they feared that Joe Biden would embrace the very policies they had left behind.

This fear was reflected in the 2020 election results, helping

Donald Trump to win the state of Florida. The large Latino communities in districts like Miami-Dade County proved crucial in deciding the outcome in the Sunshine State. Around 55 per cent of Florida's Cuban American vote went to Donald Trump, according to NBC News exit polls. His support in Miami-Dade County went from 333,999 votes in 2016 to at least 529,160 votes in 2020, while Joe Biden was unable to grow Democratic support in the county.

The Trump administration had reversed Barack Obama's policy of engagement with Cuba and had dubbed the socialist countries of Cuba, Venezuela and Nicaragua as 'the troika of tyranny'. The Trump campaign ran attack ads in Spanish casting Joe Biden as a socialist and even as a 'Castro-Chavista', referring to Fidel Castro of Cuba and Hugo Chávez of Venezuela. It proved effective and helped Donald Trump to retain Florida, but it wouldn't be enough to help him retain the White House.

'Whether you are an elected official, a pollster or a reporter, I think we are still trying to unpack Election 2020,' Democratic Congressman Brendan Boyle told me. 'Donald Trump's disastrous handling of the pandemic hurt him among white, college-educated voters who tend to live in suburban areas. He did worse among that group than any Republican nominee for a hundred years. Surprisingly, Donald Trump improved by nine points among Latino voters. How did he do better among that segment after he called Mexicans rapists and criminals?'

Congressman Boyle also believed that while the Black Lives Matter protests had majority support, when they transformed into riots in some areas it damaged Democrats because, he said, they got unfairly tagged with that negative message: '2020 was one of those all-time years that will be studied and written about, like 1968. I think when you look at the events that year, from Covid to the protests to the shutdowns, it had different effects. Some hurt Trump, but some helped him.' In an attempt to better understand the results of Election 2020, I visited a key swing state where support for the two candidates was split down the middle.

As I crossed over the state line, leaving Maryland behind, a large blue sign read: 'Welcome to Pennsylvania: Pursue your Happiness'. It was immediately followed by a portable electronic warning screen normally used to advise motorists of roadworks or poor driving conditions. This time, however, the flashing amber letters had been programmed with the message, *Out of State COVID Rules: Quarantine and Testing Required*. Crossing state lines in the US is usually a pretty seamless affair. Other than the 'Welcome' signs, you would barely know you had left one state and entered another. On family holidays, we would always make a big deal of it for the children, saying something like: 'That's another one crossed off the list.'

Out-of-state coronavirus warning signs had added another layer to normally invisible borders. But there are also other reminders as you cross from Maryland to Pennsylvania, like an enormous roadside car dealership called Mason Dixon Auto Auctions. The Mason-Dixon Line was drawn in the 1700s to mark out the borders of Pennsylvania, Maryland, Delaware and West Virginia. It would later become known as the boundary between the free northern states and the slave-owning southern states. Such divisions, thankfully, no longer exist, but some differences do remain.

The sale of fireworks is illegal in Maryland but not in Pennsylvania, so it is no surprise that retailers offering a variety of pyrotechnics have sprung up along the state line. One

such shop was hard to miss, with a giant red stick of dyna-
mite towering over the building. As the woods of Maryland
gave way to the wide, open farmland of rural Pennsylvania,
my car radio also knew I had crossed into a new territory.
The Washington DC news station I had been listening to
crackled and hissed before settling on the closest frequency.
A current affairs programme was replaced by an elaborate
radio drama on a Christian station. Actors, music and sound-
effects were used to tell the story of a young boy who
questioned how his few dollars in the collection plate at
church every Sunday could make any difference. Some
squeaky, fast-forward noises later we were in the future, when
the church was now a pile of rubble and the pastor was
homeless and begging for money. Wow, that escalated quickly,
I thought, but I would have to wait to find out the conclu-
sion of the story as I reached my destination and pulled into
the car park of the Alpha Fitness Gym in Chambersburg,
Pennsylvania.

It was a single-storey building clad in corrugated metal
that had been freshly painted in a deep red. Over the entrance
hung an American flag and on the glass panel in the doorway
a sticker showed a cartoon figure urinating on the words
'Governor Tom Wolf', the Democratic Governor of Pennsylvania. A steady flow of gym members passed through the
entrance on this Saturday morning, swiping access cards to
open the locked doors. Not possessing a card, I waited outside and called the man I was there to meet, the gym's owner,
Jeremiah Snyder.

He came out to greet me, bent his muscular arm and
we bumped elbows. We walked through the fitness studio
towards his office at the rear of the property. It felt strange
to be in a gym, having not had access to one for almost a year

due to coronavirus restrictions. Alpha Fitness was busy. Loud heavy-metal music played as more than a dozen customers lifted weights and used a variety of exercise machines. We entered Jeremiah's office and he asked if it would be OK to leave the door open, so he could keep an eye on the gym. 'No problem,' I replied as we settled into two chairs and I switched on my recorder for our interview. I wore a face mask throughout our conversation, Jeremiah did not.

He was thirty-six years old. He had a shaved head and a dark, bushy beard that was showing some flecks of grey. He was well-built and looked as you'd expect a gym owner and fitness instructor to look. 'Do you want to see my tattoo of Trump?' Jeremiah asked, as he stretched out his left leg. Covering his rather substantial calf muscle was a tattoo of Donald Trump. His mouth was open and he looked angry, as if he was shouting. Both of Jeremiah's legs were covered in tattoos. Below Mr Trump was Mike Tyson and above were Michael Jordan and Lucille Ball, who had been etched into his skin with the same dark-blue ink. There was also space for Johnny Cash and for a close friend of Jeremiah's who had passed away. And that was just the left leg.

Jeremiah didn't grow up in a particularly political house and said he wouldn't describe himself as a staunch Republican. 'My dad never really talked politics when we were growing up, but I knew he had conservative beliefs. I was raised in a Christian home and while I don't consider myself a straight Republican, I lean towards their morals and values on things like abortion,' he said.

Donald Trump was not on Jeremiah's radar during the 2016 election and he, like a lot of Americans, did not think he had a hope of winning. But win he did, helped in large part by the state of Pennsylvania. It is a key battleground, with its twenty Electoral College votes, and back in 2016 the Republican candidate defeated Hillary Clinton in Pennsylvania by the narrowest of margins: just 44,292 votes out of more than 6,000,000 cast, a difference of 0.72 per cent. Similar narrow wins in Michigan and Wisconsin secured the White House for Donald Trump and, in the end, his election win came down to fewer than 80,000 votes in those three swing states.

While his margin of victory on a state-wide level in Pennsylvania may have been tight in 2016, that certainly was not the case where I was now sitting with Jeremiah Snyder. His gym is located in the city of Chambersburg, in Franklin County, and this is solidly Trump country. He won here in 2016 with a whopping 74 per cent of the vote and won it again in 2020 by an impressive, albeit slightly reduced, margin of 70 per cent. Retaining Franklin County wasn't enough to keep Donald Trump in the White House, however. He lost Pennsylvania to Joe Biden by just over 81,000, a margin of only 1.2 per cent.

So why did a majority of voters in this part of Pennsylvania back Donald Trump again in 2020? For Jeremiah, it was because he was different and not a politician. 'I liked the fact that he was uncut and raw. Looking back on 2016, I don't think he would have won at any other time, but America was very divided following the Obama era. A lot of people were uneasy and unhappy and then someone came along who was speaking their mind and a lot of people liked what he was saying. He knows business, he knows money, and I didn't know he would look out for America in the way he did. I believe he is someone who truly cares about America.' Jeremiah also approved of Donald Trump's handling of the coronavirus pandemic. 'He was like me, caring but at the same time acknowledging that life has to go on and that we have to maintain order and business.'

The Governor of Pennsylvania, Tom Wolf, whose urine-soaked name adorned the entrance to Alpha Fitness, ordered all non-essential businesses, including gyms, to close in March 2020. Jeremiah Snyder closed for thirty days, then re-opened in defiance of the governor's orders. Police visited the premises and issued him with a $400 fine. They warned that they would continue to come back every day and continue issuing fines until the business was closed. Jeremiah told me one of the police officers was very aggressive and tried to use scare tactics. He posted about it on social media and received a very positive reaction. He says people criticized the police and praised him for taking a stand. The police never came back to Alpha Fitness, but new members did arrive, having read about it online. People came from up to two hours away to use the gym. Others came just to give Jeremiah money to help him pay the bills. He became somewhat of a local hero among business owners who refused to close their premises. They asked him for advice on how to stay open and invited him to address rallies and events.

He attended a protest in Chambersburg in late May 2020, joining other local business owners and public representatives calling for COVID-19 restrictions in the area to be lifted. The crowd chanted 'Open Up', 'Impeach Wolf' and 'Wolf Must Go'. Speakers who addressed the rally referred to Governor Wolf as a tyrant and power-hungry. When Jeremiah Snyder spoke, he described how he had been fined by the police but would fight the sanction. 'I don't really care if the fine was 50 cents because I don't believe it's correct. We have had a lot of support since we opened. We have had a lot of new members, and we've even had bikers come in from

Harrisburg just to buy T-shirts and support our business. I've had people come in and drop off cheques to help me support my family. I have two girls, a four-year-old and an eleven-year-old. This business is seven years old, and it's the baby in between,' he told the rally.

Eight months on from that protest, Jeremiah told me that he doesn't deny the existence of COVID-19 but thinks its seriousness has been exaggerated. 'I believe the pandemic to be real, but nobody got sick in my gym. We had the place deep-cleaned regularly and I didn't drag anyone in here and chain them to a machine. It was their choice to come here. The coronavirus restrictions took away people's choice, forcing them to do something they didn't want,' he said. It is an argument I had heard many times before, particularly among supporters of Donald Trump: the virus isn't as bad as the media portrays it and forcing someone to wear a mask or close their business is a breach of their rights.

Jeremiah then went on to outline another set of beliefs that he shares with millions of Trump supporters, that Election 2020 was stolen. 'Donald Trump 100 per cent got played. There was a plan for him to lose, a plan that was bigger than him and bigger than us. Machines showed spikes of thousands of votes at the push of a key or the insertion of a USB stick and Americans don't question it.'

I put it to Jeremiah that courts, the Attorney General, investigators and election officials, many of them Republicans, had found no evidence of widespread voter fraud.

'These officials are politicians, they are being paid, they only care about themselves. Look at Mike Pence, he changed quickly and let Donald Trump down.' For Jeremiah, even though they were Republican allies, the gap between Donald Trump the non-politician and the political establishment was never greater than in the immediate aftermath of the election. He believed that Mr Trump was telling the truth about rigged voting machines and altered ballots, and that everyone else was lying. Donald Trump's baseless claims of voter fraud had very real consequences on 6 January 2020, when a group of his supporters stormed the Capitol Building while members of Congress were meeting to count the Electoral College votes and certify Joe Biden's win. Jeremiah and his customers watched the events unfold on the TV screens inside his gym. His patrons put down their weights and stepped away from exercise machines to watch while an angry mob clashed with police, broke through windows and doors, vandalized offices and barged through the halls of Congress. Representatives hid under tables and chairs while others were whisked away to safety by their security details.

'I think the whole thing was a set-up,' Jeremiah told me. 'There were some Trump supporters who went along with it in the heat of the moment, but what happened was a set-up. The police just stepped back and let them into the Capitol, it almost seemed like a tour. It's almost comical. If you're going to cheat in an election, make it a little closer; if you're going to call it a storming of the Capitol, at least make it look like that.'

Jeremiah believes that the whole thing was orchestrated by dark, shadowy forces on the Democratic side who did it to damage Donald Trump. However, he fears that in the future there could be a real violent uprising, such is the level of division and unhappiness in the US.

'It could happen someday where enough pissed-off people come together who are fed-up with the lies and bullshit. They've stolen an election and they've screwed us. I just want my America back. I want 1996 back, when life was normal. It didn't use to be like this. We didn't argue on social media. Now we argue about gender stuff. We didn't argue about all these things. I was born in 1984. I remember childhood in the nineties, we didn't have to deal with all this. We played all day, but now kids can't even hang around outside because we don't know who's around, and we can't let them on their phones too long because we don't know what they're exposed to.'

Jeremiah laments a loss of innocence in America, a time when things were simpler, a time when gender roles were narrowly defined and when the US was a true superpower. He views the progressive policies of the Democratic Party as a move towards the S word, socialism, and equates it with a sort of emasculation.

'There are so many divisions now and the way everything is changing is scary. The way they are censoring social media, I fear that socialism is not far from communism. Democrats and the socialists want us to survive off the government. They don't like people like me, they don't want you to survive alone and have your business, they don't want you to be alpha males and alpha females.' The name of his business, Alpha Fitness, now had added meaning.

'Democrats want you feeding off the government. They'll tell you how much money you have every month and they'll take care of your healthcare and housing. That's not cool, that's not good. Some people push for that and I don't understand why. Yes, we were all created equal, but some people work their asses off, and why are we stealing from the rich to give to the poor? These people have earned their spot. That socialist mentality scares me.'

Jeremiah insists that he is not a bigot or a racist. He is all for equality and respects race, gender and sexuality, but he feels he's living in a world stifled by censorship and political correctness led by a liberal, mainstream media. 'They're trying to gender-neutralize everything, even in speech. For goodness' sake, we can't go through life not saying husband, wife, he, she. I think that's why Trump was loved and hated by so many, because he wasn't politically correct. He called out bullshit as bullshit, he didn't feel the need to tiptoe around every subject. That's the way he was in business – he just got things done – and he was the same as President. He didn't sugar-coat things, he just said it as it was.'

Unlike many other disappointed Trump supporters, Jeremiah accepts Joe Biden as President despite the fact that he firmly believes he cheated. He doesn't see the point of refusing to acknowledge the Commander in Chief and would view it as un-American. 'My gut tells me we're in a really bad place, but I will back Joe Biden as our President, even though I know it wasn't a legitimate win. You don't have to be a Biden fan, just be an America fan and want what's best for the country.'

Jeremiah is sceptical and downbeat about a Donald Trump run in 2024. 'What's the point? If you can rig one election, how can you ever trust one again?' He feels so much could have been achieved with another four years of Donald Trump. 'I want a leader who has a backbone, who says America is the shit and that we get it done, a leader who doesn't ask permission from others, a leader of a country that is supposed to be the greatest nation on Earth.' A leader like the angry-looking Donald Trump tattooed across Jeremiah's left leg.

After our conversation, I returned to my car and called home. As I filled my wife in on the details of the interview, my seven-year-old daughter, Erin, was shouting in the background about a wedding. Two of her teddy bears would be getting married in the woods close to our house later that day. I was told to hurry home and pick up some snacks along the way to feed the guests who would be gathering for the big day. Before I could set off for Washington, however, I wanted to explore more of Chambersburg. We had visited the area for a weekend trip the previous September, a few weeks before Election 2020. Back then, Trump signs had dominated the front yards of the homes. Five months on, most of the signs had been removed. I did see one that read 'Trump is My President', a clear denial of the recent election result. It was next to a similar sign, printed in the same colouring and font, that read: 'What happened to Seth Rich?'

Twenty-seven-year-old Seth Rich worked for the Democratic National Committee and was fatally shot in July 2016 near his home in Washington. The case went unsolved, but police believed it was a botched robbery. The killing sparked right-wing conspiracy theories that Mr Rich had been shot to silence him and that his murder was linked to the leaking of damaging Democratic Party emails in the run-up to the 2016 presidential election. Authorities dismissed the claims, saying there was no evidence that Mr Rich was involved in the leaking of emails, but it didn't stop conservative media outlets from continuing to spread the falsehoods. It was deeply upsetting for the Rich family, who were bombarded with wild claims about their son. They sued Fox News for inflicting emotional distress on them and the network settled the lawsuit in November 2020. But clearly, myths around the death of Seth Rich remained a source of concern for some people, like the homeowner in Chambersburg, Pennsylvania, who felt the need to question the motives surrounding the young man's murder on a lawn sign in front of their house.

A short distance away, I found a parking space in the town

centre, outside Greg's Bail Bonds. A flashing neon sign announced 'Open 24 Hours' and it hung over a large, framed black-and-white mugshot of a young Frank Sinatra, which stared out from the front window of the office. The infamous photo was taken in 1938 but was only made public sixty years later when the FBI released details of the files it held on 'Ol' Blue Eyes'. Sinatra had been arrested in New Jersey and charged with 'seduction', accused of having sexual relations with an unmarried woman. He was bailed on a $1,500 bond. The charge was later changed to 'adultery' when it was established that the woman was married. The case was ultimately dropped, but not before Frank Sinatra's bail was reduced to $500. I'm not sure why his mugshot was in the window of a bail bondsman's office in Pennsylvania, and I doubt very much Greg handled the case. Perhaps it was a consoling message to those who did require Greg's services: if you've been arrested and need bailing out, don't worry, there's light at the end of the tunnel – just look at Frank Sinatra.

The nearby main street is a real slice of Americana with its ice-cream parlours, diners, candy stores and traditional barber shops. The local courthouse dominates the town centre. It is a large redbrick building with a white-columned portico and topped with a domed clock tower. One could imagine Marty McFly and Doc Brown attaching cables to its spire to power their time-travelling DeLorean. There are no time-machines in Chambersburg, but there is a time capsule. It's encased in concrete and buried beneath a memorial to the town's founder, Scots–Irish immigrant Benjamin Chambers. A bronze sculpture depicts Chambers welcoming his sons home from war in 1781. At their feet, a small square plaque reads, 'Time capsule to be opened in 2081 and reopened every 100 years thereafter'. What will they speak of in

Chambersburg one hundred years from now? Some of the town's residents, like Jeremiah Snyder, long for the past, not the future, and miss a President who offered hope of a return to an America that no longer exists.

As I crossed back over the state line into Maryland, the radio, which had been playing WPFG 91.3 FM Cumberland Valley Christian Radio, crackled and hissed and returned to WAMU, the Washington-based NPR news station I had been listening to a few hours before. I never did find out what happened to the boy who questioned the importance of putting money in the church collection plate. Instead, I was now listening to President Joe Biden's Press Secretary, Jen Psaki, who was being interviewed about her first week in the job. The presenter made repeated references to the differences between the Biden and Trump administrations when it came to dealing with the press. Ms Psaki was also asked about her family life and she spoke about balancing a hectic job with having two young children. It reminded me that I had a teddy-bear wedding to attend, as Chambersburg disappeared in my rear-view mirror.

17. O Little Town of Bethlehem

Pennsylvania is the US state that I have spent the most time in, and not necessarily for work reasons. My brother has lived there since the 1990s, first in the centre of Philadelphia, before moving to the suburbs to raise his family. I made my first visit to the state in 2001 during my J-1 student visa programme. My then girlfriend, now wife, Joanna, and I had been working in Ocean City, Maryland. It is a vast seaside tourist town along the Atlantic coast. The long, straight, sandy beaches were immaculately maintained and lined by a wooden boardwalk that stretched for three miles. It buzzed with amusements arcades, ice-cream parlours, T-shirt shops and the business that would become our place of work for the summer, Flashback Old Time Photos.

It was a photographic studio where customers would dress up in old-fashioned costumes and have their pictures taken against a variety of backdrops. Joanna worked as a photographer in the back and I worked front-of-house, using my 'gift of the gab' to attract customers in, talk them through the process and try to sell them extras like photo frames and additional prints. When the clients had chosen their costume, theme and backdrop from a photo album on the counter, I rang a bell and announced to the photographers what was coming their way: 'Two gangsters at the saloon!' I would shout, or 'Two southern belles in the parlour!' It was fun. Twenty years later, while living in Washington, we returned to Flashback Old Time Photos, this time with our two daughters. A manager we had worked with two decades ago was still there and remembered us. We couldn't resist getting the girls' photo taken for old times' sake. 'A pirate and a cow-girl at the piano!'

When we finished our J-1 summer in Ocean City, we trav-elled to Philadelphia to visit my brother. At the time, he lived on Brown Street, close to the city's famous Art Museum. A statue of the fictional boxer Rocky stands close to the steps leading up to the building's entrance. It honours the iconic movie scene in which Sylvester Stallone jogs through the City of Brotherly Love in a montage that culminates with him reaching the top of the steps and raising his arms in celebration. We didn't quite manage to replicate that run, but we did visit lots of Philadelphia's well-known attractions before preparing to leave to travel to New York, where we would be staying with Joanna's aunt in Long Island. My brother persuaded us to stay an extra day so we could visit an outdoor market in rural Pennsylvania. We agreed.

The following morning, 11 September 2001, we wandered through stalls selling a variety of local produce and crafts. Many of the vendors were distracted, however, and were glued to their radios as news broke that first one, and then a second plane had hit the World Trade Center in New York. Another plane had hit the Pentagon and a fourth had crashed in a field in Shanksville on the opposite side of Pennsylvania. My future sister-in-law, Shelly, was in Washington for work and called to say that the building she was in was being evacu-ated and that everyone was leaving the city. The same was true in all major US cities that day amid fears over where the next target would be. As my brother lived in the city, we ended up driving into the downtown area while thousands were leaving. Our inbound route was empty but there were traffic jams on the outbound lanes all around us. We made it to my brother's house and, like the rest of the world, watched that day's terrible events unfold in real time on the news.

We returned to Pennsylvania three years later under much happier circumstances for my brother's wedding. It was a great day but, like the rest of the Irish guests, I was struck by a few big differences compared to weddings back home. First off, the reception ended at 11.00 p.m. as opposed to the 3.00 a.m. finishes we were used to. Second, most of the American guests drove and the first thing the bar ran out of was bottled water. We were a long way from home.

Shelly is from Bethlehem, Pennsylvania, a former steel town in the state's so-called Rust Belt. Her father worked all his life in the local steel plant before it closed. The wedding reception was held in a beautiful old mansion that was built by the one-time boss of the ironworks, which would later go on to become Bethlehem Steel. The enormous plant made parts for the Golden Gate Bridge, the Hoover Dam and the mighty US battleships that fought in the Second World War. Today, it lies idle and abandoned, having closed years ago. The tall, rusting smokestacks and blast furnaces still dominate the skyline.

When I returned to Bethlehem after fifteen years, much had changed. The area around the old steel plant has been redeveloped as an arts centre, casino and venue. We saw Irish singer Hozier perform there in November 2019. It would be one of our last live gigs before the world went into lockdown just a few months later, but it was good to go out on a high note.

A few months before, in April 2019, Bethlehem had played host to a very different live performance – a Fox News town-hall event with Democratic presidential hopeful and Vermont

Senator Bernie Sanders. A group of Donald Trump supporters gathered outside the venue and it caught the attention
of the President, who tweeted: 'Many Trump Fans & Signs
were outside of the Fox News Studio last night in the now
thriving (Thank you President Trump) Bethlehem, Pennsylvania, for the interview with Crazy Bernie Sanders.' What
caught other people's attention was not that he called Bernie
Sanders crazy, he did that all the time, but that he seemed to
be taking credit for the revitalization of Bethlehem with his
'Thank you President Trump' line. Bethlehem is often held
up as an example of a Rust Belt town that has reinvented
itself while embracing its industrial past, but that work began
long before Donald Trump took office. Many of the town's
leaders were left scratching their heads about what exactly
they should be thanking the President for.

Donald Trump has made lots of claims and promises in
Pennsylvania over the years. During his 2016 campaign, he
vowed to bring back industries like steel and coal. It was a
message that appealed to blue-collar workers, many of whom
would have been solidly Democrat for years. It helped him to
win the state and the White House. After that election there
was a belief among Democrats that they had taken Pennsylvania for granted. Hillary Clinton made some visits, but only
at the very end, when she saw the polls tightening. By then it
was too late. Donald Trump saw the state's value early on
and made lots of campaign stops there. He saw it as fertile
ground for him. Democrats quickly recognized that they had
made a big mistake by ignoring Pennsylvania.

In the 2020 campaign, however, the incumbent had a big
problem: Joe Biden. He was born in working-class Scranton,
Pennsylvania, and was seen by many in the state as one of
their own. He launched his campaign there and based his

election headquarters in Philadelphia. On the campaign trail he regularly contrasted his blue-collar, Irish-Catholic roots with Donald Trump's billionaire lifestyle, pushing an election message of Scranton versus Park Avenue. 'All that President Trump could see from Park Avenue is Wall Street. All he thinks about is the stock market,' Joe Biden would regularly tell supporters.

I returned once again to Bethlehem in October 2020, just a few weeks before Election Day. A mix of Donald Trump and Joe Biden lawn signs lined the residential streets of the town and it was a divide that was reflected in the views of the voters I met. Barbara Gallowich told me she would be supporting Joe Biden: 'I had hopes for Donald Trump, but I don't think he's come through, all the lies, he's just not a very honest man.' Robert Holland had voted for Donald Trump back in 2016 and told me he had no regrets: 'He's doing a wonderful job and is the most knowledgeable president we've had in my lifetime. He's courageous, we're going in the right direction, and I hope people give him another four years.'

Bethlehem, named after the birthplace of Jesus, markets itself as a Christmas city and every year its most prominent decoration is illuminated on a mountain overlooking the town. It is an enormous, bright star to mimic the one that guided the three wise men to the stable. But these days Bethlehem, Pennsylvania, offers a guide of a different kind. It is located in Northampton County, which is a bellwether district. The winner of the county almost always ends up winning the state, and often the White House.

Chris Borick is a professor of political science at the local Muhlenberg College and I spoke to him about Bethlehem's role in US elections. 'Since the 1920s, only once did North-ampton County not predict where Pennsylvania would go,' he told me. 'So, by the slimmest margin, it retained that sta-tus again in 2020. The county flipped back to a Democratic victory and kept its place as a bellwether. Northampton County is a great microcosm of the state and therefore the country. It has urban areas, big suburbs of people who work in Philadelphia and New York, and then very rural areas, all within a twenty-mile radius, so it acts like the state and, to a degree, the entire country.' While Northampton County switched from backing Donald Trump to Joe Biden, many other Rust Belt, working-class areas of Pennsylvania did not. 'Pennsylvania has sixty-seven counties. Overwhelmingly they voted Republican, but the small few that voted blue are where the people are. The rural–urban divide has been a feature of our politics for a long time, but it is on steroids right now.'

In general, blue-collar, largely white districts stuck with the incumbent, but what his Democratic challenger was able to do was to cut into his margin of victory from 2016 and reduce his lead in those areas. 'The reason Donald Trump was so afraid of Joe Biden, particularly in Pennsylvania, was that he had more appeal for blue-collar voters than Hillary Clinton did. In a very competitive race, everything matters. Biden made significant gains in many of those working-class areas. Donald Trump did do better in some urban areas of Philadelphia and performed better among Latino communi-ties. These were all modest, marginal changes, but they all mattered in the end,' Professor Borick said.

Although much of the state is bordered by the Demo-cratic strongholds of New York, New Jersey, Maryland and

Delaware, the voting intentions of the people of Pennsylvania have always been harder to predict for pollsters. Barack Obama won the Keystone State by a margin of over 10 per cent in 2008, but eight years later Donald Trump pulled off a shock victory there by the tiniest of margins. Pennsylvania is often described as Pittsburgh to the west, Philadelphia to the east and Alabama in the middle. The larger urban areas typically vote Democrat while Republican candidates do well in rural farm country and in the industrial Rust Belt. The electoral map of Pennsylvania resembles that of the US: pockets of blue around the edges and a sea of red in the middle. The problem for the Republicans is that those pockets of blue are cities with big populations and lots of votes. The sea of red, although vast, doesn't contain a lot of people.

The industrial Midwest was once the backbone of the US economy, the centre of a booming manufacturing sector. The imagery of white-hot molten metal and glowing furnaces is used to great effect in the classic 1978 movie *The Deer Hunter*, which tells the story of three steel-workers who leave their blue-collar Pennsylvania town to go to fight in the Vietnam War. The sounds, heat and flames of the steel mill are quickly replaced with the fire and chaos of the battlefield. In both cases, however, the power and the noise bring only misery. The film's message is that there is no glory in war, just shattered lives. Nor is there any celebration of America's place as an industrial powerhouse. The steel-workers live in rundown houses surrounded by enormous chimneys belching out black smoke. Their only relief comes when they escape to the beautiful countryside nearby to go deer hunting. Almost fifty years on from *The Deer Hunter*, the young men of the once thriving industrial towns no longer have to go to war, but also gone are the plants that once provided them with employment. The factories are now as quiet as the surrounding mountains, but in 2016 that silence was broken by a presidential candidate vowing to restore the glories of the past.

Pollsters were predicting that Election 2020 could come down to Pennsylvania and that its twenty Electoral College votes would be the difference between Joe Biden or Donald Trump in the White House. In the end, however, it was less significant than originally expected because Joe Biden also managed to flip Arizona and Georgia, meaning that even without Pennsylvania he would have reached the 270 Electoral College votes needed to win the presidency. One of the big questions after the 2016 election was how could all the opinion polls have got it so wrong? There were countless predictions from reputable polling companies, universities and media outlets that Hillary Clinton would be the winner. So, what about 2020, were the polls right this time? Well, not really. While they did predict the outright winner, the margins of victory were much closer than anyone had forecast.

'The final polls here in Pennsylvania had Biden with a four-point lead, but he ended up winning by just 1.2 per cent. Closer than expected. It was similar to what happened in 2016, but with the result going the other way,' Professor Borick said. 'In Arizona, Georgia and North Carolina the polls were pretty accurate, but in Pennsylvania the margins were off. When President Trump is on the ballot, he tends to outperform the polls. After 2016, pollsters said one of the big problems was not weighting for educational attainment, so we made some adjustments in that area.'

But even with paying closer attention to white, non-college-educated males, the polls were still off. One problem could be the so-called 'shy' Trump voter. Having been at many Trump rallies and having met hundreds of his supporters, the word 'shy' wouldn't necessarily spring to my mind, but in polling it refers to a voter who won't admit that they will be voting for Donald Trump when asked by a pollster. Professor Borick couldn't quantify this exactly, but he suggested that 'The shy Trump voter may have been more significant in 2020, or perhaps there is a wider issue with just reaching Trump supporters in general. Lots of elections that did not have Donald Trump on the ballot over the last few years came very close to what the polls were saying. It appears there is a Trump effect when he's on the ballot. In the two Georgia senate run-off elections in January 2021, the polls were pretty much spot-on and the President wasn't on the ballot.'

Donald Trump's 2016 victory in Pennsylvania's Rust Belt was forged in the shadows of abandoned steel mills and coal mines. Many who voted for him probably knew deep down that he was never really going to reopen those industries, but they backed him anyway out of a sense of nostalgia and a desire to return to an America of the past.

'Coal hasn't returned to Scranton, steel hasn't returned to Bethlehem,' noted Professor Borick, 'but despite this, his broader message still resonated with many voters. The messaging, the reach and the rhetoric attracted many of those white working-class voters. You could layer in identity issues and concerns about the country going demographically in a different direction and you have a very receptive audience. There was an idea that at least Donald Trump cared, he was interested, and he wanted to speak for them and listen to them.'

An analysis of official data reveals that the numbers of people employed in Pennsylvania's coal and steel industries did not rise during Donald Trump's four years in office.

According to the Federal Reserve Bank of St. Louis, there were 4,900 coal-mining jobs in Pennsylvania when Mr Trump took office in January 2017, and by August 2020 that number stood at 4,800. The figure hit a thirty-year low of 4,500 in April, May and June 2020, at the height of the coronavirus pandemic. The economic slowdown also hit the steel industry. There were around 11,300 people employed in iron and steel mills in Pennsylvania in January 2017. That number rose to 12,000, before falling to 10,000 in April 2020 as the economy ground to a halt.

So, if there had been no COVID-19, would Donald Trump's pledge to restore coal and steel have come to pass? Most economists agree that a move away from fossil fuels, coupled with globalization and the availability of cheap foreign labour, means those US industries would never have been restored to the levels promised by a President desperately seeking re-election.

During the presidential race, the importance of Pennsylvania as a swing state was highlighted by the number of events and rallies held there by both the Biden and Trump camps. Some days, rival campaign buses would descend on neighbouring areas just hours apart. On 9 July 2020, Mike Pence and Joe Biden both travelled to the Keystone State. Mr Pence arrived first, flying into Lancaster Airport in rural Pennsylvania on board Air Force Two. He embarked from there on a bus tour of the state, urging voters to give him and his boss another four years in office.

A crowd of supporters had gathered outside the airport and were peering through the chain-link fence surrounding the runway, trying to catch a glimpse of the Vice President. Among those who had gathered there was a man in his sixties named George. He was holding a leather folder. Inside was a large 8×10-inch colour photograph of Mike Pence. He had brought it with him in the hope of getting it signed, but it wasn't possible because of coronavirus restrictions and social distancing. It was not the first time George had been left disappointed by the administration. He had voted for Donald Trump in 2016 but told me he would not be voting for him again in November. 'I don't like that he worked with Putin and then there's the killing of US servicemen by bounty which was covered up,' George said. 'I probably do regret voting for him. I blindly put him in office.' George had voter's remorse and had come out that day, not as a Trump supporter, but as an autograph hunter.

The other people who had gathered were there to cheer for the Vice President. The visit was happening after weeks of racial unrest across the US and amid growing criticism that Donald Trump was not doing enough to tackle the coronavirus. It was damaging him in the polls. Thile Cramer, who was wearing a blue Trump/Pence hat, told me she wasn't worried: 'Who's promoting these opinion polls? It is the media. The media does not want Donald Trump in office and will do everything to get him out. The virus, the Black Lives Matter movement, none of that is going to matter. It's all politically driven and will be gone after Election Day.' Also unconcerned about Joe Biden's big lead in the polls was Trump voter Sam Smucker: 'President Trump was behind in the polls the last time and I think he'll get in again, for sure.'

Robert Rapp was in his seventies and from the local area. When I asked him to spell his last name, he told me it was Pennsylvania Dutch in origin. He had come to Lancaster that day to show his support for the Trump campaign and said he was impressed by Donald Trump's morals. 'It is the policies of a politician we should be voting on, not their personalities, unless they are outright reprobates, and Donald Trump is not. He is married and has been faithful in his marriages.' I interrupted Mr Rapp to point out that there had been accusations of infidelity and payments of 'hush money' to cover up the alleged affairs. 'Well, Melania wouldn't think that or she wouldn't have married him,' he replied with a smile. Minutes later a large, blue campaign bus pulled out of the airport and Mike Pence set off on his state-wide tour.

One area he would definitely not be visiting that day was the town of Dunmore, just outside Scranton, Joe Biden's childhood hometown. The Democratic candidate was due to visit a steel plant in the area to make a big announcement about his economic plan. He was scheduled to speak later that afternoon and Murray and I needed to get on the road as it was a two-hour drive from Lancaster to Dunmore. However, I did have one stop to make before we left the area. My wife had happened to mention to our neighbour Gupi that I would be in Lancaster, Pennsylvania, covering the Mike Pence visit and her eyes widened with excitement. 'I went to college there and they have the best spaghetti pizza!' I had never heard of such a culinary abomination, but as the name suggests it is a pizza topped with spaghetti. It is the creation of the Rosa Rosa Pizzeria in Lancaster, which describes itself as the 'home of the spaghetti pizza'. Gupi loves the dish so much that whenever she visits the area, she will buy several large pizzas to bring home and freeze for future consumption. She pleaded with my wife to ask me to bring her back a pizza. As we got ready to leave Lancaster Airport, I picked up my phone to get the address of the pizzeria, and that's when I saw the news alerts.

The US Supreme Court had just handed down major rulings in the legal battle over Donald Trump's tax returns. Mr

Trump, as in so many other areas, had broken with presidential tradition and refused to make his tax returns public, claiming he could not do so as they were under audit. New York prosecutors and Democrats in Congress both wanted to get their hands on the financial information. His lawyers had argued that he should not have to hand over the documents to investigators because sitting presidents are immune from prosecution. The Supreme Court disagreed but, rather than demanding the immediate disclosure of the information, referred the matter back to the lower courts. In a separate judgment, the Supreme Court ruled that the financial records did not have to be handed over to Congress.

The rulings were a mixed bag for the President. The court certainly hadn't handed him a victory, but it had given him time. It meant that Donald Trump's personal, and potentially controversial, financial information would not become public before the election. That was no doubt a welcome relief for a President who was already behind in the polls. The last thing he needed was a financial scandal to deal with. The President's response to the ruling was vintage Donald Trump, blaming those who were against him and portraying himself as the victim. He took to Twitter, describing it all as unfair and a 'political prosecution'. He claimed that it came down to prosecutorial misconduct and that it was his predecessor, Barack Obama, and former Vice President Joe Biden who should be under investigation.

It was major breaking news and my trip to the local pizzeria had to be cancelled. Instead, Murray and I had to find a suitable location quickly to do a live TV report into the *Six One News*. We decided to drive in the direction of the Joe Biden event but stop along the way for our broadcast.

Murray drove as I worked in the back seat, filing pieces for radio and online as well as preparing for my live TV report. The clock was ticking as we pulled over on the side of a non-descript road to set up our camera, lights and LiveU, a small device about the size of a shoebox that allows us to broadcast live back to Ireland. It was a report about the Supreme Court handing down a ruling about the President's tax returns, yet we were clearly on the side of a country road. 'It'll be OK,' Murray reassured me. 'I'll put the background out of focus and we could be anywhere.'

As I was getting ready to go live, I heard the sound of a horse's hooves behind me. A man in old-world attire was riding by in a horse-drawn buggy. We were deep in Amish Country. Lancaster County is home to America's oldest Amish settlement, where thousands still live a centuries-old lifestyle. What would the viewers at home in Ireland think if, in the middle of my report on Donald Trump's tax returns, families started riding by in the background on horses and traps? Thankfully, there was a lull in the horse traffic for the two minutes I was live on-air and the viewers at home would have been none the wiser as to our location. We had got away with it, and we even got to sample some of Lancaster's famed Amish sights. We did not, however, get to sample its weird pizza toppings, as we jumped into the car and headed for the Joe Biden campaign event in Dunmore.

McGregor Industries is a steel plant located down a narrow country lane off a busy highway. A group of Donald Trump supporters had set up camp at the junction before the plant, waving flags and chanting to show their opposition to Joe Biden. We made our way past the protesters and found a parking space close to the plant. Joe Biden had arrived a little earlier and was inside getting a tour of the metal works. John Brizinski lives across the road from the plant and, as a

Joe Biden supporter, was delighted to catch a glimpse of the Democratic candidate as his motorcade drove by. 'I didn't even know he was coming here today,' John told me.

This wasn't unusual. The Biden campaign was extremely lowkey. There were few public events due to coronavirus restrictions and while Donald Trump held big rallies in defiance of the lockdowns, his opponent kept public appearances to a minimum. When he did visit an area, it typically would not be announced in advance, to avoid encouraging large crowds to gather. It was a pleasant surprise for John Brizinski when he saw the Secret Service and the media descend on his doorstep. 'Joe Biden is for the working people, he's not for the rich,' he told me. 'He wants to keep jobs in the country and he'll be a better president than Donald Trump.'

There was a small group of Biden supporters outside the steel plant and while most of the Trump voters had remained back at the highway, some had ventured a little closer. Evan Gedrich stood out from the crowd because he was holding a Trump sign. 'This election is freedom versus tyranny. Democrats want to raise taxes, Donald Trump wants to put America first,' he said. Although surrounded by Biden supporters, Evan said he wasn't met with any hostility and the atmosphere was cordial and non-confrontational. Inside the steel plant, however, the tone was a little more combative. It was one of those 'the gloves are off' moments that the media loves to latch onto during election campaigns. Joe Biden's public addresses had been few and far between and his criticism of Donald Trump had been relatively tame, especially compared to the insults and attacks coming from the other side. On that day, however, Joe Biden ramped up his condemnation of the President.

He was there to launch his economic plan, 'Build Back Better', which he promised would create five million jobs by boosting domestic manufacturing and innovation. He delivered his big economic address before a small, socially distanced crowd in a covered courtyard to the side of the steel plant.

'When it comes to COVID-19, after months of doing nothing, other than predicting the virus would disappear or maybe, if you drank bleach, you may be OK, Trump has simply given up,' Joe Biden said. 'He promised to bring back jobs and manufacturing, but we're in a recession. Donald Trump loves to talk and talk and talk, but after three-and-a-half years of big promises, what do the American people have to show for all the talk?' he asked rhetorically. 'The truth is, throughout this crisis Donald Trump has been almost singularly focused on the stock market, not you. Not your families.'

He went on to say that even though he had had a good job as a US Senator making $42,000 a year, he knew the struggles of being a single dad who had to work with two young sons at home and he knew what it meant to bring ageing parents into your home in the last months of their lives to care for them. To underscore his 'blue-collar Joe' image, the Democratic candidate began his speech by saying how great it was to be home and name-checked locals in the crowd that he'd known for many years. After the address he visited his childhood home in nearby Scranton, saying: 'I couldn't come to Scranton without coming by the old house.'

It was no accident, of course, that Joe Biden chose Pennsylvania for his big speech on the economy. Despite all of the problems facing Donald Trump that were affecting his approval ratings, he was still polling better than his Democratic opponent when it came to the country's finances. A majority of American voters believed the billionaire businessman had done a good job of managing the economy and that the growth would have continued if not for the coronavirus. But Joe Biden's big advantage over his opponent in the key swing state of Pennsylvania was that he was from there.

The evolution of American politics is that swing states come and go. Colorado, Illinois and Oregon used to be battlegrounds, but no longer. Who knows, maybe someday soon deep red Texas will turn purple, or even blue? Pennsylvania, however, is likely to remain a swing state for some time to come because of its diverse make-up. A perfect microcosm of urban, rural, black, white, rich, poor, liberal and conservative. A state that boasts bellwethers like the little town of Bethlehem, where wise men come in search of answers about how America has voted, and why.

18. Surprises

Every four years in the US, political observers are on the lookout for an 'October surprise', a potential game-changing news event just before a presidential election. In the 2016 campaign, the first of these shockers came in the form of the *Access Hollywood* tapes. It was a 2005 recording on which Donald Trump could be heard using explicit language as he boasted about groping women. It was incredibly damaging for the candidate less than one month from Election Day. Some senior Republicans who had endorsed him withdrew their backing, others asked him to step aside. Donald Trump was already trailing behind Hillary Clinton in the opinion polls and now it looked like his campaign was toast.

But October 2016 was not yet done with its surprises and many believe the next one cost Mrs Clinton the election. With just eleven days until polling day, FBI Director James Comey announced that he was reopening an investigation into the Democratic candidate's use of a private email server. Donald Trump had attacked his opponent over her email use throughout the campaign, calling her 'Crooked Hillary', which was met with chants of 'Lock her up' from his supporters. Her repeated denials of any wrongdoing when it came to the handling of classified information were not helped by the reopening of the FBI investigation. Hillary Clinton would later blame James Comey's last-minute intervention for her election loss.

The term 'October surprise' was first used by Ronald

Reagan's campaign manager, William Casey, in 1980. The Republicans feared that the incumbent, Jimmy Carter, would announce the release of American hostages held in Iran just before the election, giving him a big bounce in the polls. The Reagan campaign decided that pre-emptively telling the electorate that their President was planning a big announcement for electoral gain would lessen the impact of any good news he might unveil. They hoped that voters would instead view it as a political tactic and that the President would be punished, rather than rewarded, at the polls.

In the end, the release of the American hostages did not happen before the election. It came instead minutes after Ronald Reagan's inauguration in January 1981. It led to accusations that the Reagan campaign had done a secret deal with the Iranian government to ensure that the hostages were not released until their candidate was president. Congressional investigations concluded that there was no plan to delay the hostages' release, but it is a conspiracy theory that has continued to this day.

The first of the 'October surprises' in the run-up to the 2020 election actually came in September. By this time, limited indoor dining had resumed in Washington DC, so my family and I decided to go for dinner in the Elephant & Castle, a British-themed pub not far from the RTÉ office. The menu of shepherd's pie, roast beef and bangers & mash contained lots of reminders of home, but the location of the restaurant could not have been more 'DC'. It is on Pennsylvania Avenue, just a few blocks from the White House and across the street from the Trump International Hotel.

Say what you like about Donald Trump's politics, but the man did run some stunning hotels. His Washington establishment was one of the jewels in his collection. It is housed in The Old Post Office, an enormous nine-storey structure that occupies an entire city block and was once the headquarters of the US Postal Service. It was built in the 1890s and its ornate façade features columns, arches and round turrets. It is topped by a tall clock tower that still dominates the Washington skyline to this day. Unlike other US cities, it has not been overtaken and dwarfed by modern skyscrapers as such buildings are not allowed in Washington due to height restrictions.

The inside of the Trump International Hotel is just as impressive as its historic exterior. The main lobby is a vast, covered courtyard housed in a soaring nine-storey atrium featuring a thousand panes of glass. The hotel run by the self-proclaimed 'law and order President' is, coincidentally, located adjacent to the Department of Justice and across the street from the FBI headquarters. The business is not just in the centre of the legal district, it has also been at the centre of multiple legal rows. Lawsuits were filed against Donald Trump claiming his ownership of the hotel breached the emoluments clauses of the US Constitution, which prohibit a president from receiving gifts or payments from foreign and state governments. It was alleged in court that officials were staying at the hotel and holding events there in order to curry favour with the President. His lawyers dismissed the cases as 'another example of presidential harassment'.

The hotel had attracted controversy from the moment it opened back in October 2016, just weeks before Donald Trump won the election. The building was still owned by the federal government and rented to Mr Trump. When he became President, he effectively became his own landlord and Democrats spent years demanding to see the details of the lease to ensure the Trump Organization was not receiving preferential treatment at the expense of taxpayers. The Trumps tried to sell the lease in 2019 but abandoned the effort when the pandemic hit and the hotel business fell off a cliff.

We were seated by a window in the Elephant & Castle, facing the Trump Hotel. 'How much would dinner cost in that place, do you think?' I wondered aloud as I paid the modest bill for our British grub. With that, my phone pinged. The US Supreme Court Justice Ruth Bader Ginsburg, affectionately known as RBG, had just died. I informed the table of the breaking news as we gathered our things, and it was my seven-year-old daughter, Erin, who was the most upset by the news. Earlier that year, she had received gifts of several children's books about RBG and I read them to her at bedtime. They were wonderful, written as inspirational tales for young people. They detailed RBG's life and accomplishments and were filled with positive messages about equality and working hard to achieve your goals. Erin and her second-grade classmates were all very familiar with the story of RBG. I had just recently helped her with a school project about the Supreme Court Justice, which involved cutting out a paper collar meant to replicate the famous and distinctive neckwear worn by Justice Ginsburg.

'The standard robe is made for a man because it has a place for the shirt to show, and the tie,' she told the *Washington Post* in 2009. She and Sandra Day O'Connor, the first woman Supreme Court Justice, 'thought it would be appropriate if we included as part of our robe something typical of a woman,' she said. The collars and necklaces she wore carried great meaning and gave an indication of how she would rule in a particular case. A black necklace with rhinestones meant she was dissenting, disagreeing with the majority view of the court. An elaborate yellow-and-gold crocheted collar would be worn when she was announcing an opinion on which she agreed with her colleagues.

Ruth Bader Ginsburg had acquired legendary status on the US Supreme Court. She was a liberal icon and a champion for women's rights and equality. From her working-class upbringing in Brooklyn, she rose through the ranks of the male-dominated legal system. As a lawyer she fought for gender equality, and as a Supreme Court Justice she backed landmark rulings securing equal rights for women, expanding gay rights and safeguarding abortion rights. The Supreme Court has enormous power in the US. Its justices are appointed for life and have the final say on a range of politically divisive issues, such as disputed presidential elections, gun control, immigration, same-sex marriage, abortion and the death penalty. The US is a country split by race, religion, party affiliation and geography. Those divisions were often laid bare on the floor of the US Supreme Court.

The nation's top judges are nominated by the president and must be approved by the Senate. At the time, the court already had a 5–4 conservative majority and RBG's passing meant it was about to move even further to the right. Donald Trump was informed of her death by reporters as he left a campaign rally in Minnesota. The song 'Tiny Dancer' was blaring from speakers in the background as the President approached the group of journalists. He put his finger to his ear as he struggled to hear what was being shouted at him by the press pool.

'She just died? Oh, I didn't know that. You're telling me this for the first time.' He paused to think of an appropriate response, allowing a few bars of Elton John's piano playing to fill the void. 'She led an amazing life, what else can you say? She was an amazing woman. Whether you agreed or not, she was an amazing woman who led an amazing life.' After another short pause, he concluded his brief remarks. 'I'm actually sad to hear that, I am sad to hear that.' It was a genuine, human, emotional response from a man who had so often upended norms and delivered stinging rebukes to opponents, even after their passing.

The morning after Ruth Bader Ginsburg's death, Murray and I made our way to the US Supreme Court to speak with those who had gathered there to pay their respects. American flags flew at half-mast overhead while people of all ages brought cards, flowers and drawings. Others just stood there, squinting in the bright autumn sun as they silently read the many tributes that had been left at the steps of the court. One woman wept. 'I'm just so worried about who will replace her,' she told her friend.

Mary Pat Cleary told me that she was devastated when she heard that Justice Ginsburg had died: 'I have an eighteen-year-old daughter who is about to start college and I can't think of a better role model for women's rights and for upholding the important elements of our Constitution. I wanted to be here today to pay tribute to her. It's a hard time for our country right now and this is just one more challenge we are facing. What I'm feeling now is beyond grief.' Christopher Kosteva said he had come to the Supreme Court to thank RBG for fighting for so many Americans throughout her life. 'It's only fitting we come out to memorialize her for all the support she has given all of us. 2020 has been a bad year and this is the icing on the cake, but we have a lot more fighting to do to make sure we can carry on her legacy,' he told me.

We were back at the Supreme Court four days later, where the sea of flowers, cards, posters and candles had continued to grow, as had the number of mourners. Pallbearers carried Ruth Bader Ginsburg's flag-draped coffin up the steps of the Supreme Court as the bright morning sun reflected off the brilliant white marble all around. Inside the court's Great Hall, a private ceremony was held for her friends and family. The coffin was then brought outside and placed under the massive columns of the building's portico for a public viewing. Large crowds queued for hours to pay their respects and say goodbye. One young woman, who was wearing an RBG face mask, told me she had been inspired by Justice Ginsburg: 'She was an amazing woman, not just a lawyer and a judge. The world has lost an amazing woman.' A man who was there with his young son and daughter described her as a rock star. 'She was a hero, but I'm really scared when I think of what happens next,' he said.

He was not the only one who was scared. The Democrats were well aware that Donald Trump now had the opportunity to tilt the balance of the court for years to come. They insisted that the nomination of a new justice should wait until after the election, which was just weeks away. They pointed to what had happened in 2016, when Republicans refused to hold a confirmation hearing for Barack Obama's nominee to replace Justice Antonin Scalia, arguing that it should not happen in an election year. Nonetheless, Republicans vowed to press ahead with confirming Donald Trump's nominee, leading to accusations of hypocrisy from their Democratic opponents. 'Why should the American people trust the Republican senators to do anything they say when they are proving right now that their speeches mean nothing the moment the shoe is on the other foot?' the Democratic leader in the Senate, Chuck Schumer, said. Republicans claimed that because they controlled both the White House and the Senate, this time was different.

Someone else who did not want to see a new justice appointed until after the election was RBG herself. Just days before her death she told her granddaughter Clara Spera: 'My most fervent wish is that I will not be replaced until a new president is installed.' But despite RBG's dying wishes, Donald Trump was getting ready to nominate his third Supreme Court Justice.

I remembered only too well the anger and divisions that followed the nomination of Brett Kavanaugh in 2018. He had been accused by university professor Christine Blasey Ford of sexually assaulting her when they were high-school students. She outlined the accusations during dramatic and emotional testimony before the Senate Judiciary Committee. Brett Kavanaugh fought back hard, denying the allegations in angry and tearful exchanges that were watched live on television by millions of people. He accused Democrats of a grotesque character assassination and as part of his defence he gave the Committee his calendar from the summer of 1982, when it was claimed the assault took place. He was a seventeen-year-old boy at the time and the entries referenced things like being grounded, going to prom and, in a nod to his Irish American roots, playing Gaelic football.

Hundreds of protesters gathered on Capitol Hill to oppose Brett Kavanaugh's appointment. Some managed to gain access to the hearing and interrupted proceedings with chants of 'Shame on you!' But Republicans stuck by their man and his nomination to the Supreme Court was confirmed by the US Senate. Now, almost exactly two years on, Donald Trump had the opportunity to choose another Supreme Court Justice. There were mixed views about what the timing of it would mean for the President politically, given that it was just weeks to the election. Tilting the court further to the right would play well to his conservative base, but they were going to vote for him anyway. On the other side, there was a sense that liberals and Democrats were so enraged by the fact that Republicans had pressed ahead with the nomination that they would come out in force to express their anger at the polls. But here again, Democrats and liberals were already enraged by four years of Donald Trump and were already planning on voting him out.

What it did offer Donald Trump was a distraction from his handling of the coronavirus, which was continuing to damage him in the polls. The President had vowed to choose a woman to fill the vacancy created by RBG's passing. Out of respect for the late Justice, he said he would wait a few days before announcing her replacement. On Saturday, 26 September, he arranged a large gathering in the White House Rose Garden to unveil his nominee. Around 150 guests attended, with little social distancing or mask-wearing on display. TV coverage of the event showed the guests hugging, kissing and shaking hands, before taking their tightly packed seats to hear the President speak. He announced from the podium that his Supreme Court nominee would be Judge Amy Coney Barrett, whom he described as one of the country's most brilliant and gifted legal minds.

As she is a conservative and a devout Catholic, liberals were worried that she would favour overturning the landmark Roe v. Wade (1973) ruling that legalized abortion in the US. In her confirmation hearing, she insisted that she would be guided by the law in all her rulings and not by her personal, political or religious beliefs. As expected, she was confirmed by the Republican-controlled Senate and Donald Trump had a victory he could relish just one week before Election Day. 'But he can't appoint a new judge,' Erin told me. 'Why do you say that?' I asked. 'Because RBG said she didn't want to be replaced until after the election,' came her confused and disappointed reply. A woman who had led so much reform and had sparked so much debate throughout her life was continuing to do so after her passing, even among those who would normally be far too young to know, or care, about such things.

In the weeks before Judge Amy Coney Barrett's confirmation, there was a lot more focus on the Rose Garden event at which her nomination had been announced than on the nomination itself. The mask-less hug-fest had been dubbed a 'super-spreader' event. In the days following the gathering, several guests tested positive for COVID-19, including the former New Jersey Governor Chris Christie and Donald Trump's former top adviser Kellyanne Conway, as well as Republican Senators Thom Tillis of North Carolina and Mike Lee of Utah. Donald Trump said he felt fine, but he had certainly been exposed to the virus at that event. Just a few days later, he stood on a stage alongside Joe Biden for their first presidential debate.

A circus, chaos and a shambles were just some of the words used to describe the showdown between the two candidates. Donald Trump started interrupting his opponent immediately and this continued for the duration of the entire debate. Joe Biden responded with frustration and insults, calling Donald Trump a clown, a liar, and telling him to shut up. 'I can't remember which of all his rantings you want me to respond to,' Joe Biden said to the debate moderator, Chris Wallace, at one point. 'I'm having a little trouble myself,' Wallace replied.

Donald Trump was asked if he would condemn white supremacists and militia groups and, when he failed to give a direct answer, was pressed further on the issue. 'I'm willing to do anything. I want to see peace,' Mr Trump said. 'What do you want to call them? Give me a name.' Joe Biden said, 'Proud Boys', referencing the far-right group. 'Proud Boys, stand back and stand by,' the President responded. 'But I'll tell you what, I'll tell you what, somebody's got to do something about Antifa and the left because this is not a right-wing problem.'

Joe Biden criticized Donald Trump for reportedly calling dead American soldiers 'losers' and 'suckers', invoking the memory of his son Beau, a decorated military veteran who died of cancer in 2015. Donald Trump quickly switched the conversation to Joe Biden's other son, Hunter. He accused him of taking money from Russia and China and of getting kicked out of the military for taking drugs. Joe Biden responded by saying that, like a lot of Americans, Hunter had a drug problem but was 'working on it' and had 'fixed it', adding, 'I'm proud of my son.' The entire debate was a complete disaster. Both sides claimed victory. Donald Trump's supporters enjoyed his loud, aggressive interruptions. The Joe Biden camp was relieved that their candidate had not made any major gaffes or missteps. Undecided voters, if there were any left at that stage, would have learned little and heard even less over the barrage of shouting.

Also raised during the debate was the perennial issue of Donald Trump's taxes. They were back in the news again thanks to another 'October surprise' pre-election bombshell. *The New York Times* published a story claiming that the President had paid little or no income tax for years before he came to power. According to the newspaper, Mr Trump paid just $750 in federal income taxes in 2016, the year he won the presidential election, and no income taxes at all in ten of the previous fifteen years. He was able to avoid paying tax because he reported losing more money than he made.

Donald Trump denied *The New York Times* story, insisting that he had paid millions of dollars in taxes. The newspaper had also reported that Donald Trump was facing more than $400 million in looming loan repayments. He dismissed the amount as 'a peanut', claiming his companies were under-leveraged with very low levels of debt. '$400 million compared to the assets that I have, all of these great properties all over the world,' he said. 'What I'm saying is that it's a tiny percentage of my net worth.'

The Trump campaign desperately wanted something else to become an 'October surprise' and that something else was Hunter Biden's laptop. It rolled off the tongue like 'Hillary Clinton's emails' and if it caught the attention of the electorate in the same way, Joe Biden's opponents hoped it would damage his lead in the opinion polls. There were unconfirmed reports that a laptop belonging to Hunter Biden was dropped off at a Delaware repair shop and that it contained incriminating information relating to his business dealings in Ukraine and China. The *New York Post* published a story based on emails it claimed had come from the laptop. The Biden campaign denied allegations of wrongdoing, the story was greeted with widespread scepticism and it did not become the scandal that the Trump campaign desperately wanted.

A story about Hunter Biden did hit the headlines in the days after the election. In December 2020 it was announced that he was the subject of a federal investigation into his taxes. 'I learned yesterday for the first time that the US Attorney's Office in Delaware advised my legal counsel, also yesterday, that they are investigating my tax affairs,' Hunter Biden said in a statement. 'I take this matter very seriously, but I am confident that a professional and objective review of these matters will demonstrate that I handled my affairs legally and appropriately, including with the benefit of professional tax advisors.'

Joe Biden's transition team released a statement saying: 'President-elect Biden is deeply proud of his son, who has fought through difficult challenges, including the vicious personal attacks of recent months, only to emerge stronger.' Donald Trump was reportedly furious that his Attorney General, William Barr, had not announced details of the Hunter Biden investigation before the election. Forget a vague, questionable story about a laptop – a federal probe into the tax affairs of his opponent's son would have fed into Mr Trump's narrative that the Bidens were in some way corrupt.

There were calls from some Republicans for the Attorney General to appoint a special counsel to investigate Hunter Biden, but William Barr said that would not be happening. 'I think it's being handled responsibly and professionally currently within the department, and to this point I have seen no reason to appoint a special counsel, and I have no plan to do so before I leave,' he told reporters. He was also asked if he planned to appoint a special counsel to investigate Donald Trump's baseless claims that the election had been stolen. Mr Barr had previously said that his department had found no evidence of widespread voter fraud that would have changed the election's outcome. 'If I thought a special counsel at this stage was the right tool and was appropriate, I would name one, but I haven't and I'm not going to,' he said.

It was his last press conference before leaving office and if Donald Trump had hoped his Attorney General was going to throw him a lifeline, it was not to be. The President had failed to manufacture an 'October surprise', but he would end up being at the centre of the biggest twist of all.

19. 'I feel like Superman!'

'Clear the park now!' the police officer screamed. We begged him to give us just two minutes. That was literally all we needed. We were about to go live into the *Nine O'Clock News* and I could hear the programme in my earpiece. There was no time to pack up and leave. I knew we were up next in the show's running order and I was going to keep my report very brief. Two minutes, that was all we needed. As Sharon Ní Bheoláin, the presenter back in Dublin, said the words, 'We can cross over live now to our correspondent in Washington', a second police officer approached Murray and added to the shouts of 'Leave this area now!'

I had no choice but to start speaking, we were live on-air. Murray continued to plead with the officers to just give us one more minute and then we would happily leave the area. I spoke at record speed, conscious that the police were getting increasingly aggressive. I had nearly finished my report and was starting to feel a sense of relief that we had managed to get through it, when suddenly one of the police officers pushed our camera, sending it spinning on its tripod. I knew instantly that it would have looked awful on-air. I was mid-sentence when suddenly the camera shuddered and ended up pointing in the wrong direction. Social media lit up with viewers asking what had happened. We were as confused.

We were reporting from the large, open green in front of the South Lawn of the White House known as the Ellipse. It was one of our regular locations as it provided the perfect backdrop for live TV broadcasts. Due to its close proximity to the White House, the area is sometimes closed for security reasons, and in the past we had been there when police officers politely told reporters and tourists to move on as the park was about to shut. This time was different. We had never seen the police behave so aggressively. There was a sense of urgency we had not witnessed before, a sense of panic. Frustrated and annoyed that our live report had been ruined, we gathered our things and moved the short distance to the footpath that borders the park. It didn't take long before we realized what was happening. The President of the United States was being airlifted to hospital and the area was being cleared so his helicopter could land.

It was Friday, 2 October 2020. In the early hours of that morning, Donald Trump had revealed that he and the First Lady, Melania Trump, had tested positive for COVID-19. Though at first they downplayed his symptoms, the President's condition had clearly worsened throughout the day and now he was being hospitalized.

The White House and the Washington Monument were bathed in golden light in what would have been a stunning sunset on any other evening. But the onlookers who had stopped were not there to witness an autumn dusk, they were there to see something else. Media and members of the public gathered as the President's helicopter, Marine One, landed on the South Lawn. Once he was on board, the rotor blades roared loudly and Donald Trump was carried into the cloudless sky. Ten minutes later he would land at the Walter Reed Medical Center in Bethesda, Maryland.

It was one of those *Reeling in the Years* moments, of which there were many during my time in Washington. The President was being taken to hospital suffering from a deadly virus that had claimed so many lives. It was also a rare moment of unity in a divided America. Republican or Democrat, there was a collective sense of worry about the health of a man who, love him or hate him, was clearly in medical distress.

Steve Tabor had stopped outside the White House to watch events unfold. 'It's painful for me as a Trump supporter,' he told me. 'I know there is a lot of division in our country, but this is heart-breaking for everyone, I hope, at this point. If we don't unite over this situation, there will be no unity in this country ever again,' he said. Stan and Patty Orlaski looked on as the helicopter departed. 'Our thoughts and prayers are with the President, that he will get well quickly and get back to the campaign,' Stan told me. 'I was surprised he got the virus, but I think he'll pull through pretty well, he seems like a vigorous guy,' he added. 'We just wish the best for him and his family,' Patty said.

It was another bombshell in what had been a year of bombshells. The previous day, 1 October 2020, US media had started reporting that one of Donald Trump's closest advisers, Hope Hicks, had tested positive for COVID-19. It sparked immediate concerns about the President's potential exposure to the virus because she had travelled with him on board Air Force One earlier in the week. I filed the story about Hope Hicks for the morning radio bulletins and was thinking about going to bed, but decided to stay up a little later so I could hear an interview the President was due to do with his friend Sean Hannity on his Fox News show. He was asked about Hicks. 'She did test positive. I just heard about this. She tested positive,' Mr Trump said.

He then revealed that he and the First Lady had been tested. 'I just went out with the test, I'll see, 'cause, you know, we spend a lot of time, and the First Lady just went out with a test also.

So, whether we quarantine, or whether we have it, I don't know,' he said. At that point, I knew I wasn't going to bed. I suspected something was up. Donald Trump sounded tired and a little congested and also uncharacteristically downbeat about it all. He spoke about how it was difficult for him and those close to him to avoid the virus since so many people, including members of the military and law enforcement, tried to interact with them. 'It's a tough kind of a situation,' he said, 'it's a terrible thing. So I just went for a test, and we will see what happens. I mean, who knows? I will get my test back either tonight or tomorrow morning, but I spend a lot of time with Hope and so does the First Lady, and she's tremendous,' he said.

He repeatedly referenced how he had been in close contact with a confirmed case and that he was now awaiting his own test results. It was almost as if he was preparing us for what was to come. Perhaps he wasn't feeling well and suspected the worst, or maybe he had already tested positive and was waiting for a second test result before confirming the news. Three hours later, just before 1.00 a.m. Eastern Time, he tweeted that he and the First Lady had tested positive for COVID-19. 'We will begin our quarantine and recovery process immediately. We will get through this TOGETHER!' he wrote. Of all the Donald Trump tweets I had read and reported on throughout his presidency, this was the most significant as it related to the President's own personal health. It was 6.00 a.m. in Ireland and the *Morning Ireland* team was just beginning its day. I called the editors with the breaking news, filed stories for our online and radio platforms and prepared to report live into the programme.

A letter had been released from the President's doctor saying that Mr Trump and the First Lady were both well and would remain at the White House. 'Rest assured, I expect the

President to continue carrying out his duties without disruption while recovering,' Dr Sean P. Conley wrote. Anyone who had been in contact with Donald Trump, or his staff, had to be tested. Ireland's Minister for Foreign Affairs, Simon Coveney, had been in Washington earlier that week for meetings at the White House and on Capitol Hill. He tested negative for the virus on his return to Ireland and restricted his movements.

It was all happening exactly one month before the US presidential election. A campaign that had already seen countless twists, turns and surprises had now been hit with the biggest shock of all. At age seventy-four, Donald Trump was in the higher risk category of developing serious symptoms. It brought renewed focus on safety protocols within the White House and on the President's downplaying of the virus, including his belittling of mask-wearing. There would be no more rallies or public appearances for the foreseeable future, raising big questions over what the final month of campaigning would look like.

Donald Trump's condition deteriorated rapidly throughout Friday, 2 October. He had a fever and his oxygen levels were falling. That evening, the White House said that while he remained in good spirits and had mild symptoms, 'out of an abundance of caution' his doctors had recommended that he work from the presidential offices at Walter Reed Medical Center for the next few days.

Walter Reed is a large military hospital in Bethesda, Maryland, just outside Washington DC. It is traditionally where US presidents go for their annual check-ups and for any medical treatment they may require. A tall Art Deco tower rises from the centre of the complex. At its base is a set of large, gold-framed double doors. In early October 2020, the world watched as those big doors swung open and teams of doctors emerged to give daily updates on the President's condition. The information was often vague and confusing, however. At one point, Dr Conley said his patient was 'doing great'. Minutes later, White House Chief of Staff Mark Meadows gave what was supposed to be an anonymous briefing to reporters but was captured on camera speaking to the assembled journalists. It was a contradictory assessment. 'The President's vitals over the last twenty-four hours were very concerning, and the next forty-eight hours will be critical in terms of his care,' he said. 'We're still not on a clear path to a full recovery,' he added.

In the days that followed, the medical updates did not get any clearer. Direct questions about oxygen levels, lung damage and the exact timeframe of the diagnosis went unanswered. The messaging from Donald Trump's doctors about his health mirrored the communication from the White House throughout the pandemic: confused, contradictory and vague. It was never clear when Mr Trump had last tested negative. This was important as it would have given the public an indication of how long into his illness he was.

Murray and I were camped outside Walter Reed for that entire weekend, waiting for updates. So too were large groups of Trump supporters. Some drove by the gates in their pickup trucks, honking horns and waving flags. Others stood at the hospital entrance, holding posters and chanting. One woman held a sign that read: 'Prognosis: four more years in the White House'. Other placards simply read: 'Get Well Soon'. Similar tributes and cards had been left alongside bunches of flowers at the hospital gates. At one point, a group of supporters bowed their heads as a man on a loudspeaker prayed for the President's health.

Ken Deibler was holding a large poster depicting Donald Trump as the action hero Rambo. 'I have faith that he is a strong warrior and that he will defeat the virus and make short order of it,' he told me. A woman who was carrying an American flag said she rejected criticism that Donald Trump had not been taking the virus seriously. 'We don't know when that bug entered him. He could have had a mask on and maybe he touched a surface and touched his eye. It is unfortunate, but he is human, just like us,' she said.

A man wearing a Donald Trump hat and face mask told me he was confident the US President would be fine. 'He's going to recover and frankly, to be a little tongue-in-cheek, I thought he needed the break,' he said. The President's supporters cheered with delight when Donald Trump briefly left the hospital at one point to drive by the crowds that had gathered. He had earlier announced that he would 'pay a little surprise to some of the great patriots that we have out on the street'. A masked Mr Trump waved from the back of his SUV. It led to widespread criticism that he had put the health of those around him at risk for the sake of a publicity stunt. Among the critics was a doctor affiliated with the Walter Reed Medical Center. 'Every single person in the vehicle during that completely unnecessary Presidential "drive-by" just now has to be quarantined for fourteen days,' Dr James P. Phillips tweeted. 'They might get sick. They may die. For political theater. Commanded by Trump to put their lives at risk for theater. This is insanity,' he wrote.

Earlier that day, I had actually begun to think that Donald Trump had a newfound appreciation of the scale of the COVID-19 crisis and of the seriousness of the virus, now that he himself had become infected. He had posted a video to social media in which he said he now got it. 'It's been a very interesting journey. I learned a lot about COVID,' Mr Trump said. 'I learned it by really going to school.' He added, 'I get it, and I understand it.' His reckless drive-by came a short time later and made it clear that he had learned nothing and would continue to flout safety guidelines and downplay the seriousness of the virus.

The following day, Donald Trump was discharged from hospital and what played out was a made-for-TV moment from the master of reality TV. Those massive, gold Art Deco doors swung open and a masked President appeared at the top of the steps. He initially went to grab a gold banister alongside the stairs in front of him, but he thought better of it, tapping it instead. He clearly did not want to give the impression that he needed any support while descending the steps. He then boarded Marine One.

After flying for ten minutes across Washington, the helicopter arrived at the White House. Donald Trump walked across the South Lawn and ascended the steps, stopping on the Truman Balcony. He removed his mask and appeared to be taking deep breaths. He posed for photographs while waving, saluting and giving the thumbs-up. He then went inside the White House and recorded a video for social media. In it, he told people not to be afraid of the virus because they could beat it. He spoke about how he was now better and might be immune, adding that vaccines and treatments would soon be on the way. 'Don't let it dominate you. Don't be afraid of it,' the President said. 'We're going back, we're going back to work. We're going to be out front. Don't let it dominate your lives. Get out there, be careful.'

After his release from hospital, his team posted a campaign-style video with dramatic music showing Marine One landing and Donald Trump returning, triumphant, to the White

House. There were media reports that the President had suggested a plan that would involve him pretending to be frail as he left the hospital but then opening his shirt to reveal a Superman T-shirt underneath. That stunt did not go ahead, but when he returned to the campaign trail shortly after his release from hospital, he told his packed rallies that he felt like Superman and boasted about the fact that he was now immune. 'They tell me I'm immune! I could come down and start kissing everybody, every man and woman. Look at that guy, how handsome he is. I could kiss him, not with a lot of enjoyment,' he said to loud cheers and laughter from his supporters.

The narrative that the President was a warrior and a fighter played well to his base. They saw him as someone who had taken on Washington, the Democrats, lawlessness, the mainstream media, and now the coronavirus. But the President's message of 'I beat the virus, so can you' ignored the fact that he had received round-the-clock treatment from the best doctors in the world, as well as experimental medicines that were not available to the general public. It was a package of care that would have cost hundreds of thousands of dollars, unaffordable for the vast majority of Americans.

That did not matter to his devoted followers, however. He continued to speak about his conquering of the virus in those final weeks of campaigning and the crowds lapped it up. I recall speaking to a Trump supporter named Gregory at one of the President's final rallies in North Carolina. He told me that he agreed with Mr Trump's handling of the pandemic: 'I like the balance he struck because he has allowed people to have freedom and states to have rights and make their decisions for themselves and I'm pro-freedom.' I pointed out that Trump had caught the virus and some would say that he should have taken more precautions with his own health. 'He bounced back quickly, though,' Gregory replied, a smile spreading across his unmasked face. 'It makes me question the validity of the hype and hysteria around the virus.' Many of Donald Trump's supporters had refused to accept the seriousness of the pandemic and, taking their cue from their President, had downplayed the need for mask-wearing, social distancing and business closures. Now, they had another reason to dismiss the pandemic: if Donald Trump had recovered so quickly, it couldn't be all that bad.

In the early days of October 2020, the news was dominated by claims about Donald Trump's personal finances and by the fallout from the disastrous first presidential debate, but these stories were eclipsed by the President's coronavirus diagnosis. It had come hot on the heels of the passing of Ruth Bader Ginsburg, which had triggered a divisive political showdown over the fate of the Supreme Court. We were in the final weeks of an election campaign that had been dominated by a devastating pandemic and unprecedented racial unrest. What impact would all of these seismic events have on voters as they went to the polls?

Outside Walter Reed Medical Center, I had met a young Donald Trump supporter. He was wearing a red 'Make America Great Again' hat and a faded blue 'Reagan Bush '84' T-shirt, a campaign that had played out years before he was born. 'What impact do you think Donald Trump's illness will have on the campaign? Will it weigh on the minds of voters?' I asked him. 'Absolutely. This is a super-liberal area. I've never been able to come out here with my Trump flag and my MAGA hat. I'd get yelled at. But now there are so many of us out here that I feel comfortable. I feel like all the conservatives in Bethesda and Washington DC are able to come out of the woodwork and show their support.'

He made an interesting point. I had never seen Trump supporters gather in that way in Washington or its suburbs. They had come to wish their President well and to pray for his recovery. Just a few weeks later, they would be back in the US capital, but for very different reasons. They would accuse the Democrats of stealing the election and would insist that Donald Trump was the real winner. They would chant, they would march and, ultimately, some would even launch an attack on the heart of US democracy.

20. Red mirages and blue shifts

The effects of the pandemic saw record numbers of people cast their ballots in the days and weeks leading up to Election Day either by using early in-person voting or mail-in ballots. For months, Donald Trump had claimed, without evidence, that this would lead to widespread voter fraud, suggesting at one stage that the election date should be moved because of the coronavirus. But to no avail.

When the results came in on election night, it played out as many had predicted. Donald Trump surged ahead in several states in what had been dubbed the 'red mirage', a lead caused by the fact that Republican voters were more likely to vote in person on Election Day and therefore have their votes counted first. In the days that followed, however, the mail-in ballots were counted, votes that typically favoured Joe Biden. This was known as the 'blue shift', which saw the Democratic candidate overtake Donald Trump and win crucial swing states like Pennsylvania, Michigan and Wisconsin. He even flipped red states like Arizona and Georgia. Although it wasn't all bad for Donald Trump, who managed to hold on to battlegrounds like Florida, North Carolina, Ohio and Iowa.

It took the US TV networks much longer than usual to project a winner. It finally came on Saturday, 7 November, four days after the election. There had been small crowds of Joe Biden supporters outside the White House all week, waiting for the results. When the projections finally came, those who had gathered made a lot of noise. They cheered, danced and waved flags and posters. Within minutes, more and more people started to appear, pouring onto Black Lives Matter Plaza from the surrounding streets. Before long, the numbers had swelled to thousands. They clattered pots and pans. A man alongside me was banging a large gong just as I was about to go on-air live into the opening of the *Six One News*. I was thinking, if this guy doesn't move, it is going to sound like a continuation of the Angelus, but he left just as I started my report.

There was a carnival-like atmosphere and one of those who had gathered, Bradley Baker, told me it was a wonderful day for America. 'There's a sigh of relief here in Washington DC and across the nation. There are lots of children here and I think it is going to be a better country for them,' he said. Erin Uritus came to the White House with her two young daughters. 'My girls are half-Arab Muslim, their father is Egyptian. For four years we have been waiting to restore integrity to government and I want my girls to know that no matter who you are, you can be treated fairly in this country,' she said. Most of the signs being waved carried Joe Biden's name but others were messages to Donald Trump, with slogans such as 'You're fired' and 'Time to go'.

Many of those who gathered outside the White House said they believed Donald Trump would not leave without a fight. Mark Joseph Stern said he did not think Mr Trump would concede and fully expected him to launch legal challenges: 'As a lawyer, I can say that his lawsuits have no merit. They will fail and he will be gone on January twentieth.'

It was a mild November evening as the sun set on Washington. The cheering Biden supporters wore shorts and T-shirts as they danced in front of a White House that would soon be occupied by their candidate. His poor caucus result in a freezing cold Iowa just nine months before seemed like an eternity ago. So much had happened in that time. A devastating pandemic, shutdowns, protests, racial unrest and a bitterly divisive election. But much more drama was to come.

Donald Trump was at his golf course in Virginia when TV networks projected that Joe Biden would be the next US president. As Mr Trump returned to the White House, he was greeted by thousands of people calling for him to go. Their cheers could no doubt be heard inside the West Wing, but they fell on deaf ears as he refused to accept defeat and vowed to fight the election results.

Many of those who worked for Donald Trump believe he would have been re-elected were it not for COVID-19, among them Mick Mulvaney. 'Oh, I'm 100 per cent sure he would've won if not for the virus,' he told me. 'Before the pandemic we fully expected Bernie Sanders to be the opposition. The pandemic played particularly well to Joe Biden because his weakness was campaigning and remains campaigning. He is mistake-prone, he is gaffe-prone. He lost the first three or four primaries, some of them badly. But when COVID kicked in, and the campaign changed, the atmosphere was different, and he did better. In February 2020 we had a booming economy, record low unemployment and we were facing the possibility of Bernie Sanders as our Democratic opponent. We fully expected to win – forty to forty-two states, a Reagan-like landslide re-election – but obviously it didn't work out like that.'

In the early days of the election campaign, Donald Trump spent a lot of time talking about the pandemic but frequently used those opportunities to advance core policy objectives, with an eye on his re-election. Whether it was ventilators, protective equipment or medicines, the coronavirus outbreak had put a sharp focus on supply-chain issues within the US. Mr Trump used these concerns to highlight his 'America First' policy and push his desire to see US companies move their foreign operations back to the United States from countries such as Ireland.

In March 2020, as hospitals were beginning to suffer from a shortage of equipment and supplies, Donald Trump was asked about access to medical devices. 'Ireland does a lot of work for us in that world, in the pharma world. A very tremendous producer,' he said. 'We are looking to bring a lot more back home.' In May of that year, he made an unprompted, specific reference to Ireland once again when asked a question about America's dependency on drug manufacturing in China. 'It's not only China, you take a look at Ireland. They make our drugs. Everybody makes our drugs except us. We're bringing that whole supply chain back,' he said. In August 2020, Mr Trump's top trade adviser, Peter Navarro, described Ireland as a 'tax haven' that was 'punching very high above its weight' in the pharmaceutical sector because of its low taxes.

Whenever Donald Trump, or members of his team, made such statements, the Irish government and IDA Ireland were always quick to point out that the presence of US pharmaceutical companies in Ireland wasn't just about low corporation tax. It was also of huge benefit to those firms as it gave them access to EU markets and a talented workforce.

Donald Trump could well have won Election 2020 if not for the pandemic. At the start of the year, the economy was strong and a big field of Democratic candidates were tearing each other apart in the primaries. Then, in March, the world changed. A major crisis can make or break a political career. For Donald Trump, it turned out to be the latter.

His usual tactics of downplaying, blame, insults and martyrdom had got him through the scandal of the *Access Hollywood* tapes, hush money claims, the Mueller Report and his first impeachment, but the Trump playbook did not work when the coronavirus hit. But what were the alternatives, and would a different approach have saved him? Federally ordered mask mandates and widespread closures would have angered his base and could have cost him some of those 74 million votes he managed to get on Election Day. On the other hand, a greater focus on the pandemic early on could have saved lives and resulted in more moderate voters re-electing a leader they felt had done his best to tackle the virus.

Also, it would be wrong not to acknowledge that there were some coronavirus successes under the Trump administration. His international travel restrictions were maintained by the incoming Biden administration and its Operation Warp Speed helped bring about the speedy development of vaccines. Unfortunately for Donald Trump, the fruits of that effort did not emerge in time for the election. On Monday, 9 November, less than one week after polling day, Pfizer announced that its COVID-19 vaccine was 90 per cent effective, based on early test results.

Mike Pence was quick to ensure that the outgoing administration would get the credit, tweeting that the good news from Pfizer was 'thanks to the public-private partnership forged by President Donald Trump'. The President took a different approach, however, alleging that the announcement of the test results had been delayed deliberately until after the election for political reasons. He tweeted: 'As I have long said, Pfizer and the others would only announce a vaccine after the election, because they didn't have the courage to do it before. Likewise, the FDA [Food and Drug Administration] should have announced it earlier, not for political purposes, but for saving lives!'

Pfizer denied that it had delayed the release of test results until after the election. If anything, the company said, the data had become available earlier than expected. But it all played into Donald Trump's victim complex. As the non-politician outsider who had promised to 'drain the swamp', he consistently claimed that the establishment was against him. This included Washington's political elite on both sides of the partisan divide, as well as big tech and big media. Now he could add big pharma to that list. In November 2020, after the election defeat, Donald Trump made an announcement from the White House on lowering drug prices. He took the opportunity to attack the pharmaceutical industry, accusing it of using armies of lawyers and lobbyists. 'Big Pharma ran millions of dollars of negative advertisements against me during the campaign, which I won by the way, but you know, you'll find that out, almost 74 million votes,' Mr Trump said. But, despite his claims to the contrary, Donald Trump did not win the election.

It meant that in November 2020 the media spotlight switched from Washington DC to the hometown of the new President-elect, where Joe Biden was preparing for his move to the White House. The Queen theatre in downtown Wilmington, Delaware, has an old-world feel. Its front entrance and box offices are topped by an ornate marquee with back-lit signage that normally carries details of the current show or upcoming performances. Instead, the black letters had been arranged to spell out a public health message, telling people to stay safe amid the pandemic. The Queen, like every other theatre around the world, had been forced to close because of COVID-19, but now the venue had a new star attraction.

There were no tickets or audience members, but what played out on stage was watched by millions. The Queen theatre had become Joe Biden's base for his transition to the presidency. It was from there that he held virtual Zoom meetings with advisers and delivered his addresses to the nation. It was late November, less than three weeks after he had been projected to become the next US President, and Joe Biden took to the Queen's stage to unveil his new foreign policy and national security teams.

'America is back, ready to lead the world,' he said as he announced his nominees for top jobs such as Secretary of State, National Security Advisor and UN Ambassador. Many of his candidates had come from the Obama era and had plenty of government experience. They vowed to be loyal to the country rather than the President and to be led by facts and the truth. Joe Biden announced the first female Director of National Intelligence and the first Latino Secretary of Homeland Security. He said his team would restore America's global leadership and moral leadership and that the US would 'once again sit at the head of the table, ready to confront our adversaries and not reject our allies'.

For the previous four years, Donald Trump's foreign policy was based on his vow to put 'America First'. It led to a move away from multilateralism and saw the US withdraw from international treaties and alliances. Relations with traditional allies, like the European Union and NATO, became strained, while traditional adversaries were embraced, such as Russia and North Korea. 'America is back, ready to lead the world, not retreat from it,' Joe Biden said.

It was just before Thanksgiving, and while the President-elect was unveiling his foreign policy team, the President was participating in the rather bizarre tradition of pardoning a turkey at the White House. Although still challenging the election results and refusing to concede, Donald Trump did appear to acknowledge that a major shift in US foreign policy was coming. 'As I say, America first. We shouldn't go away from that. America first,' he told the assembled guests before going on to pardon a turkey named Corn.

I had also taken part in a Thanksgiving tradition that day. Every year a Belfast-based charity called the Flax Trust holds a Thanksgiving Breakfast on the top floor of Washington's Hay-Adams hotel, which is across the street from the White House. The function room is surrounded by a rooftop terrace with stunning views of DC's landmarks. It was an opportunity for the charity to thank those who had supported its work throughout the year and to honour well-known Irish Americans. It was an event I looked forward to every year but in 2020 the breakfast, like most in-person gatherings that year, was held virtually. Guests were encouraged to click on the Zoom link and raise a cup of coffee or a glass of orange juice from our homes.

I attended the virtual breakfast from the back of Murray's car. Sipping a takeaway Starbucks, I listened to the various speeches and musical performances as we drove from Washington DC to Wilmington, Delaware, a journey of 108 miles. The Flax Trust call ended just as we arrived at Barley Mill Road. There was no rooftop view of the White House this year, but I was outside a presidential home of a different kind.

Joe Biden's three-storey mansion overlooks a lake and is located in Greenville, Delaware's priciest suburb. The neighbouring homes are large with perfectly manicured lawns. Locals jogged and walked dogs, paying little heed to the Secret Service vehicles and armed guards that blocked the country lane leading to the Bidens' compound. Murray filmed some footage of the area, but I was disappointed that we couldn't get a better view of the house. It is, by all accounts, a luxury property, with a jetty, outdoor swimming pool and lots of terraces from which to enjoy the views.

When we had finished recording, we took the short fifteen-minute drive to downtown Wilmington and found a parking space close to the Queen theatre. As we reported live into the *Six One News*, police cars and blacked-out SUVs pulled up behind us. Joe Biden's motorcade was arriving. Surrounded by his newly unveiled nominees on the stage of the theatre, Joe Biden outlined his foreign policy vision for America and then exited stage left.

Murray and I were waiting outside. We were behind a barrier but close to the motorcade, close enough to shout a question and get it answered, we hoped. The door swung open and a cameraman emerged, followed by a small group of reporters. This was the press pool that accompanied the President-elect everywhere. If they were leaving, I knew Mr Biden wouldn't be far behind. The journalists rushed past us and boarded a nearby bus. This was a bad sign. They had clearly decided not to wait for the departure and the chance to shout questions – perhaps they had been told that Joe Biden would not be speaking?

Additional police cars pulled up and the door of one of the black SUVs was held open by a waiting Secret Service agent. I was watching the stage door closely when suddenly there was a flurry of activity behind us. It was the press pool. 'We were looking at you and your cameraman from the bus,' one reporter explained to me. 'Someone saw your RTÉ microphone and knew it was Irish TV. Joe Biden loves Ireland, so we decided we'd better wait with you in case he spoke and we missed something.' With that, the newly arrived photographers started snapping furiously as Joe Biden emerged from the theatre.

At first, he seemed to be veering away from the waiting media, and was about to get into his car when I shouted a question about Ireland that caught his attention. He approached the group of journalists. 'Can I ask you a question about Ireland?' I repeated. 'You can ask about Ireland any time you want,' he replied. 'With Brexit negotiations underway right now, what is your message to those negotiators, particularly when it comes to Northern Ireland?' I asked.

'We do not want a guarded border,' Joe Biden told me. 'We want to make sure; we've worked too hard to get Ireland worked out. I've talked with the British Prime Minister, I've talked with the Taoiseach, I've talked with others, such as the French. The idea of having the border north and south once again being closed, it's just not right, we have got to keep the border open.'

It was the first time that Joe Biden had spoken about Brexit since his election win. I attempted to get in a second question, but I was shouted down by the US reporters and their queries about various domestic issues. After he walked away, the American journalists who were there joked that from now on they would shout the word 'Ireland' to get interviews with their new President. A similar tactic had been used in the 1990s. Back then, reporters soon learned that questions about the Northern Ireland peace process or the Good Friday Agreement were the best ways to get the attention of President Bill Clinton.

Murray and I sent our Joe Biden interview back to Dublin, relieved that our trip to Wilmington had not been in vain. We had managed to get access to the man who was preparing to take over the most powerful office in the world. But many Americans believed he was not the legitimate winner of the election and their anger was growing.

21. 'Stop the Steal!'

On 14 November 2020, the Million MAGA March was held in Washington DC. It was the second Saturday in a row that I found myself in the city centre covering a political rally. Just one week before, thousands of Joe Biden supporters had gathered outside the White House to celebrate his election win. Today it was the turn of Donald Trump's followers.

The turnout did not meet the 'million' touted in the name of the event, but there were still huge crowds on the streets. Tens of thousands of people gathered with Trump flags, hats and signs. Before that day, I had never seen that many 'Make America Great Again' logos in Washington DC. It is largely a Democratic city, but on that afternoon the nation's capital resembled a Trump rally in North Carolina or Alabama.

The crowd size was no doubt helped by the fact that Donald Trump had hinted that he might make an appearance, tweeting the night before: 'Heartwarming to see all of the tremendous support out there, especially the organic rallies that are springing up all over the country, including a big one on Saturday in D.C. I may even try to stop by and say hello.' His motorcade drove through the crowds while he was on his way to play a round of golf in nearby Sterling, Virginia. Wearing a red baseball cap, he waved to his supporters, who cheered and snapped photos as he drove by.

The crowds gathered at Freedom Plaza, near the White House, and marched along Pennsylvania Avenue, past the Capitol Building and on to the US Supreme Court. They chanted 'USA', 'Four More Years' and 'Stop the Steal'. A man shouted into a loudspeaker: 'America will never be a communist country!' Minutes later there was the crackle of another loudspeaker, this time held by a woman who was shouting: 'We don't want satanic paedophiles running the country. We want good ol' American boys!' This was a reference to the QAnon conspiracy theory that was embraced by many of Donald Trump's supporters. It claimed that Mr Trump was engaged in a battle against a powerful group of devil-worshipping child-abusers.

When the President was asked to condemn QAnon and distance himself from the movement he refused to do so, telling NBC in October 2020 that he agreed with their anti-child-abuse stance. 'Let me just tell you what I do hear about it is they are very strongly against paedophilia and I agree with that,' Mr Trump said. The previous August he had told reporters: 'I don't know much about the movement other than I understand they like me very much, which I appreciate.'

Back at the Million MAGA March, the protesters I met were all in complete denial that he had lost the White House. Trish Haight was holding a poster of a cute, smiling baby surrounded by the words: 'Trump 2020, the Pro-Life Choice'. She told me that the Democratic machine had taken over the election and engaged in fraud. She insisted there was evidence of this and dismissed claims to the contrary as fake news from a corrupt media. 'The media doesn't get the luxury of picking our president, the people do. Americans won't accept Joe Biden as president until the constitutional process is completed,' she said.

Chip Bauer was a man in his sixties wearing a red Trump hat. He said he was hopeful that the various legal challenges and recounts that were still ongoing at that time might change the election outcome: 'If nothing else, today's march will send a message that we will not tolerate what appears to be voter fraud. We want the other half to know that we are serious.' I pointed out to Chip that there wasn't any evidence of widespread voter fraud. 'Well, that's your opinion. I see differing opinions about that. I guess it depends on where you get your news from.' Chip also told me that if Donald Trump failed to overturn the election result, he should run for the White House in 2024 and that he would definitely vote for him again.

A young woman in a red 'Stop the Steal' hoodie told me the election had been overtaken by outside forces. 'If you were watching on election night, Trump was leading and then all of a sudden it seemed like they stopped counting, it flipped for Biden and he was winning,' she said. I pointed out that the mail-in ballots take longer to count. 'And that's the problem,' she replied. 'In the county where I live, we were still getting mail-in ballots even after Election Day. Something has definitely gone wrong. If you watch the rallies, the patriotism and the boat parades all across the country, there is no way that Trump lost.'

Before I could speak to any more protesters, I was distracted by a new round of chanting. It was coming from a side street leading to the main route of the march on Pennsylvania Avenue. There were angry shouts of 'All Lives Matter' and 'Fuck Joe Biden!' from a group of around thirty men dressed in black and yellow. Some of them wore military-style helmets and bulletproof vests. These were the Proud Boys. It was my first time seeing them in the flesh. Murray ran towards them for a better camera angle while I called after him, urging him not to get too close. The right-wing extremist group is known for its anti-immigrant views and for violent clashes with rival groups on the far-left.

When Donald Trump infamously failed to condemn them during the first presidential debate, he told them to 'stand back and stand by'. The phrase was embraced by the Proud Boys, who incorporated it into their logo and had it printed on T-shirts and flags. As they joined the Million MAGA March that day, I noticed that one of them was also carrying a sign that read: 'Kyle Rittenhouse did nothing wrong'. Rittenhouse was a teenager accused of fatally shooting two men and wounding a third in August 2020 during a Black Lives Matter protest in Kenosha, Wisconsin.

The Million MAGA March made its way through Washington and ended at the US Supreme Court, the same place Donald Trump was hoping his election fight would be decided in his favour. It wasn't to be, however. On 11 December 2020, the court rejected a legal challenge backed by the President. The state of Texas had tried to sue Pennsylvania, Georgia, Wisconsin and Michigan, claiming, without evidence, that there had been voter fraud. In a one-page order, the Supreme Court denied the complaint due to 'lack of standing'.

The ruling was very much on the minds of the thousands of Donald Trump supporters who gathered in Washington the day after the court decision for another 'Stop the Steal' rally. It wasn't as big as the Million MAGA March the previous month, but those who were protesting were just as adamant that Mr Trump was the real winner of the election and that the Democrats had cheated. They took photos in front of a Trump-branded bus and bought T-shirts, flags and posters from street vendors. They carried signs with slogans such as 'We love you Supreme Court but we won't tolerate lawlessness', 'Stealing is not winning' and 'Trump Won'.

A rather convincing-looking Donald Trump impersonator stood on the steps of a nearby building. He was unmasked, hugging and shaking hands with those who posed for photos with him. He pulled a mask off a young woman's face as her friend snapped a photo, but she didn't seem to mind and just laughed. A line started to form of people wanting to get a picture with the super-spreader-in-chief, but then another attraction turned up at the carnival. There were loud cheers and people started filming something on their phones. It was the Proud Boys, and their arrival was greeted with great excitement. Those who had gathered appeared pleased to see them, except perhaps the Donald Trump impersonator, who lost his audience to the new arrivals.

While the Proud Boys represented extremist views, a casual observer would have been struck by the diversity on display among the many banners and flags being carried by the other protesters: 'Chinese Americans for Trump', 'African Americans for Trump', 'Gays for Trump' and 'Latinos for Trump'. A young woman named Casey was wearing a pink 'Women for Trump' baseball cap. 'We have to stand up and fight, even if you don't like Trump. Voter fraud can't happen on either side. The liberals should also be worried because it could happen to them next time,' she told me. I pointed out that the courts and election officials had said there was no evidence of widespread voter fraud. 'Of course they'd say that, it's just what they want you to believe. They haven't produced any proof that there wasn't fraud,' she said. 'But there isn't any proof that there was fraud, there's a lack of evidence,' I replied. 'Evidence for a court of law, or evidence beyond reasonable doubt? We all believe there was fraud,' she concluded.

Meg Tracey was in her sixties, at least I think she was. It was difficult to tell behind her stars-and-stripes hat, scarf and face mask. 'I believe in democracy for America, but we are headed towards socialism,' she told me. 'I believe the election was stolen. They changed the rules and allowed mail-ballots to come in days later. They stopped the counting in the middle of the night. Back in the old days, we used to stay up all night counting.' But what about the fact that officials say there was no widespread fraud? 'Ha! And if you believe that, there's a bridge in Brooklyn I'm gonna sell you!' she replied.

I was unfamiliar with the saying, so I looked it up that evening. It is a New York expression based on the story of conman George C. Parker who, in the early 1900s, repeatedly 'sold' the Brooklyn Bridge, and many of the city's other landmarks, to unsuspecting victims. One hundred years later, here we were talking about another New Yorker who was telling tall tales as he tried to sell his theory that he had won an election he had lost.

Among his supporters, Donald Trump had found plenty of eager buyers. People like Michael Willett, a grandfather who had travelled to Washington from New Jersey for the Stop the Steal March. 'I'm here to support my President because this election was stolen from him . . .' I pulled my microphone back. 'But there's no evidence of that,' I interrupted. 'That's not true, that's a media talking point. There's plenty of evidence and affidavits but the courts don't have the backbone to rule, so this march is an opportunity for me to show my support for the President, whatever happens. Even if he's not elected, we still go on because he started a movement of people who love their country and we think we are headed in the wrong direction.'

Michael told me that he believed US politics was at a crossroads: 'The Democrats are off on the far-left and most of the Republicans don't have backbones, so a lot of us are wondering if there is a need for a reform party or a patriot party because the Republicans are not representing the people who voted for them.' He described Donald Trump as a refreshing change. 'You can love or hate him. He can be arrogant, he can be brash, but he is not a politician and he has done what he said he was going to do. I hope he stays around, or maybe some of his family members might run for office. Donald Trump's supporters aren't going anywhere!' he told me.

A few feet away, we came across Zoe sleeping happily in her buggy. She was an eleven-year-old black Pomeranian, and on the side of the children's stroller in which she sat hung a poster that read: 'All Aboard the Trump Train'. On top of the dog's head was a tiny 'Make America Great Again' hat. Her owners were Greg and Robin Pressley from Tennessee, no relation to that state's most famous son. 'It's spelt P-r-e-s-s-l-e-y, like Elvis but with one more s,' Greg told me. He claimed there was plenty of evidence of voter fraud. 'I'm out here to support my President and stop Joe Biden from stealing this election. Donald Trump is going nowhere for the next four years.'

Robin predicted that election fraud was also going to be an issue in the upcoming Georgia senate races where two Democratic candidates were taking on Republican incumbents. 'I've already got a text message from Georgia wanting to send me a ballot and we live in Tennessee. There's already fraud in that election.' A Pressley from Tennessee casting a ballot in a Georgia senate race could well have sparked allegations of dead people voting, even if the spelling was slightly off. Suspicious minds, indeed.

We left the Pressleys and their hound dog Zoe behind and made our way to our live position. When we finished our report into the *Six One News*, a young Donald Trump supporter started shouting at us. He was in his twenties and wearing a green hunting vest over a blue T-shirt. He claimed we were spreading 'fake news' and, picking up on my Irish accent, told us to 'go back to your own country, you're not welcome here'. That last part annoyed Murray, who was born in nearby Maryland and has lived there all his life.

The man followed us for several blocks through Washington, shouting abusive comments and trying to rile up his fellow Trump supporters. 'Hey guys, these liars are saying that Donald Trump lost the election and that there was no fraud!' Fortunately, no one seemed to care and they ignored him. It was still unnerving, though, and our anxiety levels rose as he followed us onto a quiet, empty street. A large group of men marching together suddenly rounded the corner. I instantly recognized their black-and-yellow clothing.

'Hey, Proud Boys,' our heckler called out to them. 'These guys are lying about Trump!' It was a scary moment as we were surrounded by members of an extremist group known for violence. Thankfully, they kept walking and ignored the annoying Trump supporter, just as everyone else had done that day. We emerged onto a busier street that had a large group of police officers standing at a roadblock. We stood alongside the officers, who laughed as the Trump supporter continued to shout at us from across the street.

'Are you all right, lads, do you want to come inside?' It was an Irish accent. We were standing in front of The Hamilton restaurant on H Street, close to the White House. Its general manager, Irishman John Grace, had seen what was going on and offered us a safe place, if we needed it. It was a welcome offer of Irish hospitality, but fortunately our nagging Trump supporter had finally got bored and wandered off, so we started walking in the direction of the RTÉ office. On our way, we came across dozens of police officers running towards a crowd. The Proud Boys were fighting with a group of counter-protesters. Murray started filming from a safe distance, both of us relieved that we were covering the violence from afar rather than being on the receiving end of it.

Throughout that day, the supporters chanted 'Four More Years!' But by mid-December and into early January it was becoming a case of 'four more weeks' as the clock ran out on Donald Trump's time in office. Despite this, many of his followers firmly believed that he had something 'up his sleeve' or would 'pull something out of the bag' that would see him remaining in the White House. They expected him to produce some shocking piece of evidence of voter fraud that could not be ignored by the courts, or perhaps to convince state legislatures in key battlegrounds won by Joe Biden to throw out the results and declare him the victor instead. Of course, in the end, he had nothing 'up his sleeve', just more false claims and baseless accusations. His words of anger and division could not force judges or politicians to overturn an election, although they could incite his supporters to try to take matters into their own hands.

22. 'Fight like hell!'

'I was just inside the Capitol,' he told me proudly. He had a beard, was in his thirties and was wearing an olive-green army helmet, a green rain jacket and a backpack on his shoulders. He approached Murray and me as we were finishing a live report into the *Nine O'Clock News*. We were standing in front of the Capitol Building, which had just been stormed by a mob of Donald Trump supporters. Some were still inside, others had started to leave, and there was a steady flow of people passing our live position on Pennsylvania Avenue carrying Trump flags and wearing 'Make America Great Again' hats and scarves. Police reinforcements were arriving from across Washington DC and from neighbouring Maryland and Virginia. Emergency vehicles whizzed by, sirens blaring.

'What network are you guys with? Are you fake news?' the man asked. I told him we were with an Irish TV station called RTÉ. 'I'm Irish!' he said. 'You can interview me, but only if you use everything I say.' I hadn't asked him for an interview, he had approached us, and I would never promise editorial control to someone just so they would speak to me. 'You're probably recording all of this anyway,' the man said as he gestured into the camera.

Looking down the lens, he was about to explain why he had just stormed the Capitol Building. I stopped him and said that if we were going to do an interview, he would need to look at me. I then asked him why he had joined today's protest. 'As Americans, we are completely fed-up with politics as usual. We feel like our sovereignty has been subverted. We've had enough. We've gone through every legal recourse possible. We've been shit on. Our economy has been completely debased by the communist Chinese party,' he said.

A line of police cars was fast approaching behind us and their sirens were getting louder and louder. As the background noise rose in volume, so too did my interviewee's voice. He also grew more animated, gesturing and pointing wildly as he spoke. 'Enough is enough! We, as Americans, feel that the prosperity of the world rests on the shoulders of our ancestors. Ancestors that I share with you from Ireland, my last name is Shalvey. There is going to come a reckoning and the American people will lead, as usual.' The loud sirens were almost upon us now and Mr Shalvey was almost done. 'We are not violent, we do not seek to kill. We seek to re-establish righteousness in the world for Jesus Christ. Thank you!'

He walked off and disappeared into a crowd of his fellow protesters as they made their way down Pennsylvania Avenue, away from the Capitol Building. Murray was busy filming footage of the dramatic scenes playing out all around us. I was on my phone, trying to find out the latest information on the riots. We did a second live report into the *Nine O'Clock News* and as I was wrapping up, I could see a group of Donald Trump supporters gathering behind Murray. They were listening to every word I was saying. Just as I finished speaking, they started screaming 'Fake news!', clearly angered by the honest, factual account of events I had just delivered. I was used to hearing the President's followers echo his words, but now those words were being used by some as an excuse for violence and disorder. It marked another dark chapter in those final days of the Trump presidency.

Murray and I quickly started gathering our equipment so we could leave the area, aware that members of the media had been targeted by the mob earlier in the day. Their aggressive shouts of 'Fake news!' grew louder and we were getting worried. A police officer, who had been watching it all from his squad car, approached us. 'Everything OK here?' he asked. 'These fucking assholes are telling lies!' one member of the group claimed. 'Why don't you come with me, gentlemen?' he said to us and we walked towards his squad car. Our tormentors didn't follow and instead went to join the steady stream of demonstrators that continued to ebb away from Capitol Hill. The police officer was on his own and had shown great bravery in coming to our aid. We thanked him for his help and went on our way.

In the days that followed, dramatic images from inside the Capitol Building started to emerge. Some of the most striking footage was recorded by journalist Luke Mogelson, a veteran war correspondent and a contributing writer for *The New Yorker* magazine. He had spent months reporting on radical elements within Donald Trump's support base. He followed the rioters into the Capitol Building and recorded the unbelievable scenes on his phone.

The video showed the protesters breaking into the building and wandering through the halls and chambers of Congress chanting, 'Whose house? Our house!' and 'Treason! Treason!' as they stormed the Capitol. One rioter told a police officer: 'If you will not stand down, you are outnumbered. There's a fucking million of us out there. And we are listening to Trump, your boss.' Another man shouted into a loudspeaker, 'Defend your liberty, defend your Constitution!' as he made his way through a corridor, his fellow protesters banging on the office doors they were passing.

Luke Mogelson also captured footage of a group of rioters making their way onto the floor of the Senate chamber. They rifled through desks, reading and photographing documents left behind by the fleeing Senators. 'There's got to be something in here we can fucking use against these scumbags,' one man said as he flicked through a folder of notes. On the balcony above, the bare-chested rioter in furs and horns known as the 'QAnon Shaman' yelled and chanted while banging a flagpole on the floor. 'This is a good one, him and Hawley or whatever. Hawley, Cruz,' one of the rioters said as he read a document. He was referring to Republican Senators Josh Hawley and Ted Cruz, who had objected to the certification of the Electoral College votes in a bid to please Donald Trump and his support base. 'Hawley, Cruz?' asked another man. 'I think Cruz would want us to do this . . . so I think we're good.'

A third man had found another document belonging to Senator Cruz. 'He was gonna sell us out all along, look!' He proceeded to read the words from the page. 'Objection to counting the electoral votes of the state of Arizona.' He paused. 'Oh, wait, that's actually OK.' The man was wearing a backpack and a green army helmet. I recognize that guy, I thought as I watched the footage. It was Mr Shalvey, the Irish American man who had stopped to tell me why he had invaded the Capitol as he left the scene of the riot. According to court records, Dale Jeremiah 'DJ' Shalvey was charged in February 2021 with trespassing on Capitol grounds, violent entry, disorderly conduct and obstruction of Congress. He turned himself in to the authorities and joined the hundreds of people who were charged for their part in the storming of the Capitol.

The attack that day was the culmination of the Stop the Steal campaign that had begun after Donald Trump's election defeat. Believing his falsehoods that the election had been stolen from him, the President's loyal supporters took to the streets in massive numbers to object to the outcome. They embraced conspiracy theories about dead people casting ballots and rigged voting machines. There was no evidence of widespread voter fraud and the claims were dismissed by courts, the US Attorney General and election officials.

It was all building up to 6 January 2021, the day that members of Congress would gather on Capitol Hill to formally count the Electoral College votes and ratify Joe Biden's win. A massive rally, dubbed Save America, was planned for that day and would see thousands of Donald Trump supporters converge on Washington. The President would address the gathering outside the White House, followed by a march to Capitol Hill. For weeks beforehand he had been encouraging his supporters to attend, tweeting on 19 December: 'Big protest in D.C. on January 6th. Be there, will be wild!'

Several smaller events were organized on the days leading up to the big rally and throughout that week Donald Trump supporters started to arrive in Washington from all across the US. On the evening of 5 January, the eve of the storming of the Capitol, a protest was held on Freedom Plaza, close to the White House.

Caroline Kyle had travelled from Fort Worth, Texas, and was wearing a red 'Make America Great Again' cowboy hat. She claimed there was widespread election fraud and laughed when I said there was no evidence of this. 'Oh, there's a considerable amount of fraud evidence and they have displayed this. You just won't see it on mainstream media. I think there are a lot of people in DC who are not real Republicans, they are RINOs [Republicans in name only], and they don't have the Constitution in mind when they are making their decisions,' Caroline told me.

She was with Anna Mason, a young African American woman who was also wearing a similar Trump cowboy hat and waving a flag that depicted Donald Trump as Superman over the word 'SuperTrump'. She told me, 'Stevie don't have to Wonder that this election was stolen. I'm here for God, country, freedom, liberty and justice for all.'

Linda Chalk had travelled from Dallas. 'We were at the rally last month and you are never among better people than at a Trump rally. Patriots and people who love God and country. Donald Trump won this election, and you can tell that by the rallies and events like this. Joe Biden doesn't have the ability to be president.' I pointed out that the reason Joe Biden didn't hold any big rallies was the pandemic, but Linda tutted and shook her head. 'Oh dear, the pandemic has nothing to do with the election, it's just a "plandemic", that's why I don't wear masks when I don't have to,' she replied, referring to an anti-vaccine, anti-mask conspiracy theory that downplayed the seriousness of the coronavirus.

'Don't count Donald Trump out,' Linda continued. 'He has a lot up his sleeve, and he is a very smart man. He knows what is coming, he knows what they have planned and that is why he has called us here because he will show the truth. There's a lot more coming, for those of us who follow. We know it will all be exposed soon,' Linda told me. It struck me that there were religious connotations in her use of terms like 'he has called us here' and 'show the truth'. It was as if she expected the President to reveal some great mystery or divine wisdom that the rest of us mere mortals could not see. As if he were some sort of spiritual rather than political leader, a Pope rather than a President. And in the eyes of his supporters Donald Trump was, just like the Pope, infallible. He could do no wrong.

A male Trump supporter I spoke to had high expectations when I put it to him that the President had run out of legal options to overturn the election result. 'Well, we'll have to see about that. There's supposed to be big news coming, so we'll just have to see what happens tomorrow.'

The following morning, 6 January, Murray and I made our way to the Ellipse, the large green area in front of the White House. A stage and big screens had been erected under signs that read 'Save America'. Thousands of Donald Trump supporters gathered there, the crowd stretching back to the Washington Monument. 'Donald Trump can do this, he's got this, he is our man,' a woman from Arkansas told me. A man named Mark, who had travelled from Ohio, said he was there to show his support for the President. 'This election has not gone well. We believe it's been stolen and it's not fair to anybody in our country. It should be one legal vote per person. That hasn't happened and that is unacceptable,' he told me.

Before Donald Trump addressed his supporters, other speakers took to the stage, including his lawyer, Rudy Giuliani. He told the crowd, 'Let's have trial by combat!' He later denied that this was a call to violence and said it was a *Game of Thrones* reference. Perhaps he was inspired by the man standing next to me in the crowd who was holding a large poster depicting Donald Trump as Jon Snow, the series' main character. Under the picture were the words 'Cross the Rubicon Mr Trump'.

It was the culmination of a bizarre few months for Rudy Giuliani that had provided more drama than any episode of *Game of Thrones*. On 7 November 2020, just days after the election, Mr Giuliani had called a press conference to make unfounded claims of voter fraud. Donald Trump tweeted that it would be held at the Four Seasons Hotel in Philadelphia, but it was later clarified that it would in fact take place in the car park of a business called Four Seasons Total Landscaping, which provides gardening services. It is located in an industrial area of Philadelphia, close to a sex shop, a crematorium and a jail. The strong suspicion was that the wrong venue had been booked by the Trump campaign. Four Seasons Total Landscaping became famous on the back of it and started selling T-shirts and other merchandise with slogans like 'Make America Rake Again' and 'Lawn and Order'.

Worse was to come for Rudy Giuliani. During a press conference just over a week later, he appeared to be sweating profusely as he made more wild, unsubstantiated claims about rigged voting machines and fraudulent ballots. In an apparent hair-dye mishap, lines of black liquid started trickling down his face and onto his shirt collar. Donald Trump's lawyer was happy to claim fraud at a podium in front of the cameras, but when the allegations were put before the courts they were dismissed repeatedly due to lack of evidence. Dominion, a voting machine company that was a repeated target of Mr Giuliani's baseless accusations, filed a defamation lawsuit against him, seeking $1.3 billion in damages.

Back at the Save America rally in Washington, Rudy Giuliani had finished his address and it was time for the main event. The crowd erupted in cheers as Donald Trump took to the stage. He claimed his election loss was an egregious assault on democracy and had to be confronted by Congress. 'We fight like hell and if you don't fight like hell, you're not going to have a country any more,' he told them. He also claimed he would join them on their march to the Capitol Building, something which never transpired.

'We're going to walk down, and I'll be there with you . . . and we're going to cheer on our brave senators and congressmen and women, and we're probably not going to be cheering so much for some of them because you'll never take back our country with weakness. You have to show strength and you have to be strong. We have come to demand that Congress do the right thing.'

Donald Trump also urged the crowds to make their voices heard 'peacefully and patriotically', but what followed was anything but peaceful as a group of his supporters stormed the Capitol Building where Congress was meeting to confirm Joe Biden's presidential election win. There were unimaginable scenes of chaos inside the chambers and halls. Security guards were involved in armed stand-offs and elected representatives were forced to shelter under desks while protesters smashed windows and vandalized offices. Shots were fired. Lives were lost. It was bedlam.

As we made our way to the scene, our phones pinged with an alert from the mayor of Washington DC warning that a curfew would be enforced from 6.00 p.m. that evening. It reminded me of similar messages that flashed on our phones six months earlier during the unrest that surrounded the Black Lives Matter demonstrations. But there was a stark contrast between the heavy-handed police action during those mainly peaceful protests and the delayed response of authorities to this attack.

Also delayed was Donald Trump's condemnation of the rioters. Initially, he called them patriots and told them he loved them. Eventually, he encouraged the mob to go home and attempted to distance himself from the violence. But by then, the damage was done. Members of his staff started to resign in protest, like his Northern Ireland Envoy Mick

Mulvaney, who quit two weeks before his term of office was due to conclude.

'It's mostly symbolic,' Mulvaney admitted, 'because of the short period of time left, I recognize that, but it's a direct result of what happened in Washington DC and it's the only official act I can take to express my displeasure with what happened. It was unforgivable and inexcusable, and I simply don't want to be part of an administration that contributed to it,' he told me at the time. 'You cannot have a President of the United States encouraging people to go up and, essentially in an armed riot, try to prevent the constitutional processes of our government from taking place. That's unforgivable. What happened was uniquely terrible within this administration.'

Mick Mulvaney had previously said that he believed Donald Trump could run for President again in 2024, but now said he no longer thought that would be the case. 'Certainly, I think his political career is over and most likely that of his family. He will go down in history now, not as the President who had a great economy, not as the President who had the lowest unemployment rate among black Americans, he will go down in history essentially as the President who encouraged people to rise up against the government. That historical penalty will be there, and there may also be criminal penalties after what happened.'

I spoke to Mick Mulvaney again a few weeks after Donald Trump left office. Did he still feel that Trump's political career was over? 'I think that while he might be able to manage a credible campaign, he is no longer electable. There's a saying in religion: the converts have greater passion. If you convert to Catholicism, sometimes you are more passionate than those who are raised in the faith. The flip side of that is true: there's no disappointment and cynicism more deep than among those who were in the faith and have left. Donald Trump created a large number who believed in him very fervently and deeply and they've been very disappointed in his conduct surrounding the riots and it would be nearly impossible, if not impossible, to win a national election having turned off that many people.'

Mick Mulvaney believes that all the achievements of the Trump administration will now be forgotten because of the storming of the Capitol. 'We had full employment for an extended period of time without inflation. We had no new overseas war during the President's term and that's a tremendous achievement, something we should all be proud of. But that will all be lost because of what happened on January sixth. You don't get to say, "Yes, there was a riot, but we had a great tax policy"; it doesn't work like that. They are not close to being of equal importance and what happened on January sixth will taint the administration forever and it is hard to argue that it shouldn't.'

He was still trying to process the scenes from the Capitol that day. 'I shake my head and wonder what happened in those final weeks in the White House to allow January sixth to happen the way that it did. I'm not talking about the riot itself but the President's conduct and response to it was different to the President I had worked for. I don't know who was advising him, but his behaviour on that day surprised me.'

Mick Mulvaney said that Donald Trump's treatment of Mike Pence was one of the biggest disappointments. That was a sentiment echoed by many Republicans and White House staff. In the days leading up to the counting of the Electoral College votes, the President was putting massive pressure on Mr Pence to intervene and refuse to certify Joe Biden's victory. The Vice President, as the president of the US Senate, does have a role in the counting of the votes but it is largely a ceremonial one. He was there to oversee the count, hear objections and announce the results, but had no power to change the outcome. Donald Trump disagreed and repeatedly said in tweets and public statements that his VP should step in and save the day. 'I hope Mike Pence comes through for us,' he told supporters at a rally in Georgia. 'I hope our great Vice President comes through for us. He's a great guy. Of course, if he doesn't come through, I won't like him very much.'

When Mike Pence didn't 'come through' on the day of the count, Donald Trump tweeted: 'Mike Pence didn't have the courage to do what should have been done to protect our Country and our Constitution, giving States a chance to certify a corrected set of facts, not the fraudulent or inaccurate ones which they were asked to previously certify. USA demands the truth!' The message was posted just as a mob of the President's supporters were smashing their way into the Capitol Building. Some of them chanted 'Hang Mike Pence' as they searched for him in offices and hallways. He and his family members had been moved to a secure location by Secret Service agents just minutes beforehand.

Donald Trump never called his Vice President while he sheltered in the Capitol to check if he was OK. Nor did he call him in the days that followed. The President was seemingly unconcerned about the welfare of a man who had spent the last four years defending his boss with unbreakable loyalty throughout multiple controversies. It was telling that, on Inauguration Day, Mike Pence chose to attend Joe Biden's swearing-in ceremony rather than Donald Trump's farewell event.

23. The moderate radical

Washington DC is usually a walkable city, laid out in a grid of numbered and lettered streets intersected every now and again by wide avenues. It is normally easy to get around, but not in January 2021. The streets around the White House, Capitol Building and National Mall were all closed, blocked by large military trucks surrounded by armed National Guard troops in camouflage uniforms. At one point, Murray and I struggled to walk just a few blocks. Convinced we had worked out the best route, our hopes were dashed by yet another roadblock and a disapproving look from an armed guard who was unimpressed by the yellow media credentials hanging around our necks.

We asked a police officer for guidance at one barricade. 'I don't know, man,' he answered with a sigh and a shrug of his shoulders. 'I have no idea which roads are open and which are closed, it keeps changing.' It was new territory for everyone, even the officers on duty. There had never been a presidential inauguration like this before. It was always going to be a scaled-back event because of COVID-19, but the storming of the Capitol Building had led to an unprecedented security lockdown.

On the morning of the inauguration, we loaded our equipment into an Uber before dawn and told the driver where we wanted to go. 'No, it's all closed,' he said in broken English. 'It's OK, we have media credentials that will get us through the roadblocks,' I said, hoping that this would be the case.

We did have the appropriate ID badges and accreditation, but we were still nervous that we wouldn't get through.

I was due to be interviewed by Neil Prendeville on Cork's RedFM, the local radio station where I had begun my broadcasting career as a college student. I did the interview over the phone while sitting in the back of the Uber. While I was live on-air with Neil, describing the atmosphere in Washington, Murray and the driver started arguing. I raised my voice, hoping the row wouldn't be audible to the radio listeners of Cork. The driver, still adamant that all the roads were closed, was insisting that he had to drop us off several miles from where we needed to be. Murray knew better and urged him to follow the directions we were giving him. Eventually he did and, thankfully, our credentials allowed us through a series of security checkpoints.

We unloaded the car and walked through metal detectors. Our equipment was checked by sniffer dogs, our bags were searched, our temperatures were taken, and we were given face masks. 'Please put this on over your existing face covering,' we were told as staff informed us that double-masking was being encouraged. We finally got through the multiple layers of security and made our way to our live position on the National Mall in front of the Capitol Building where, in a few hours' time, Joe Biden would be inaugurated as the 46th President of the United States.

The Mall is a long, rectangular park in the middle of Washington DC. It stretches for two miles from the Capitol Building to the Lincoln Memorial and is lined by some of the best-known museums and monuments in the world. On Inauguration Day, it would normally be packed with thousands of people, but not in 2021. That year it was eerily quiet, with no members of the public allowed to gather. Streets that would usually be lined with crowds were instead lined with armed National Guard troops and barbed-wire fences.

The National Mall was transformed into a field of flags, 200,000 of them, to represent the people who could not be there. Inauguration Day was windy, and the long, straight Mall acted like a tunnel, amplifying the force of the gales. Smaller flags from individual states that had been planted into the soil were able to withstand the gusts and fluttered in waves. It was a striking image and the sound of the flapping cloth echoed in the empty park.

Larger US flags had been placed on the gravel pathways alongside the lawns and were no match for the high winds. One by one, they started to fall over. Staff were quick to replace them or, in some cases, take them away in their golf carts and wait for the winds to die down. The image of toppled American flags is the last thing organizers would want the world to see on Inauguration Day.

Before the swearing-in ceremony, Joe Biden's morning began with Mass. He attended a service at the Cathedral of St Matthew the Apostle in Washington. Irish violinist Patricia Treacy performed at the service. Also in attendance were Congressional leaders from both sides of the political divide.

While senior Republicans and Democrats were at Mass, Donald Trump was leaving the White House for the last time. In a break from tradition, he refused to attend the inauguration of his successor. Instead, he delivered a farewell address at Andrews Airforce Base in Maryland before he boarded Air Force One for his final flight as President. 'We've accomplished a lot,' he told the crowd. 'What we've done has been amazing by any standard.' He didn't mention Joe Biden by name, but he did wish the new administration 'great luck and great success'.

'I think they'll have great success. They have the foundation to do something really spectacular,' he said. 'Have a
good life. We will see you soon. Goodbye. We love you. We
will be back in some form.' Mr Trump boarded the aircraft
and it took off to the sounds of Frank Sinatra's 'My Way',
transporting him to Florida to begin his life as a former
president.

Back at the National Mall, the winds started to pick up and
there was a light fall of snow as Joe Biden took to the podium
to deliver his inaugural address. These speeches are typically
about unity and healing. Given how divided America was and
the fact that millions of voters did not see him as their legit-
imately elected leader, it was important for Mr Biden to make
such appeals. But his address wasn't just about unity, it was
also about perseverance and survival. He spoke about how
democracy had come under attack, but survived. Truth had
been undermined, but prevailed. 'Politics need not be a raging fire destroying everything in its path. Every disagreement
doesn't have to be a cause for total war,' Mr Biden said. It was
an appeal for a spirit of togetherness, in spite of everything.

Mr Biden was kept busy in his first days in office, signing
a series of executive orders. The measures would see the US
rejoin the World Health Organization and the Paris Climate
Accord. Funding was cut for Donald Trump's border wall
and his travel ban affecting Muslim-majority countries was
ended. Many of the actions related to the coronavirus crisis.
The Defence Production Act was invoked to ramp up vaccine
manufacturing and distribution. Mask-wearing was ordered
in federal buildings, airports and on public transport. Directives were issued on reopening schools.

There was another big difference under the new administration: Joe Biden let the scientists speak for themselves and

hold their own press briefings without interrupting them or trying to take over. When America's top infectious disease expert, Dr Anthony Fauci, spoke to the press for the first time as Joe Biden's adviser, he noted the difference between the two presidencies. 'The idea that you can get up here and talk about what you know, what the evidence is, and let the science speak, is somewhat of a liberating feeling,' he said.

In his first days in office, Mr Biden warned that things would get worse before they got better. He spoke of dark days ahead and predicted that the number of US deaths from the virus would continue to rise. It was a very different approach from that of the previous administration. Donald Trump admitted downplaying the virus and was eager to embrace quick-fix solutions and unproven cures.

My first time entering the White House under the Biden administration came on 12 February 2021 and was a complicated affair. Further COVID-19 restrictions had been imposed in a bid to reduce the number of people in and around the complex. Only a handful of reporters were allowed inside the briefing room to ask questions at the daily updates given by the White House Press Secretary, Jen Psaki. Journalists were spread out among rows of empty, socially distanced seats and had to undergo a COVID-19 test before being allowed near the West Wing.

The outer perimeter of the White House was expanded to include Lafayette Park, a square in front of the north entrance of the building. A gap had been left in a long metal fence for a white tent. I went inside, where a security guard checked my ID and radioed ahead to the next checkpoint to let them know I was coming. 'You need to go to 718 for your COVID test,' he told me. I had no idea what he was talking about. 'Excuse me?' I replied. '718 Jackson Place, it's down there on the right.' I walked through, only to find myself entering a second white tent. Here, my bag was checked and I passed through a metal detector. 'Where's 718 Jackson Place?' I asked the security guard. 'I have no idea, man,' came the reply. I would just have to find it on my own.

Jackson Place is a row of beautiful redbrick townhouses which leads to the White House. Given their close proximity to one of the most secure buildings in the world, it is no surprise that they are now all owned by the federal government. Some are still homes, used by visiting dignitaries, but most of them are offices. I ascended the steps of number 718 and pressed an intercom next to the locked door. 'Yes,' crackled a voice from the speaker. 'Ah, I'm here for a COVID test, I'm a—' but further explanation wasn't required as the door buzzed and clicked open. A burly, masked Secret Service agent greeted me. 'Hi, I'm here for—', but just like the intercom outside, he didn't need to hear my backstory. 'Follow me please, sir,' he said as he led me into an office reception area. 'Fill in this form, please.' He handed me a clipboard. It had the feeling of a dentist's office or GP surgery, if not for the armed guards sitting at the desks.

I was then led into another room where the agent asked me a series of questions, the same questions I had just answered on the form at reception: name, phone number, social security number, etc. I was led behind a grey partition where a gloved, masked man in a black suit directed me to a leather swivel chair. 'You can sit or stand,' he said. I decided to stand and instantly regretted it when I realized the man was more than a foot shorter than me. I had to squat awkwardly so he could reach my tilted head. The cotton buds tickled as he scraped the insides of both nostrils. He deposited the swabs in a small packet with my name written across it in marker. 'If you don't hear from us, assume everything is fine,' he told me.

Back at reception, a woman handed me a fluorescent orange wristband to prove I had been tested. I left and descended the steps, my nose still tickling as I walked towards the White House. 'Excuse me, sir!' came a shout from behind me. It was the Secret Service agent from the COVID-19 testing centre running after me. Oh Christ, I've failed the test, I thought. 'I forgot to ask your date of birth,' he said. 'No problem,' I said as I rattled off the numbers. You could have read it off the fecking form you made me fill out, I thought, but that probably wouldn't have helped my chances of getting in. Armed with my bright orange wristband, I went through another layer of ID checks and metal detectors and then, finally, I was inside President Joe Biden's White House.

He had promised to be a unifying president, but Washington remained as divided as ever. Republicans accused Joe Biden of running as a moderate but ruling as a radical. The party's most senior member in the House of Representatives, Kevin McCarthy, told Fox News that the President had pulled a 'bait and switch' in his first hundred days in office. 'The bait was that he was going to govern as bipartisan, but the switch is he's governed as a socialist,' he said. Those accusations of socialism came as the President announced plans to spend $4 trillion on infrastructure, climate action measures and family supports. He said it would be paid for by taxing high earners and making corporations pay their fair share. His plan for a new global minimum tax rate for American multinational companies caused concern in Ireland, amid fears it would impact the country's attractiveness as a location for foreign direct investment by US firms.

President Biden's first legislative win came in March 2021

with the passage of the American Rescue Plan through Congress. The massive $1.9 trillion coronavirus relief bill included extended unemployment benefits, stimulus payments for taxpayers, as well as funding for COVID-19 vaccines. This was the new President's signature piece of legislation and the first test of the razor-thin Democratic majorities in Congress. But despite lots of talk of bipartisanship and unity, Joe Biden could not get one single Republican to vote for his bill.

That month, March, was the annual Irish American Heritage Month. Usually, it is announced in a short press release with a few lines about the historic links between Ireland and the US. The proclamation issued by President Biden in March 2021 was very different. He praised the contributions of Irish immigrants. They had, he said, helped define America's soul and shaped the country's success across generations. He made reference to his own Irish roots, saying that it was hope and faith in the possibility of a better life that had brought the Blewitts of county Mayo and the Finnegans of county Louth to the United States: 'By 1909, my grandparents Ambrose Finnegan and Geraldine Blewitt met and married in Scranton, Pennsylvania, and passed on to my mother, Catherine Eugenia Finnegan Biden, a pride and a passion that run through the bloodstream of all Irish Americans.'

In his statement, he spoke warmly of cultural contributions: 'Irish American writers pollinated America's literary landscape with their love of language and storytelling, while Irish lyricism has brought poetry, art, music and dance to nourish our hearts and souls.' He also referred to a previous visit he had made to Ireland: 'As I said when I visited Dublin in 2016, our nations have always shared a deep spark, linked in memory and imagination, joined by our histories and our futures.'

Ambassador Dan Mulhall was struck by the wording of the proclamation. 'It is usually a bland, low-key, prosaic document, but this time it was infused with the personal enthusiasm of the President for his Irish heritage and I found it to be quite moving and poetic in the way it paid tribute to his Irish roots,' he said. 'Remember, he is the most Irish president since John F. Kennedy. Ten of his sixteen great-great-grandparents were born in Ireland. Two of his great-grandparents were born in Ireland, and also in his life, upbringing and identity he has always projected himself as an Irish American, and that is something special for an Ambassador, to be here at a time when the President who holds that high office has such a passion for Ireland.'

The former Taoiseach Leo Varadkar similarly saw Joe Biden's Irishness as genuine and important. 'I have met him on numerous occasions over the years. We have spent hours together. I would have seen him as a former Vice President, telling me about the political battles he had fought, and I did not think at that time that I would lose an election and he would win one and he'd be the President and I'd be the Deputy Prime Minister. It shows how unpredictable politics is,' he said. 'One thing that is so important is that he has a genuine interest in Ireland and genuinely emotionally supports Ireland beyond anything I've seen. He does actually have our back, and we'll never have that again. We didn't have it with Barack Obama or with Donald Trump.'

Naturally, there was going to be a lot of focus on President Biden's first St Patrick's Day. As 17 March 2021 approached, there was much speculation about whether Taoiseach Micheál Martin would travel to the US for the traditional shamrock ceremony. At the time, Ireland was under the strictest of lockdowns following a surge of coronavirus cases and deaths after

Christmas. I knew from speaking to family and friends back home that people had had their fill of the restrictions and patience was running out. News stories I posted to social media about a possible visit by the Taoiseach to the US were met with angry replies like, 'I can barely go outside my own front door and he thinks he can swan off to America!' Micheál Martin said he would go to the White House if he was invited, but he was in a lose-lose situation. If he went, he would attract the ire of an angry, frustrated electorate. If he turned down an invite, it could be seen as a diplomatic snub. In the end, the matter was taken out of the Taoiseach's hands. All of Joe Biden's first meetings with world leaders would be virtual, and the St Patrick's Day celebration would be no different.

The Biden administration had incredibly strict COVID-19 safety protocols, as I had found out on my first visit. Only a small number of journalists and officials would be allowed inside the Oval Office for the opening of the President's virtual meeting with the Taoiseach. Fortunately, I was able to secure one of the coveted places. I was nervous as I made my way to 1600 Pennsylvania Avenue on the morning of 17 March. If I tested positive, I would not get to cover Joe Biden's first St Patrick's Day in office.

Before making my way through security, I checked my phone. There was an email from our health insurance company informing me that I was eligible for a vaccine and I was invited to book an appointment. I called my wife. She had received the same email. We were both pleasantly surprised, as this was far sooner than we had expected. Was this St Patrick's Day 'luck of the Irish'? I signed up for a slot the following day.

At that time, the US had a massive stock of vaccine supplies and was well ahead of its targets. Joe Biden had vowed that 4 July 2021 wouldn't just be Independence Day, it would mark the start of America's independence from the virus. It was a very different situation in Ireland and the rest of the European Union at the time, where there was a desperate shortage of doses leading to a much slower vaccine rollout. Taoiseach Micheál Martin had vowed to bring up the issue of vaccine supplies in his meeting with Joe Biden. As I made my way through the first layer of White House security, I realized that I would be spending that day reporting on vaccines and spending the following day getting vaccinated myself.

Before passing through the metal detector, I removed my watch and belt, placing them with phone, keys and bag on the conveyor belt leading to the x-ray machine. Once I was through, it was time for my COVID-19 test. I prayed everything would be OK as the tester placed my sample into an envelope and wrote my name on it. 'If you don't hear from us, assume everything is fine,' he said. It was just like my last time entering the White House, except on this occasion I was given a blue wristband. 'Shouldn't this be green for St Patrick's Day?' I asked. My poor attempt at humour was met with a grunt and I went on my way.

I felt a sense of relief to be inside the White House press briefing room. I chatted with fellow journalists as we awaited the first of the Taoiseach's virtual engagements with the administration that day, a meeting with Vice President Kamala Harris. 'How do you pronounce Taoiseach?' one American journalist asked me. 'How do you pronounce Micheál?' another inquired.

As I flicked through emails on my phone, a new message appeared with the subject line: 'Your lab results are ready'. My heart sank and I felt a knot in my stomach. I had been tested just thirty minutes earlier and they had said they would only get in touch if something was wrong. Did the fact that I had received an email so quickly mean that I was positive? Would my name be called out over the intercom? Would Secret Service agents be dispatched to escort me off the premises? A million thoughts ran through my head as I opened the email.

My test result was negative. Thank God, I thought as I stood up to pull my laptop from my bag and begin my day's work. It was then that I realized my trousers were loose and my shirt had become untucked. In my haste to get through security and testing, I had forgotten my belt in the x-ray machine. I would have to wait until the end of the day to retrieve it. I spent the next few hours having to adjust my clothing every time I stood up, but I didn't care. I was in the White House and that was all that mattered.

As we were led into the Oval Office, the room felt a lot bigger than I remembered. The last time I had been in there was one year previously, for the St Patrick's Day meeting between Taoiseach Leo Varadkar and President Donald Trump, and it was bedlam. The Oval Office was packed with journalists from the US and Ireland shouting questions at the two leaders about travel bans and restrictions.

This time was different. The small number of reporters and officials allowed into the room made the office seem a lot more spacious. I looked around and noticed that there was nothing on the Resolute Desk. Presumably all the important documents had been taken away ahead of the arrival of the journalists. At the far end of the curved room, Joe Biden sat alongside a TV screen showing Micheál Martin back in Dublin. Despite the fact that the two leaders were 3,000 miles apart, there was a closeness and a connection between them. The monitor on which the Taoiseach appeared was tilted at an angle in the direction of the shamrock bowl. Joe Biden leaned in towards the screen as he addressed the Irish leader, almost as if he were there alongside him.

There was a second bowl of greenery on a larger table in front of the President and a garland made of a similar plant had been draped across the mantelpiece. It looked like shamrock, but the leaves were much more prominent. 'It looks different, but do you think that's also shamrock?' I whispered to a US journalist who was standing alongside me. 'Oh yes, I believe it's American shamrock,' she replied knowingly. 'The leaves are larger.' 'Everything's bigger in America!' I said drily, but she did not react. The President had begun talking.

Mr Biden spoke with fondness about Ireland. Perhaps with another president there might have been a danger that a virtual meeting would have led to a downgrading of the event or lessened its diplomatic impact, but that certainly wasn't the case with a US leader who was so proud of his Irish ancestry. The meeting itself was longer than usual, running for an hour and twenty minutes. It was described as incredibly positive, with Joe Biden telling Micheál Martin that he was only a phone call away.

The politicians may not have been able to travel from Dublin to Washington DC, but the city felt very Irish that day. The fountains outside the White House were dyed green in the morning and, as night fell, the building itself was illuminated in green light. It was a glow that had also been felt inside the West Wing earlier that day as the two leaders met, separated by an ocean but connected by shared values and traditions.

The following day, I went to get my vaccine shot. 'Where's

that accent from?' the nurse asked as she directed me where to sit. When I said Ireland, she didn't mention Conor McGregor, but she did wish me a belated Happy St Patrick's Day. As we chatted, I told her about my visit to the White House the day before and about how people wanted our Prime Minister to ask Joe Biden for some of America's vaccine supply. 'Ha!' she laughed. 'That ain't gonna happen. He's gonna make sure Americans are vaccinated first.' Ouch, I thought as the needle went into my arm. It wasn't the injection, but the painful reality that she was right. The President was never going to send vaccines to other countries until he was sure he had enough for his own people.

I was glad to be getting my jab, but on one level it felt wrong. Here I was, a healthy forty-year-old getting vaccinated because in America it was my turn, but back home in Ireland my parents, in their seventies, were still weeks, if not months, from getting theirs. Having spent the previous day celebrating the connections between Ireland and the US, the two countries suddenly felt very distant again as major gaps emerged in the vaccine rollout effort.

Irish heritage is not the only thing that Joe Biden has in common with JFK. Kennedy was America's first Catholic president, Joe Biden is the country's second. When my family and I first arrived in Washington in 2018, we started attending Mass at Holy Trinity Catholic Church in the Georgetown area of the city. It is a beautiful building and the oldest Catholic church in Washington. A plaque at the front entrance commemorates the fact that President Kennedy worshipped there frequently. Sunday morning Mass in Holy Trinity was not short. Lengthy sermons and a full programme of hymns, performed by an impressive choir, meant a service could last well over an hour. Our daughters would complain about the duration but were delighted to avail themselves of the doughnuts that would be served in the parish centre after Mass. They also attended Sunday school at Holy Trinity. At first, they were not too pleased about having to go to school at weekends, but they loved the lessons and would skip out of class holding the latest drawing or project they had completed.

When I first started going to Mass in Holy Trinity, I realized that the church was also attended by senior members of Congress, including the Speaker of the House, Nancy Pelosi. There were politicians in the congregation and political references in the sermons and prayers. The priests would often talk about the latest developments in the White House or on Capitol Hill while explaining and analysing the messages contained in that week's gospel. I recall one 'prayer of the faithful' that began along the lines of: 'Dear Lord, please stop the Trump administration from separating immigrant families at the border.' It was met with the usual response from the congregation: 'Lord, hear our prayer.' In Washington, even Mass was political. I soon realized that my Sunday mornings would be just like the rest of my working week, spent listening to people talking about Donald Trump.

Then came the year of the coronavirus and, like everything else, Mass and Sunday school had to go virtual. When restrictions eased, only a handful of families were allowed to attend services that were governed by strict mask-wearing and social distancing rules. Online sign-up for in-person Mass opened at noon on Wednesdays and the small number of places would be snapped up in minutes. In January 2021, the winds of change blew through Holy Trinity as well and I found out that we had a new member of the parish.

A White House press pool report pinged on my phone,

informing me that President Biden would be attending Sunday morning Mass at Holy Trinity. 'That's our church!' I said to my wife. 'Now it's going to be even harder to get a place at Mass,' she replied. In a letter to parishioners, the priest wrote: 'We are living in a time of significant changes in our nation with the arrival of a new president and a new administration, several of whom are Holy Trinity parishioners.' The letter noted that this had brought 'increased visibility' for the parish. Yes, I thought as I read the letter, the US President sitting in the back row of the church will definitely bring additional attention.

Joe Biden may be a practising Catholic and a regular churchgoer, but many conservatives are unhappy with the fact that he is a supporter of abortion rights. In his first days in office, he signed an order overturning a ban introduced by the Trump administration that blocked federal funds going to international aid groups that perform or provide information about abortions. According to the order that President Biden signed, 'It is the policy of my administration to support women's and girls' sexual and reproductive health and rights in the United States, as well as globally.'

He also ordered a review of rules from the Trump era that blocked government funding for family-planning clinics in the US that refer women for abortions. The directives were issued on the eve of the annual March for Life anti-abortion rally in Washington DC. Every year, a protest is organized that coincides with the anniversary of Roe v. Wade, the landmark Supreme Court decision that legalized abortion in the US. Organizers have vowed to march every year until the ruling is overturned. It usually attracts tens of thousands of people and, in 2020, Donald Trump became the first US President to address the March for Life.

In 2021, it was very different. The event was mainly virtual, with only a handful of protesters gathering outside the US Supreme Court. They had to assemble at the back of the court. The front of the building, which faces the Capitol, was still in lockdown since the 6 January riot. Armed guards looked on from behind barbed-wire fences as protesters left flowers in front of the court and said prayers. Many were lamenting Donald Trump's election defeat and the end of his pro-life policies.

I spoke to a young man in a red 'Make America Great Again' hat who had joined the march. 'The difference is like night and day between Joe Biden and Donald Trump when it comes to abortion. Even though President Biden is a Catholic, he goes completely against the Catholic faith by openly endorsing abortion,' he told me. A woman I spoke to described Donald Trump as the most pro-life President America had ever seen. 'I feel with Joe Biden as our new President the pro-life movement is just going to get more difficult and it is not time to give up, it's time to push back harder,' she said.

Those words encapsulate the division that undercuts the Biden administration – the President wants to pull people together, but many of those people want to push back. He was elected by a broad coalition of voters, with strong support from African American communities, suburban families and blue-collar workers in the Rust Belt. Disillusioned by Donald Trump, they put their faith in a new leader, expecting big changes. He will also have to be a unifier and address divisions within his own party, where the splits between progressives and moderates are growing ever wider. He has inherited a divided nation, a fractured America, where people stand at opposite ends of the political spectrum, staring at one another with incomprehension.

This means there will be a long road ahead for Joe Biden, who is faced with a difficult path to navigate, as tricky as the maze of roadblocks that lined the route to his inauguration ceremony. As the wind battered and knocked US flags on an empty National Mall, a new President spoke about the resilience of America and Americans. A toppled flagpole is easily righted, but restoring a country battered by a devastating pandemic and deep political divides is going to be a far greater challenge.

As for meeting Joe Biden at Mass, for a while it appeared it was destined not to be. We normally attended the twelve noon Sunday service, but on the weeks we missed Mass, we would hear that Joe Biden had been there. On the weeks we were there, he would inevitably have attended the 5.00 p.m. Saturday service or he would be in his hometown church in Wilmington, Delaware.

Then, one Sunday morning in June 2021, Joanna dropped me and the girls off at Holy Trinity. As I took my seat and switched my phone to Silent, I noticed a text from her. It was a photo of blacked-out SUVs and a team of Secret Service agents outside the front door of the church. 'Looks like you are getting a special visitor,' she wrote. I watched the door. It swung open and two agents entered. They stood at the back of the church, surveying their surroundings. They spoke into their wrists and pressed their fingers to their earpieces. The door opened once more and I, like everyone else in the socially distanced pews, watched and waited. Two women passed through the entrance and were directed to a seat at the back of the church.

'Who is it?' Lucy asked, as she craned her neck to see. 'Is it Joe Biden?' Normally, I would scold her for looking around in Mass, but I was guilty of doing the same thing. 'No,' I informed her when it became clear that no one else was coming. A ripple went through the congregation as we all realized that it was Nancy Pelosi who was joining us for that day's service. Comments were murmured behind masks and, without seeing people's faces, it was difficult to tell if they were excited to see the Speaker of the House or disappointed that it wasn't the President.

As was usual, the Prayers of the Faithful contained political references. This time it was the migrant crisis on the US–Mexico border, which had become a big problem for the Biden administration. 'We pray that governments and peoples welcome the stranger, protect the vulnerable, reunite separated children and families, and promote justice,' the reader announced. 'Lord, hear our prayer,' we all responded. The President was not there to hear it, but perhaps Speaker Pelosi would pass on the message. Although, with immigration reform already on Joe Biden's very long To Do list, I guessed she might have been preaching to the converted.

24. Where it all began

The former Vice President Mike Pence disappeared from public view after he left office, until early March 2021, when he wrote an op-ed for the conservative publication *The Daily Signal*. Did he use it as an opportunity to attack his former boss and criticize him for sending a mob of supporters to hang him? No, Mike Pence chose to echo Donald Trump's baseless, divisive claims of voter fraud.

'After an election marked by significant voting irregularities and numerous instances of officials setting aside state election law, I share the concerns of millions of Americans about the integrity of the 2020 election,' he wrote. 'That's why when I was serving as presiding officer at the joint session of Congress certifying the Electoral College results, I pledged to ensure that all objections properly raised under the Electoral Count Act would be given a full hearing before Congress and the American people. The tragic events of January 6th, the most significant being the loss of life and violence at our nation's Capitol, also deprived the American people of a substantive discussion in Congress about election integrity in America.'

In the immediate aftermath of the storming of the Capitol, Democrats called on Mike Pence to invoke the Twenty-fifth Amendment of the US Constitution and remove Donald Trump from office. When he refused to do so, they quickly moved to impeach the President for an unprecedented second time. They accused him of assembling a mob of his supporters, whipping them into a frenzy and inciting an insurrection. The Article of Impeachment said the President had 'gravely endangered the security of the United States and its institutions of Government. He threatened the integrity of the democratic system, interfered with the peaceful transition of power, and imperilled a coequal branch of Government.'

The accusations did not just relate to Donald Trump's role in the storming of the Capitol, the Article of Impeachment also made reference to his prior efforts to overturn the election results, which 'included a phone call on January 2nd, 2021, during which President Trump urged the Secretary of State of Georgia, Brad Raffensperger, to "find" enough votes to overturn the Georgia Presidential election results and threatened Secretary Raffensperger if he failed to do so'.

An audio recording of the hour-long phone call had been leaked and it gave listeners an insight into a President who was seeing his grip on power slip away. He moved from desperation, to flattery, to threats and to anger as he pleaded with election officials in Georgia to declare him the winner in the swing state where Joe Biden had claimed victory. 'So, look. All I want to do is this. I just want to find 11,780 votes, which is one more than we have because we won the state. So, what are we going to do here, folks? I only need 11,000 votes. Fellas, I need 11,000 votes. Give me a break,' Mr Trump said.

A president threatening state officials on a phone call was bad enough, but also worrying were the threats being received by election workers in districts where Donald Trump had falsely claimed there was voter fraud. 'It has to stop!' an emotional Gabriel Sterling told a press conference in December 2020. A senior election official in Georgia, he spoke about the fear being felt by his colleagues. 'Someone's going to get shot. Someone's going to get killed. And it's not right,' he said.

Just over a month after those comments, people did get killed during the storming of the Capitol Building. In the aftermath of the attack, senior Republicans criticized Donald Trump for his role in the riot but few voted to impeach him and he was acquitted by the Senate. The small number of Republicans who did vote to impeach or who dared to speak out against the former president's falsehoods were punished by the party. With an eye to regaining control of the House and Senate in the 2022 Midterm Elections, Republicans made a calculated, political judgement that sticking with Donald Trump was their best chance of winning.

In many ways, the assault on the Capitol Building was the culmination of four years of divisive politics under Donald Trump. He had always been a divider. There had to be an enemy in an 'us versus them' world of his own creation. During his 2016 campaign, it was Mexicans and Muslims. When Black Lives Matter protesters took to the streets in 2020, he focused on the 'angry mobs' that were looting and vandalizing. When the coronavirus pandemic hit the US, it was China's fault. When he lost the election, it was because the Democrats cheated with rigged voting machines and fraudulent ballot papers.

Donald Trump ticked a lot of boxes for his support base. He cut taxes and oversaw a booming economy until the coronavirus hit. He kept his 'America First' promises by pulling out of international treaties and accords. His pro-gun, pro-religion, pro-life policies pleased the conservatives who helped put him in the White House. But by peddling falsehoods about a rigged election, he did his followers a grave disservice and heightened tensions, anger and distrust.

The launch of Donald Trump's political career will forever be associated with that famous moment in June 2015 when he descended the golden escalator at Trump Tower in New York to announce that he would be running for the Republican nomination. His first major rally took place two months later, on 21 August, in Mobile, Alabama, and saw 30,000 supporters gather in a football arena. The event was originally supposed to take place in the city's Civic Center but was moved to the much larger Ladd-Peebles Stadium to accommodate the crowd. Before the event began, Donald Trump flew over the arena in a private jet as his supporters below cheered loudly. He delivered an hour-long speech while wearing a red 'Make America Great Again' baseball cap.

It was an auspicious start. Alabama loved Donald Trump and he loved Alabama. He revelled in the cheering crowds and on that hot August evening, the phenomenon of the Trump rally was born. After his election win, the president-elect returned to Mobile in December 2016 for a victory rally. 'There is no better place to celebrate than here,' he said. 'This is where it all began. I just want to thank the people of Alabama.'

I wanted to see the place where it all began. I made my way along the multi-lane highway that leads into downtown Mobile. The route was lined with big advertising billboards, most of them for personal injury lawyers. Smiling and suited, they urged you to call their 1-800 number if you had been injured at work or involved in a car accident. One poster simply asked: 'Have you been wronged or hurt?' It sounded more like a counselling service than an attorney's office.

I was following directions to the Ladd-Peebles Football Stadium using the sat-nav on my iPhone, which I had plugged into the hire car I was driving. The American phone was linked to an Irish Apple account and this was clearly confusing for the CarPlay system in the rented Toyota Camry. When I first plugged it in, the voice giving me directions was a very posh-sounding English lady. The following day it had switched to an American man. Today's voice was that of a young woman with an Irish accent. That's nice, I thought, until she started mispronouncing my destination. A former French colony, it is pronounced 'Moh-beel' and not 'Moh-bile', like a cell phone. My friendly Irish sat-nav was unaware of this, but I forgave her as the voice reminded me of home.

Two mispronounced exits later and I had left the highway and the personal injury lawyers behind. Their large billboards gave way to small, handwritten advertisements hanging from lampposts offering to buy houses and cars for cash 'with no questions asked'. The streets were lined with small clapboard bungalows and cottages. Many of the houses were rundown. Others were completely abandoned with boarded-up windows and doors. Some of the driveways were filled with old, rusting cars and broken kitchen appliances. I was in the predominantly black working-class neighbourhood of Maysville which surrounds the football stadium.

I couldn't help wondering how many of these locals had gone to Donald Trump's first major rally, even though it was happening on their doorstep. The only reminders of politics I could see were two yard signs in front of a house, one for Biden–Harris, the other for Black Lives Matter. Suddenly, my Irish sat-nav sounded right at home as she directed me down Dublin Street, which ran parallel to Belfast Street and Waterford Street. Curiously, at the back of the football stadium there was a network of roads named after Irish locations. There was a Sligo, a Limerick and a Wexford Street, but I was unable to find one named after my native Cork.

There were other European destinations, too, with streets named after Amsterdam, Brussels and Antwerp.

Outside the stadium, fresh-looking posters advised attendees to wear masks and practise social distancing. Older signs warned that weapons were not permitted inside and that umbrellas were also banned. For some reason, the umbrella advisories were larger and more prominent than the ones relating to weapons. I guess in the Deep South, where the Second Amendment right to bear arms is sacrosanct, umbrellas pose a greater threat than guns. Next to the stadium was a large, disused factory with faded letters on its crumbling, redbrick façade that read: John A. Lamey Milling Company. Perhaps this once provided badly needed employment in the local area, but not any more. The old mill is dwarfed by the large football arena that has been built alongside it. While many of the locals may not have attended that first Donald Trump rally, in some ways I suppose it was the ideal location for him to launch his promise to 'Make America Great Again'. A rundown working-class area with faded reminders of an industrial past. There were few signs of rejuvenation, however, when I visited six years after Donald Trump had first flown over this area in his private jet to launch a political campaign like no other.

As I made my way towards downtown Mobile, the small crumbling houses of Maysville were replaced by the impressive mansions of the city's Oakleigh Garden Historic District. The colonial homes, with their columns, wraparound porches and window shutters, reminded me of another historic city of the Deep South: Savannah, Georgia. There are similarities with other neighbours, too. Every year, Mobile hosts America's oldest Mardi Gras festival. While it may be the original, it is not nearly as well known as the annual Carnival held in New Orleans, which is just two hours away in Louisiana.

I drove out of the city centre, heading east over the bridges and causeways that span the vast Mobile Bay. As my sat-nav informed me that I was merging onto Battleship Parkway, I noticed a cluster of warships, tanks and fighter jets occupying a large park on the western shore of the bay, built to honour America's military might. I was on my way to interview someone with a military history of their own, a retired career-Marine and Gulf War veteran by the name of Dr Louis Campomenosi. We had arranged to meet at the Original Oyster House, a seafood restaurant on the waterfront. Its website promised Southern hospitality and local specialities, such as fire-grilled oysters, homemade gumbo, grits and its signature dessert, chocolate-chip peanut butter pie. The building was as colourful as the menu, with plastic sharks, alligators, turtles and fish protruding from the walls.

Louis Campomenosi had arrived before me and was waiting in the restaurant's reception area. He was a man in his seventies and was wearing a US flag face mask. There were more stars and stripes on the lapel of his navy blazer: a pin of the American flag and another displaying the flag of the US Marine Corps. Under this, he wore a large white badge that read 'Common Sense Campaign', the name of the local Tea Party organization of which he is the Chairman. The Tea Party is a conservative movement within the Republican Party that was formed in 2009. It called for an end to excessive taxation and government interference, as well as greater immigration controls.

A waiter led us to our table and handed out menus, looking disappointed when we said we would just be having coffee. 'And bring me the bill,' Louis added to his minimal order. 'Absolutely not,' I replied, 'I'm paying.' The waiter said he'd leave us to 'fight it out' between ourselves. I was about to make a comment about Mrs Doyle and her friend in *Father Ted* but stopped myself in time, remembering that the reference would be lost on someone whose knowledge of Irish sit-coms was probably limited. Louis Campomenosi did, however, know a lot about politics, history and world affairs.

As a child in the 1950s he had spent time in Cambodia, where his father was posted as a military adviser to the government. After he retired from the Marines he became a professor of political science, teaching a variety of courses on international relations, American foreign policy, political philosophy and military history. He was attracted to the Tea Party movement because he saw it as the antidote to the Obama presidency, which he viewed as moving the US towards socialism. I asked him what was wrong with a government stepping in to help people with healthcare or housing. 'America has always been able to accommodate moving people from the bottom to the top without forcing them to do things they would otherwise not do,' Louis said, echoing one of the central points of his movement, a call for 'big government' to keep their noses out of people's lives.

Louis was sceptical of Donald Trump when he started to emerge on the political stage with those big rallies. 'I thought he was going to be a disaster. We had to beat Hillary Clinton and stop this movement towards socialism. I couldn't believe he was running, but after he won and when I saw what he started to do in terms of policy, I thought this is the best way to go. He did what conservatives had been talking about doing for a long, long time. The religious right was sceptical of Trump because of his background and scandals like the

Access Hollywood tapes. His bona fides as a cultural conservative religious right person were questioned, but it didn't matter. What mattered was that he was a conservative in policy orientation.'

His flow was interrupted by the arrival of our coffees. Louis dumped two sugars into his. 'Where was I?' he asked. 'Donald Trump's conservative policies,' I reminded him.

'Yes. But even before that, his first order of business was to figure out how to stop China from stealing from the United States, because the reality is China has been taking advantage of us in many ways, like intellectual property and trade. Secondly, he was focused on trying to become energy independent, freeing us from being reliant on overseas oil.' He moved on to consider Donald Trump's immigration policies. As he stirred his coffee with a small plastic straw, he acknowledged that he, a Campomenosi, is descended from Italian immigrants and that he was speaking to an Irishman. 'Look, I know this country was built by immigrants, but when it comes to immigration it has to be legal and has to meet some sort of standard of who is coming over. Does that translate into a racist statement? Well, to the people on the left, anything I say on immigration will be construed as racist. I disagree with that fundamentally. We need to find the best people who can come here, regardless of colour. That's it.'

When he heard Donald Trump's campaign speeches on building a wall and beefing up border security, he had found his ideal candidate. 'I think what Trump was trying to do was move in a direction in which we look at the types of people coming in and making sure they fit. It was an issue that he focused on and the symbol of it was the border wall. He was absolutely right and what Biden is doing today is letting all of these folks in who wanted to come as asylum-seekers,' he claimed.

But what about all the Trump controversies? The insults, the nicknames and the angry tweets? Louis saw these not as negatives but as effective communication tools. 'The lesson from his campaign was that he was able to destroy his opponents with nicknames that stuck. As far as he's concerned, it was working, so that fed into his tweeting strategy. He was hemmed in by a mainstream media that hated him, so this was his breakout approach.' After the storming of the Capitol, his 'breakout approach' was taken away and Donald Trump was suspended from social media. 'It was amazing that Twitter allowed him to do it as long as they did,' Louis said. 'Twitter was a way for Donald Trump to strike back at his enemies both on the left and the right. There is an element of the Republican Party that is very upper-class orientated, the country club crowd. They like decorum, the coat-and-tie approach, they go to church, and that's who they are; but there are times when you have to get dirty in politics and Trump understood that from having to deal with New York politics all his life, so he was ready to fight these people.'

Louis Campomenosi does not blame Donald Trump for the storming of the Capitol Building. He believes, like many of the former president's diehard supporters, that the whole thing was a set-up, a plan executed by the far-left to damage Mr Trump. He believes the conspiracy theories that claim that Antifa and Black Lives Matter activists were the real perpetrators of the riot and that the police were involved in it too, which was why they allowed the protesters to enter the building without putting up a fight. 'The broad establishment had to deal with President Trump, but the accommodation only went so far, and deep down they were done with him. It wasn't just Democrats; senior Republicans accused him of telling lies about the election and accused him of being responsible for the storming of the Capitol.'

Louis also believes that Donald Trump's election loss was a result of widespread fraud. He organized a Stop the Steal rally in his local area to protest against what he says was a rigged election. There was a good turnout for the demonstration, which is no surprise given its location. In Baldwin County, Alabama, Donald Trump defeated Joe Biden by 76.2 per cent to 22.4 per cent. Louis believes there were unconstitutional changes to the election laws in key swing states to facilitate the use of mail-in ballots. The measures were enacted because of the pandemic, but Louis claims it allowed for widespread voter fraud to take place.

'But there's no evidence of that,' I said as we drained the last drops of coffee from our mugs. 'The courts, the Attorney General and election officials all said that there was no evidence of widespread voter fraud.' 'Well, election officials are never going to admit that the fraud happened on their watch,' he replied.

For Louis, it was just another example of the establishment ganging up on a president they could not handle any more. He also believes that Republicans will regret turning their backs on the former president. 'It is a risky business for establishment Republicans to stray too far from Donald Trump's policies,' he concluded as I snatched the bill from the waiter. I made a big deal of paying, in true Mrs Doyle fashion, but then realized it was a bit of an overreaction when I saw that the charge was only $5.

As the sun set on Mobile Bay, I made my way back into the city centre, once again passing the Alabama stadium where Donald Trump's presidential journey had begun. In an arena surrounded by street signs that read Dublin, Belfast, Limerick, Brussels and Antwerp, he had set out a vision that would fundamentally change how the US dealt with the outside world, promising to put 'America First'.

Over the course of four years, the Trump presidency dug deep into the fissures that ran through American society and pulled them wide. His style, his temperament, his bombast and his constant tilting towards his conservative base created an environment where those divisions felt unbridgeable. I was at the Capitol Building as the House of Representatives etched Donald Trump's name into the history books by making him the first ever president to be impeached twice. Outside, a lone protester stood holding a sign that read, 'Stop Hating Each Other Because You Disagree', and from a speaker he was playing Bob Marley's 'One Love'. It was a strong message of unity, but the demonstrator was surrounded by stark reminders of the deep divisions that had been laid bare in Washington.

As members of Congress gathered to cast their impeachment votes, construction crews were installing tall, unscalable metal fences around the perimeter of Capitol Hill. Hundreds of armed National Guard troops looked on as workmen hammered and drilled the railings into place. Exactly one week before, the Capitol Building was under siege. A week later, Joe Biden was inaugurated at that same location. Soldiers in camouflage uniforms gripped their rifles while forklifts and trucks delivered additional fencing and rolls of barbed wire. Barely audible above the roar of the engines, Bob Marley pleaded, 'Let's get together and feel all right'. I hope they do, after the tumultuous time America has been through, I really hope they do.

Postscript

Growing up, I watched US TV shows and movies in which the characters hung out in enormous shopping malls, years before such developments were built in Ireland. The mass vaccination centre in Sterling, Virginia, used to be a department store, located in a dilapidated retail park. Its neighbouring businesses were still operating as shops, but they looked deserted, suffering no doubt because of COVID-19 and the move towards online shopping.

Outside, the long queues of people and the packed car park resembled the first day of a big sale that had attracted shoppers eager to bag a bargain. They had not come to buy shoes or electrical appliances, but they were there for the season's must-have item. Inside, COVID-19 vaccines were being administered in what used to be the make-up and fragrance section of the store. Patients and staff sat in front of cosmetic counters panelled with mirrors. Those waiting for their shots lined up alongside disused dressing rooms and bare shelves that once displayed the latest fashions.

It struck me as another chapter in the American story, the plot twist at the end of a tale of disaster and chaos. This department store, this symbol of US consumerism and capitalism, had died, but had been reborn anew as something more powerful that offered hope to a nation devastated by the pandemic. America was supposed to be the great superpower but when the coronavirus hit, it quickly became the worst affected country in the world and an example of what not to do. Now, the tables had turned.

While Europe and much of the rest of the world were struggling, the US vaccine rollout was surging ahead. Under the Trump administration, the government had invested billions of dollars early in the pandemic on vaccine development, testing and production. Red tape was cut and approvals were fast-tracked, guaranteeing quick access to supplies once the vaccines were ready. America had thrown billions and billions of dollars at the problem, and it had worked. When US infection rates and deaths were soaring, the country had been pitied by its neighbours. Now, its vaccine rollout was the envy of the world.

When the Trump administration departed and the Biden administration took over, a sort of silence, a calmness descended on the US for a while. But as things returned to 'normal' in Washington, we also saw the re-emergence of some of the bleakest problems that continue to beset America. They had been there all along, but they had been shouted down by the constant noise of the Trump years. When the silence returned, so too did the darkness. Gun violence and racism reared up again in all their ugliness. Epidemics for which there are no vaccines.

The Hennepin County Courthouse is located in an impressive twenty-four-storey skyscraper in downtown Minneapolis. The glass and steel towers are designed to resemble the letter H, after the county over which they loom, but in April 2021 the building resembled a military fortress. Concrete barricades topped with barbed-wire fences were erected around the complex. Military vehicles were parked on the surrounding streets and armed National Guard troops patrolled the outer perimeter. The streets were deserted. Minneapolis was a city on edge. Tensions were high and there was a sense of anticipation.

The previous evening, the jury in the Derek Chauvin trial had retired to consider its verdict. The court proceedings had been broadcast non-stop by US TV networks for three weeks. Americans were glued to their screens as the prosecution and the defence laid out their cases and questioned forty-five witnesses. Some of those who testified were bystanders who had witnessed George Floyd's death. They broke down in the stand as they recalled the horror of watching him taking his final breaths while he begged for his life.

Other witnesses were medical experts, like Irishman Dr Martin Tobin. As a pulmonologist, a specialist in the study of lungs and breathing, the Kilkenny man testified that George Floyd had died from a lack of oxygen. He had analysed the video footage of Mr Floyd being restrained on the ground with Derek Chauvin's knee pressed to his neck for more than nine minutes. By watching the victim's breathing patterns, he was able to pinpoint the moment of death. 'One second he's alive, and one second he's no longer,' he said. 'That's the moment the life goes out of his body.'

The defence had argued that George Floyd might have died from drug use, an underlying health condition or even carbon monoxide poisoning from the exhaust pipe of the police vehicle close to where he was being restrained.

The prosecution's strongest piece of evidence did not come from a medical expert or police witness. It came from the mobile phone video footage recorded by seventeen-year-old Darnella Frazier. Her video went viral, sent shockwaves through the world and sparked a global protest movement. Darnella Frazier told the court that the death haunts her still and keeps her awake at night. 'It's been nights I stayed up apologizing and apologizing to George Floyd for not doing more and not physically interacting and not saving his life,' she said.

In closing arguments, the prosecution told the jurors to trust their judgement and use their common sense. They were asked to remember how they felt when they watched the video for the first time. 'This case is exactly what you thought when you saw it first. You can believe your eyes. It's what you felt in your gut. It's what you now know in your heart. This wasn't policing. This was murder,' prosecutor Steve Schleicher said. It was a simple message.

As the jurors retired to consider their verdict, I made my way to Minneapolis. It is a three-hour flight from Washington DC and many of my fellow passengers on board the plane were journalists and camera crews embarking on the same mission as me. At the luggage claim area in Minneapolis airport, the conveyor belts were filled with hard, black cases containing cameras and broadcast equipment. My small, red suitcase stood out among the professional gear. I had been unsure what to pack. Jury deliberations are unpredictable. The trial judge, Peter Cahill, had told the jury to 'plan for long and hope for short'. I took his advice and brought enough clothes for five days.

As I was getting ready to report live into the *Six One News* from outside the Hennepin County Courthouse, there was an unprecedented intervention from the US President Joe Biden. 'I can only imagine the pressure and anxiety they are feeling,' Joe Biden told reporters, referring to the family of George Floyd. 'I'm praying the verdict is the right verdict. I think it's overwhelming in my view. I wouldn't say that unless the jury was sequestered now, not hearing me say that.'

The jury may have been isolated from the outside world, but it was still a surprise to hear a sitting President give his personal views on a trial before a verdict had been reached. White House Press Secretary Jen Psaki defended the comments and insisted the President was not trying to influence the outcome of the case. 'I don't think he would see it as weighing in on the verdict. He was conveying what many people are feeling across the country, which is compassion for the family.'

After just ten hours of deliberations, we were told the jury had reached a decision. The verdict would be announced between 9.30 p.m. and 10.00 p.m. Irish time. It would not make the *Nine O'Clock News*, but *Prime Time* would still be on-air and I prepared to do a live report into the show as soon as the verdict was handed down. The streets surrounding the courthouse, which had been deserted all day, started to fill with people. I could hear sirens in the distance and helicopters overhead. A state of emergency had been declared amid fears that acquittal would result in riots and unrest. But as the three Guilty verdicts were announced, the helicopters and sirens were drowned out by loud cheers from those who had gathered outside the court.

The next sound I heard was a voice in my earpiece. It was Miriam O'Callaghan, back in the studio in Dublin. 'Breaking news, the jury has just come back in the Derek Chauvin trial. Brian, bring us up to date. What's the story?' she asked. 'Guilty on all three counts – second-degree murder, third-degree murder and manslaughter,' I replied. As I finished my live report, the crowds outside the courthouse were continuing to grow. 'Say his name – George Floyd!' they chanted as armed National Guard troops looked on from behind the barbed-wire fences and concrete barricades. People hugged, cried and danced. Passing drivers beeped their horns.

The smell of cooking began to fill the air as a group of men prepared burgers and hotdogs on a large barbecue. Music played from speakers. Vendors sold Black Lives

Matter T-shirts and flags from stalls. On the surface, it looked like a street party, but many of those who had gathered said it was a bittersweet moment. They spoke about hope, but also about a difficult road ahead in the struggle for racial justice. 'This has only cranked the car up for the very long journey that we have to take,' a young African American man named Devante Hill told me. 'America has to finally acknowledge what it has done to people of colour. This wasn't the be-all and end-all, but it was a step in the right direction to dismantle systems of oppression that black people have been living under.'

It was a glimmer of hope for a community that had suffered so much for so long. It would not erase years of oppression and racial injustice. Nor could it be ignored that as the verdict was being handed down, more black lives were being lost at the hands of police. It was never going to stop gun violence or heal political and social divides but, just like the vaccine rollout, Chauvin's conviction and subsequent 22-and-a-half-years sentence were signs that sometimes in America, things can go right.

As the crowds gathered on the streets ahead of the verdict, the sense of anticipation and tension brought me back to St Peter's Square in Rome eight years earlier, as we watched for the white smoke to curl from the Sistine Chapel. I was 5,000 miles from the cathedrals and churches of the Vatican. Instead, outside a Minneapolis courthouse, the faithful turned to a higher power as they begged for justice. When it finally came, they knew their prayers had been answered.

Acknowledgements

Thank you to Michael McLoughlin and Patricia Deevy from Penguin Random House Ireland and to my wonderful editor, Rachel Pierce.

Thank you to my RTÉ colleagues for their support, including Jon Williams, Hilary McGouran, Eimear Lowe, Roisín Duffy, Colm Ó Mongáin, Fiona Mitchell, Eleanor Burnhill, Jonathan Rachel Clynch and my fellow podcaster Jackie Fox.

A big thanks to a talented cameraman and great friend Murray Pinczuk. I want to mention our 'lockdown buddies' in Washington DC, Suzanne Lynch and Barton Macfarlane, and our 'virtual lockdown buddies' Donal and Una Bradley. Thank you to all my family and friends back home in Ireland whose Zoom calls and WhatsApp groups helped overcome all those cancelled visits.

Thank you to my parents, Mary and Jim, for their constant support and encouragement, and to my siblings, Gary, Ruth and David, and their spouses. I also want to thank my in-laws, Sheila and Joe Griffin, Nana T and the Kierce family.

The biggest thanks of all goes to my wife, Joanna, and my daughters, Lucy and Erin, for their love, patience and understanding. They have been with me every step of the way throughout our big adventure in the USA.

He just wanted a decent book to read ...

Not too much to ask, is it? It was in 1935 when Allen Lane, Managing Director of Bodley Head Publishers, stood on a platform at Exeter railway station looking for something good to read on his journey back to London. His choice was limited to popular magazines and poor-quality paperbacks – the same choice faced every day by the vast majority of readers, few of whom could afford hardbacks. Lane's disappointment and subsequent anger at the range of books generally available led him to found a company – and change the world.

'We believed in the existence in this country of a vast reading public for intelligent books at a low price, and staked everything on it'
Sir Allen Lane, 1902–1970, founder of Penguin Books

The quality paperback had arrived – and not just in bookshops. Lane was adamant that his Penguins should appear in chain stores and tobacconists, and should cost no more than a packet of cigarettes.

Reading habits (and cigarette prices) have changed since 1935, but Penguin still believes in publishing the best books for everybody to enjoy. We still believe that good design costs no more than bad design, and we still believe that quality books published passionately and responsibly make the world a better place.

So wherever you see the little bird – whether it's on a piece of prize-winning literary fiction or a celebrity autobiography, political tour de force or historical masterpiece, a serial-killer thriller, reference book, world classic or a piece of pure escapism – you can bet that it represents the very best that the genre has to offer.

Whatever you like to read – trust Penguin.